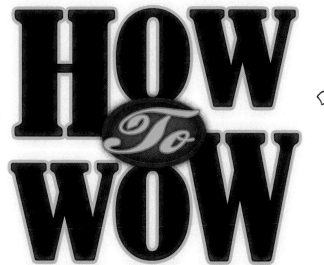

HOW *To* WOW

W9-BNT-017

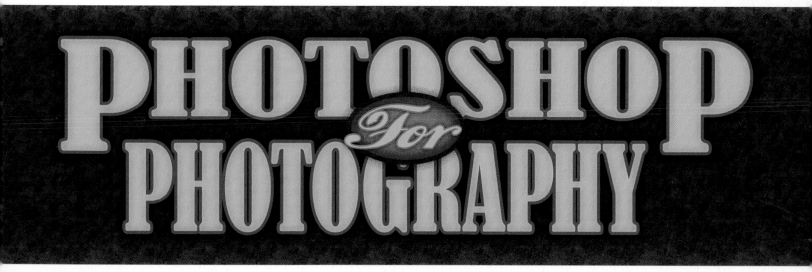

PHOTOSHOP *for* PHOTOGRAPHY

Jack Davis & Ben Willmore

Peachpit Press

How to Wow: Photoshop for Photography
Jack Davis & Ben Willmore

Peachpit Press
1249 Eighth Street
Berkeley, CA 94710
(510) 524-2178
(510) 524-2221 (fax)
Find us on the World Wide Web at:
http://www.peachpit.com
Peachpit Press is a division of Pearson Education

ISBN 0-321-22799-9

0 9 8 7 6 5 4 3 2
Printed and bound in the United States of America.

To George Lepp and Dewitt Jones — two world-renowned photographers and all-around great guys. You have graciously shared with me your time, expertise, encouragement and most importantly, your passion for exploring new ways to capture the incredible beauty that is all around us. Mahalo!

–Jack

To each and every person who has attended one of my seminars or bought one of my books—you've given me the best "day job" I could ever hope for.

–Ben

Acknowledgments

First I thank Ben, my Photoshop World speaking buddy of many years, for throwing himself into the very deep end of this (sometimes painful) project. His incredible virtuosity with Photoshop and his invaluable expertise as an educator and a writer made the creation of this book not only possible, but pleasurable as well! He even tackled rough lay outs and wrote copy to fit, thus giving Jill very clean pages to work with. Muchas grácias, mi amigo! It was an added bonus to work with his assistant Regina Cleveland. Her strong work ethic and efficiency not only helps Ben sound good, but she lightened the load for Jill, my wife and loving partner-in-crime. Since our kids are now school-aged, Jill came off "sabbatical" to attack the design, layout and production of this book. She's the best in the business (*and* I get to sleep with her)!

For years I've relied on many people for their support and constructive encouragement to help me become a better teacher, writer, and creative professional. To Software Cinema (www.software-cinema.com), especially Dean Collins, thanks for working with me to try to create the best instructional resources possible. The pages of this book are the "Cliff's Notes" of one of those resources: the *How to Wow: Photoshop for Photography* set of training video discs. For putting up with my relentless requests for critiques, I'd like to thank my fellow NAPP Dream Team photographers Kevin Ames, Jim DiVitale, Julieanne Kost, and Vincent Versace. To Nikon, specifically Richard LoPinto and Steve Heiner, you've supported me with access to the very best tools in the world for capturing life on film – sorry, on "chip." To a sculptor without a set of sharp chisels, a stone is just a stone.

I'd also like to thank Aaron Chang, Robin Robertis and Matthew Eisenberg for letting me use their exceptional photographs, and the many friends and associates that have put up with my incessant shooting of them for use as "stock." And, thank goodness for Val Gelineau and Denise Davert at PhotoSpin.com, who allowed me access to their beautiful and readily available on-line image library, especially for times when the scope of my own work wasn't up to the task.

To Tim Grey, author, teacher and demented dynamo at the Lepp Institute of Digital Imaging, thank you for "beta testing" the book, images and presets for us, and for your welcomed suggestions so we wouldn't miss a trick. Also, we owe much gratitude to the whole programming and marketing teams at Adobe for giving us the most phenomenally creative tool since the pencil, especially Julieanne Kost and Russell Brown, our fellow psychopathic speakers-in-arms.

Finally, thank you Peachpit Press and Nancy Ruenzel for catching the vision of the *How to Wow* series; it's been 12 years since we first embarked on a book together, and you haven't missed a beat! Thanks also to our editor Rebecca Gulick for putting up with the never-ending delays and the anal-retentive nature of us creative types; and for helping us dot our i's and cross our t's, thank you to production manager David Van Ness, proofreader Liz Welch, and Rebecca Plunkett, our indexer.

–Jack Davis

It's been said that too many cooks spoil a broth, but Jack Davis and his wife Jill are living proof that this isn't always the case. As a first time *co*-author, I had my trepidations about sharing the kitchen with another chef. Would we fight over the dessert? Come to blows over the hors d'oeuvres? Well, it turned out to be quite the opposite, and I want to thank both Jack and Jill for being such gracious co-conspirators and making this experience such a rewarding one. They are truly awesome folks to work with.

As is often the case with books of this nature, we dutifully put in our share of all-nighters so I'd also like to thank the makers of Jolt gum for their contribution to my wakefulness, and I can indeed attest that their slogan "Chew More, Do More!" is truth in advertising.

Finally, I'd like to say thanks once again to Regina. She has painstakingly edited darn near every word I've ever uttered in print, and she always goes to great lengths to make sure that my writing doesn't turn into gibberish.

–Ben Willmore

Contents

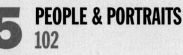 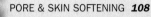
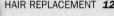

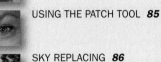
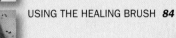

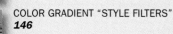

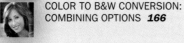

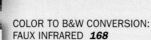

9 COMBINING & COLLAGING 218

Introduction

WE LIVE IN EXCITING TIMES. Over 20 years ago the graphic design and publishing industries experienced a major revolution as the personal computer and desktop publishing era unfolded. Sometimes it's easy to forget that the digital tools we now take for granted have completely changed the way we produce creative communications. Life-altering change is occurring once again—this time in the world of photography. The marriage of Photoshop and digital cameras is a match made in heaven; it is revolutionizing every aspect of how we capture, process and print our beloved photographs.

In the past, it often took considerable time, energy and money to experiment with the photographic process. Now we can shoot to our heart's content *and* get instant feedback, which equates to a fantastic opportunity to learn and grow in our art. And, all this experimentation is free until you're ready to print (if you don't count the thousands you spend on new computers, cameras and various other sundry digital accoutrements). Once you've captured the images,

Photoshop provides a breathtaking range of options. You can not only reproduce a vast majority of tradi-tional darkroom effects, but you are now free to stretch your creative wings and fly beyond the darkroom's restricting chemically scented walls to produce imagery that wasn't even imaginable (let alone possible) in years past.

The Birth of *How to Wow*

As with all revolutions, it takes time to acclimate. For many, there's a steep learning curve which can lead to frustration. We are here to guide you through the obstacle course and make sure you have all the phenomenal capabilities of Photoshop at your disposal when your next commercial job or personal project comes in, or when the next lightning bolt of creativity hits you right between the eyes.

Both of us are established authors, speakers, instructors and all-around Photoshop and photography nuts. Jack is best known for his *Photoshop Wow!* books, and Ben for his *Adobe Photoshop Studio Techniques* books.

Our goal is to help you quickly master the many creative opportunities available within a Photoshop-centric workflow: what file formats to choose before you click the shutter release; how to work with your plethora of potential award-winners in the File Browser; how to best optimize your images' color and contrast; how to fine-tune the final masterpiece; and even how to combine those masterpieces into an elegant collage. Our mantra is, *"Quality, Flexibility and Speed,"* which you will experience for yourself as you work through the projects in this book.

What's in it for You?

To help you speed toward that goal (quality, flexibility and speed), we wanted to give you the biggest bang for your buck by making it incredibly easy for you to get immediate, hands-on experience with the features in Photoshop. We provide you with the mouth-watering recipes (as well as heaps of helpful tips and insights), but in order to turbo-charge your experience, we've complemented each "dish" by including the complete supporting files on this book's companion CD. This multi-pronged approach will get you working at peak performance levels faster than you can say, "How'd you *do* that?"

If you're experienced at working in a conventional darkroom, you'll enjoy learning alternative techniques for creating some of the traditional effects you're familiar with (such as Dodging, Burning, Vignetting, etc.), as well as some new treatments that wouldn't have been an option with darkroom alchemy.

If you're new to photography, we'll introduce you to many of the industry terms and techniques, and help launch you (as painlessly as possible) into your all-digital adventure. No matter which flavor of operating system you prefer (Mac or Windows), you'll be at ease because we cover the shortcuts and location of features for both platforms.

How to Use This Book & CD

To make your experience as enjoyable and trouble-free as possible, we ask that you NOT give in to the temptation to skip the first two chapters (the foundational nuts and bolts part) before you dive into the fun stuff in later chapters. Once you've worked through Chapters 1 and 2, you'll be well equipped to tackle the rest in any order you'd like.

The How to Wow companion CD at the back of this book contains an incredible assortment of custom Wow Presets, as well as all the photographs used in the projects showcased throughout the book. These images can be found, organized by chapter, in the **HTW Project Files** folder on the CD. There you will also find a folder called **HTW Preset Sampler,** which contains literally hundreds of custom tools, swatches, shapes, styles, patterns, gradients and actions. We will use some of them in this book; the rest are there for you to explore at your leisure. Make sure to review the part called Working with Presets (page 19) in Chapter 1, "Workflow Foundations," to ensure that the presets get loaded properly. It will just take a minute or so to learn how to use the presets, and if you don't, *you'll be missing out on an invaluable resource.*

Prepackaged vs. Garden Fresh

To get you going as quickly as possible, we have taken on the role of both prep cook and master chef, not only preparing some of the ingredients for you, but also holding your hand through the step-by-step recipes as well. This is a bit of a double-edged sword. While we want you to get as comfortable as possible with the techniques in this book, we don't want to turn you into a "prepackaged" junkie, relying solely on what we've prepared for you. What we really hope for is that you will receive the inspiration, insights, and skills needed to produce your own fresh and original creations.

The projects in this book range from tasty little appetizers to nourishing main courses and even some decadent desserts, all of which we know will feed your creative appetite. Hopefully, when you have made it through our recipe book and completed the hard labor necessary for crafting a Photoshop gourmet meal, you can push away from the table and contentedly sigh… wow! ▥

1

WORKFLOW FOUNDATIONS

*Workflow as Time,
Energy & Sanity Saver*

YOU BOUGHT THE BOOK. You've finally got a few moments to call your own and now you're revving your engine, impatient to mash down the accelerator and burn rubber all the way to the land of Wow. You're just about to take off when you look up and see Jack and Ben standing on the center line, staring you down through their mirrored Ray-Ban Aviators like two Alabama State Troopers after a bad morning at the Krispy Kreme. They don't look happy. They suspect that you're going to go straight to the eye candy and skip Chapter 1!

OK, so you're caught. Don't worry, we're not going to write you a ticket, but we are going to detain you just long enough to tell you why you're going to want to take the time to read this chapter.

For a moment, ignore the mind-numbing phrases like "digital workflow" and "optimal exposure" and look at it this way: If you are a fledging chef and go straight for the gourmet soufflé recipe without first knowing some essential cooking basics (say, knowing the difference between "folding in" an ingredient instead of "stirring" it in), you might find that your soufflé never quite looks like the one on the cover of *Bon Appétit.* This is also the case with the recipes in this book. There are some things you will want to have implanted in your brain before you start the cooking process; a foundation of information that will help you avoid headaches later and set the stage properly so that you can sit back, relax and enjoy building your masterpieces. In essence, you need to get some of the "how" before you can successfully do the "wow."

Putting the "Flow" Into Workflow

To get you started, we'll give you a tour of our recommended workflow for folks using digital cameras. You'll learn how to manage your images during every step of the process, from taking the photo and creating the original file to preparing it for handling in Photoshop. Not only will you learn the proper order of each task, you'll get tips on how to use the settings on your camera to achieve maximum quality and optimal exposure, and how to transfer, catalog and archive your images.

Once your image is prepared for Photoshop, you'll be ready for the next phase of the workflow. You'll get the complete answer to one of Photoshop's most pressing questions, which is, "Where do I start?" You'll learn how to use file formats to protect your files, and why it's important to perform certain tasks

in a specific order so you don't degrade the quality of your image. You'll learn at what stage you should perform retouching and apply creative effects, as well as when it's safe to sharpen your image.

Managing the Color Monster

Next, you'll be ready to tackle color management: how you achieve *consistent color* between what you see on your monitor and what you get with your final output, whether it's a printing press, an inkjet printer, or the Web. In truth, the subject of color management can be a snarly ball of yarn and many books of great girth have been written on the subject (a new one we recommend is Tim Grey's *Color Confidence*). We've chosen to give you a highly streamlined version of the process that will get you started on the path to successful color management. At the very least you'll understand what *Profiles* are, how to use them and what to do when those annoying Missing Profile warning boxes pop up in Photoshop.

Tackling Camera Raw

If you shoot digital and haven't been taking advantage of the *RAW* format (assuming your camera offers it), you're invited to take a look into Photoshop's Camera Raw dialog box with us. The benefits of using a RAW format are enormous, and once you've ventured through the process at least once, you'll find that it will be easier than opening up a jar of Cheez Whiz.

So, while we want you to get to the fun stuff as soon as possible, we hope you'll take your foot off the accelerator for just a moment and give this chapter a read-through while you rev your engine.

Starting Your Digital Camera Workflow

If you're shooting with a digital camera, you may need to rethink your approach to opening and working with your images in Photoshop. An image coming straight from a digital camera is a bit different than a regular image (one that has already been scanned or provided by a source other than your digital camera).

The differences might seem subtle at first, but if you ignore them you are likely sacrificing image quality and subsequently setting yourself up for some headaches down the road. Understanding these differences and knowing how to deal with them will help you avoid future frustrations and give you an edge as you develop your digital imaging skills.

So, you digital shooters, take the time to read through this section. It will be worth your while.

1. Choose File Format

Many digital cameras offer you a choice of file formats. High-end cameras usually offer a choice between **JPEG** and **RAW**, while medium-end cameras might offer JPEG and TIFF. In general we usually stay away from the TIFF option because it creates huge, memory-hogging files which quickly fill storage cards and severely limits how many shots you can take in rapid succession. The choice between RAW and JPEG is a personal one and here's our take on it: If you prefer to get it right "in camera" and not make radical changes in Photoshop; need to fit a large number of images on a storage card; or need to take many shots in rapid succession, then consider using JPEG (example: wedding photographer). If on the other hand, you don't shoot action photos; like to make large changes to brightness or contrast in Photoshop; and don't mind spending a little extra time in an attempt to get the highest quality image possible, then consider using a RAW format (example: landscape photographer). Some Nikon digital cameras also offer a **Lossless Compressed RAW** format which combines the small file size of a JPEG file with the added versatility of the RAW file format.

2. Choose Color Space

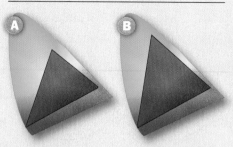

When shooting in the JPEG file format, it's especially important that you choose an appropriate color space (for example, **Adobe RGB** or **sRGB**). In essence, the color space determines the exact colors of red, green and blue your images will be made out of, and therefore determines the range of colors that your images will be capable of containing. If the only use of your images is for on-screen viewing, i.e., the Internet, then choose sRGB A. For all other uses, the Adobe RGB B option will usually deliver better results. This setting isn't as critical when shooting in RAW format because it can be easily changed when opening the file in Photoshop through Camera Raw.

> **T I P**
>
> **sRGB Flavors.** If you are mainly shooting for the Web, or you don't plan to work on the image in Photoshop (boy, do you have the wrong book!), you can use the sRGB color space. Some camera manufacturers (Nikon, for example) offer different flavors: **sRGB I** slightly warms an image (making it good for portraits); **sRGB II** emphasizes the cool colors in a photo (making it good for landscapes).

3. Choose ISO Setting

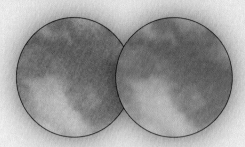

Most medium to high-end digital cameras allow you to choose an **ISO** setting, which determines how sensitive the camera will be to light (the equivalent to film speed in traditional photography). You'll want to check this setting each time you turn on your camera to make sure it's at the lowest usable setting for your particular shooting situation. Higher settings produce noisy images which can be objectionable especially after the image has been adjusted, which will often exaggerate any noise contained in the image. If your camera offers an Auto ISO setting (below is Nikon's Auto ISO camera option), consider using it in challenging lighting conditions because it will attempt to maintain the lowest ISO setting possible for the aperture or shutter speed setting you have chosen.

4. Set White Balance

The **White Balance** setting in your camera determines how the overall color in your image will look—warm, cool or neutral. When the White Balance setting reflects the current lighting situation, then the colors in the image are rendered accurately. When the White Balance setting doesn't reflect the lighting conditions, your image will contain a color cast that will make it appear warm (yellow-red) or cool (blue-green). The White Balance setting isn't critical when shooting in RAW format because you can change the setting when you open the image in Photoshop. This setting is much more critical when shooting in JPEG format because it gets locked into the file and is not as easy to correct after the image is opened in Photoshop. When that's the case, we prefer to set up a custom White Balance setting (although most cameras' **Auto** setting often produces the correct setting). When shooting RAW images, we leave the camera set to Auto White Balance unless we'll be shooting a large series of images under consistent lighting conditions (like in a studio).

5. Make Exposure

If you're used to shooting with negative film and have the habit of overexposing with the thought that negative film can hold the highlight detail, then you're going to need to adjust your thinking. Also, if you've been shooting digital for a while and you have been intentionally underexposing your images (trusting Photoshop to save your shadows – *and your posterior*), stop. Generally, when shooting digitally or with film, you don't want to over- or under- expose your images, otherwise you will lose precious highlight or shadow detail. If you do need to weight your exposures one way or the other, lean toward a lighter exposure (lighter areas of a photo have more detail than darker areas), just don't overdo it or you may "blow out" or "clip" your highlights. Fortunately most medium to high-end digital cameras offer a **Histogram** review feature that indicates if you've lost highlight or shadow detail (which shows up as spikes on the ends of the histogram). Many cameras also offer a flashing highlights feature which will indicate where you've lost highlight detail. Lost highlight and shadow detail can usually be corrected by adjusting the exposure compensation setting on your camera and reshooting. See page 15 for more on determining the optimal exposure.

6. Transfer

After you've finished shooting, it's time to transfer your images to your computer's hard drive. You have the choice of using the cable that came with your camera, or using some sort of card reader. If your camera comes with a standard USB cable, we recommend using a card reader because it will often be up to four times faster than using the cable. Firewire on the other hand offers very fast transfer speeds, but since your camera has to be turned on in order to transfer the files directly, we still prefer a card reader since we can transfer multiple storage cards without depleting the camera's battery.

If you plan on shooting a large number of images and don't want to lug around a laptop, then look into the different battery-driven hard drives that are available, which allow you to transfer your images without needing a laptop or power source.

INSIGHT

RAW File Extensions. Each camera manufacturer uses a different file extension to designate their particular flavor of a RAW file format. For example: Canon uses .crw, Nikon uses .nef and Kodak uses .dcr.

7. Catalog

Photoshop's **File Browser** allows you to view your images as thumbnail images, sort them and perform automated tasks. If you work with a large number of images, then you'll want to look into the different photo cataloging software packages like **iView Media Pro** or **Extensis Portfolio.** Unlike Photoshop's File Browser, these photo cataloging packages allow you to keep track of images that are archived on CD or DVD and allow you to quickly search within a permanent catalog of images which can be much faster than working with the File Browser in Photoshop.

TIP

CD/DVD Handling. When working with CDs and DVDs, try to hold the discs only by their edges as the top and bottom surfaces are very fragile. Use only acid-free felt-tip markers on the label side (like the newest Sharpies) and keep in mind that the label side is closest to the data layer of the disc so be extra careful not to scratch that side. Remember to always store your discs away from the light because the dyes used in them can fade and make them unreadable.

8. Archive

When working with an image in Photoshop, we often end up with three versions of the file. We suggest you archive the original JPEG or RAW images to a CD or DVD soon after transferring them to your computer so that you can retrieve them in the event of a hard drive failure. Then after opening an original image and adding layers, save the image in Photoshop (.psd) format because that is the best file format that supports layers. Then if we need to send an image to be output or to be inserted into a page layout program, we'll flatten the layers in our Photoshop file and save the image in the TIFF format.

By using this system, we can quickly glance at a folder full of images and by looking at the file extension, we can easily tell which ones are the untouched originals (JPEG or RAW), which are our working files (PSD) and which are ready to be sent for output (TIFF). 🖫

Determining the Optimal Exposure

Your camera's Histogram feature is an essential tool in determining the proper exposure for a scene. We'll explain how to think about histograms more in Chapter 7, "Color & Tone Treatments"; for now, let's concentrate on how the histogram in your camera can help you change your approach to getting a good exposure.

Underexposed

Whenever a tall spike appears on the absolute left edge of the histogram, it's telling you that a large area of your image is solid black. That's usually an indication that you've underexposed the image, which has caused a loss of shadow detail. If shadow detail is important, than change the **exposure compensation** setting on your camera to a positive number to use more light when exposing the image and reshoot. If a spike still appears, then increase the exposure compensation setting and reshoot the image again. If you're not able to find an exposure that gets rid of the spike (on either end of the histogram) without introducing another one of the far right of the histogram, then consider taking two exposures as described at the bottom of this page.

Overexposed

A spike on the absolute right of a histogram indicates that a large area of your image is pure white, which is usually an indication that you've overexposed the image and lost (or "clipped") highlight detail. If highlight detail is important to your image, then change the exposure compensation setting in your camera to a negative number to use less light when exposing the image and reshoot. If you are shooting in a challenging situation and you know you will be needing to adjust your image in Photoshop, remember it's better to darken lighter images and hide artifacts than it is to lighten darker images and reveal artifacts (like noise), just be sure that your highlights aren't clipped.

Difficult Exposures

Sometimes the scene you're attempting to photograph is beyond the exposure range that your camera is capable of capturing. These are the instances when no matter which exposure compensation setting you use, you end up with a spike on the right, left or both ends of the histogram. In that situation, consider placing your camera on a tripod and taking two exposures: Shoot one exposure trying to retain highlight detail **A**, and a second exposure attempting to retain shadow detail **B**. (Be sure to only change the shutter speed on your camera, otherwise the two images might end up having slightly different **depths of fields**—areas that are in focus—and will be difficult to align in Photoshop.) Then combine them in Photoshop **C** (as we'll show you on page 62 in Chapter 3, "Adjusting & Optimizing").

Photoshop Workflow

Now let's look at a start-to-finish workflow that will help you in creating the highest quality images possible in Photoshop. That way, when we get to the nuts and bolts of adjusting our images in later chapters, you'll be ahead of the game and will already know how to combine those ideas into a professional workflow.

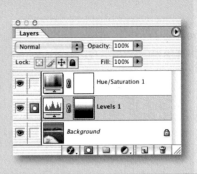

1. Preserve the Original

Our #1 priority when editing an image in Photoshop is to always preserve the original image. By doing so we'll be able to make multiple changes to the image without fear of permanently altering or degrading the original. At any time we'll be able to bring any portion of the image back to either its original state or any other state we've created while working with the image. We'll accomplish that by working with features such as **Adjustment Layers**, **Layer Styles**, **Layer Masks** and **Duplicate Layers**. This will allow us to work with great speed and versatility while maintaining the highest quality possible.

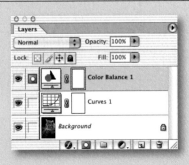

2. Fix the Biggest Problem First

When adjusting an image in Photoshop, it's best to start off by tackling the largest problem and then go on to applying more subtle changes to the image. That usually means adjusting either overall tonality or color. If nothing jumps out at you as an obvious problem with the image, we suggest that you start by performing tonal correction using a Levels or Curves adjustment layer, then move on to adjusting the color in your photo using, for example, a Hue/Saturation adjustment layer.

3. Start Global, Then Go Local

When you begin working on an image, you might be tempted to start making selections and adjusting small areas of your image. We suggest the opposite: start by making **global** adjustments (ones that affect the entire image) before you move on to **localized** adjustments. These global adjustments can often fix the entire image, thus rendering it unnecessary to make any local adjustments. Moreover, they may expose other problems with your image that can be fixed simultaneously with other adjustments.

4. Perform Retouching

Once you have the overall color and tonality of the image adjusted, it's time to analyze the image to see if it needs any retouching. The reason we retouch at this stage instead of the beginning is that adjusting the color and contrast of the image often exposes areas that need to be retouched that were not obvious when you first opened the image.

5. Perform Spotting

So far we've just been thinking about the big picture, but now it's time to concentrate on the smallest details. You might not notice dust, noise, scratches and other tiny defects that might not show up until you spend the time and money to output a large print. To avoid being disappointed, zoom into 100% view and scroll around every square inch of your image looking for small defects and use the Healing Brush to remove them.

6. Apply Creative Effects

At this stage we'll start thinking about any creative effects that we might want to apply. Retouching an image after creative effects have been applied can be very difficult, which is why we wait until this stage to think about applying them.

7. Archive Project File

Once the image feels pretty much complete, it's time to save the layered image in Photoshop (.psd) file format and archive it to CD or DVD for safekeeping. Using the Photoshop file format ensures that you'll retain all the layers, masks and adjustments that we've created and will allow us to return to the file at any time to make refinements.

8. Scale & Sharpen for Specific Output

Once our master project file has been archived, it's safe to start modifying a duplicate of the image to prepare it for various types of output (Web, inkjet, commercial printing, etc.). Each type of output might have different requirements for size, sharpness and color mode. To make sure we don't change our master project file, we'll duplicate the file (by choosing Image>Duplicate) before making changes that are specific to an output device. It's best to perform sharpening on an image after it has been scaled to the size it will be when printed or displayed on-screen. Choose Image>Image Size and specify the exact dimensions and resolution that are appropriate for your particular output device. Since filters work on only one layer at a time, it's important that you choose Layer>Flatten Image before applying sharpening to the image. After sharpening, you'll need to make sure it's in the proper mode for the type of output you plan on using. In general, images that will be printed on a desktop printer or displayed on the Internet should be kept in RGB mode. Any image that will be printed on a commercial printing press will need to be converted to CMYK mode by choosing Image>Mode>CMYK Color (after inputting the Color Settings provided by the printing house).

9. Save Output Specific Files

Now that we have an image that is scaled and sharpened, it's time to save it for the specific output device we plan to use. If you'll be sending the image out to be printed, then we suggest using the TIFF file format because most programs designed for dealing with photographs can open that format. If, on the other hand, you'll be using the photograph on the Internet or attaching it to an email, then you'll need to choose JPEG. ▥

Color Management

Getting your screen to match your printer is a universal need for most Photoshop users and that's what color management is all about. When you have everything set up properly, your screen will give you an accurate view of your image, your printer will reproduce an accurate print of your image and if both are set up as they should be, your screen will match your printer. Let's take a look at what's necessary to set up a proper color management workflow.

Accurate On-Screen View

For Photoshop to accurately display your images, your operating system needs an accurate description of how your monitor displays color (saved as a Profile). Specifically it needs to know the exact shades of red, green and blue your monitor uses to create images as well as the brightness of your screen. The best way to obtain this information is to use a hardware device known as a *colorimeter*, which costs less than $150. If that's too rich for your blood, you can use the Calibrate button under the Color tab of the Displays system preference in Mac OS X, or the Adobe Gamma control in Windows. Using the built-in software is nowhere near as accurate as using a colorimeter, but it's better than nothing.

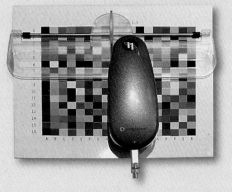

Accurate Desktop Prints

To accurately reproduce your images on your desktop printer, Photoshop needs a description of how your specific printer reproduces color on specific papers. That description comes in the form of an *ICC Color Profile*. You can often find a profile for your printer on the CD that came with the device or on the manufacturer's web site. If you find that the "canned Profiles" that come with your printer don't deliver acceptable results, then you should consider having a custom profile created for your specific printer and paper combination. An inexpensive way of doing that is to visit a web site like chromix.com where you can send in a special print sample and be emailed a printer profile. If you'd rather create your own custom Profiles, then you'll need to look into a device known as a *spectrophotometer* which can set you back around $2000! Once you have a profile for your printer, you'll need to place it in the proper location on your hard drive so Photoshop can use it when printing. In Mac OSX, place the profile in the Library/Colorsync/Profiles folder. In Windows, just right-click on the profile and choose Install Profile from the pop-up menu that appears.

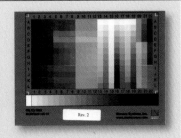

Accurate Scans

You can also use a profile to obtain more accurate scans on a desktop scanner. But since most scans will be color corrected and adjusted after opening them in Photoshop, profiling a scanner is optional. To create a profile for your scanner, look into software programs such as MonacoEZColor. This type of software comes with a sheet of paper that contains sample color swatches that you scan and then run through the software.

Working With Presets

This book relies heavily on presets to save you time and effort. So before you start wowing your neighbors with the techniques found in the more creative chapters, let's take a moment to learn how to load and use those presets. You'll be amazed at how fast and easy techniques will become once you get comfy with these presets and start creating your own!

Copy Presets & Project Files

In the CD at the back of this book you'll find two important folders: **HTW Presets Sampler** and **HTW Project Files**. You're welcome to work with these files directly off the CD, but we think you'll find them essential as you progress through this book. We suggest you copy both folders to your hard drive for easy access. You can double-click on any of the files in the HTW Presets Sampler folder to load a particular preset into Photoshop, but to make things even easier, copy the HTW Presets Sampler folder into the Presets folder that is found within the Photoshop folder on your hard drive. By doing that (and restarting Photoshop), you'll be able to quickly load the presets from Photoshop's palettes.

Exploring the Presets

Once you've copied the HTW Presets folder, the presets will be available from various palettes and dialog boxes in Photoshop. The most obvious places to find them are in the Styles, Actions and Tool Presets palettes. But, as you will learn in later chapters, the presets will also show up in various dialog boxes that offer patterns, gradients and styles. When you load presets using the side menu of a palette A. You'll be asked if you'd like to Replace or Append the current presets B. Appending will add the presets to the existing ones, while Replacing them will clear out the list before adding the new presets. Once you've loaded some presets, you can control how they are previewed by choosing from the side menu of the palette C. The following choices are available:

Large Thumbnail   **Small Thumbnail**   **Large List**   **Small List**

The Preset Manager

The Preset Manager, which is found under the Edit menu, allows you to do the following:
- Drag a preset to change the order in which the presets are sorted.
- Option/Alt-click a preset to delete it.
- Command/Ctrl-click on multiple presets and save them as a new preset file.

For more on working with the Wow Presets, see the "Read Me" file on the top level of this book's companion CD.

Using Profiles in Photoshop

Obtaining Profiles for your monitor, printer and scanner is not enough to get accurate color between devices. Let's take a look at how Profiles can be used to obtain more predictable results when scanning, printing and working in Photoshop.

Color Settings

Your first stop in getting Photoshop to accurately display and print images is the Color Settings dialog box. Choose Photoshop>Color Settings in Mac OS X, or choose Edit>Color Settings in Windows.

The RGB pop-up menu in the Working Spaces area determines the range of colors you'll be able to create when working on an RGB mode image. Choose *sRGB IEC61966-2.1* if you primarily reproduce your images on the Internet or in newspapers. For most other uses, including printing on inkjet printers and commercial printing presses, choose *Adobe RGB (1998)*.

If you'll be printing your images on a commercial printing press, be sure to talk to the company that will be printing your job to make sure the CMYK pop-up menu is set properly for each printing situation.

Next, set all three of the pop-up menus in the Color Management Policies area to Preserve Embedded Profiles, so Photoshop doesn't mess with images that are set up differently than yours.

Finally, turn off the Profile Mismatches checkboxes and turn on the Missing Profiles checkbox so Photoshop only bothers you about color when it really needs to.

Assigning Profiles

Every once in a while you'll open an image and get a Missing Profile warning **A**. When that happens it means that Photoshop does not have enough information to accurately display the image you are attempting to open (in other words, it doesn't have an ICC Color Profile attached to it).

In the Missing Profile dialog box, Photoshop is asking you to guess which profile would be appropriate for the image. Since your image isn't actually open yet, this is a challenge because you can't see the consequences of your actions. We suggest that you not be concerned with the setting specified and just click OK in the Missing Profile dialog box. Then to assign the proper profile and get the image to look its best, choose Image>Mode>Assign Profile **B** which will present you with the same choices that were available in the Missing Profile dialog box, but now that your image is open you can see how the setting will affect it. All you have to do is cycle through the first four choices found under the Profile pop-up menu until you find the one that makes the image look its best.

You can also use the Assign Profile dialog box to assign your scanner profile right after scanning an image.

Converting to Profiles

If you plan on giving an image to someone who might use software that is not designed to use **ICC Color Profiles** to accurately display images (like database programs and most web browsers), then do the following: Choose Image>Mode>Convert to Profile, set the Profile pop-up menu to sRGB IEC61966-2.1 and click OK. Many programs that ignore ICC Color Profiles will display your image as if it was made using sRGB. By converting to sRGB before saving your image, Photoshop will adjust the numbers that make up your image so that it will look appropriate in programs that assume sRGB. Your image won't look any different on-screen in Photoshop, but it will often look better in database programs and web browsers.

Printing with Profiles

To accurately print an image from Photoshop, choose File>Print with Preview, turn on the **Show More Options** checkbox and choose **Color Management** from the pop-up menu. Next, set the Source Space setting to **Document**, choose your printer profile from the **Profile** pop-up menu, set the Intent to **Relative Colorimetric** and turn on the **Use Black Point Compensation** checkbox. Those settings will usually give you the most accurate prints if you have an accurate printer profile. Some people prefer the look they get when the Intent pop-up menu is set to **Perceptual**, so experiment until you find the setting you like best.

When you click the Print button in the Print with Preview dialog box, you'll be presented with a dialog box full of printing options that are specific to your brand of printer. In that dialog box search for any color management options and set them to either No Color Adjustment, None, or Off (the location and name of the setting will depend on the brand of printer you own). That way Photoshop will be in charge of producing accurate color when printing and your printer driver won't accidentally adjust the image after Photoshop already has done the job.

Converting to CMYK

To prepare an image for commercial printing, choose Image>Mode>CMYK Color before you save your image and send it off to be printed. There are many settings involved when converting to CMYK mode. You can find those settings by going back to the Color Settings dialog box we talked about earlier and clicking on the CMYK pop-up menu in the Working Spaces area. If your printing company has supplied settings, then you'll want to choose Custom CMYK from that menu and type in the settings they've specified **A**.

If you'd like to simulate the look of a commercial printing press on your desktop printer, then choose Window>Proof Setup>Working CMYK before printing. Then in the Print with Preview dialog box, set the Source Space to Proof, set the Intent to **Relative Colorimetric** and turn off **Black Point Compensation B**. 🖩

Camera Raw Adjustments

Adjust and optimize the brightness, contrast and color of an image using Camera Raw.

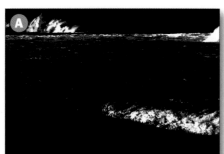

Exposure   +0.90

INSIGHT

Where to Start. When using Camera Raw, we usually start by adjusting either the White Balance or the Exposure/Shadows settings. It's best to begin with the feature that will make the largest improvement to your image. So, just because we start with Exposure in the technique shown on this page, that doesn't mean we'd start that way with every image. A quick glance at your image is usually enough to know where to start.

INSIGHT

Specular Highlights. *Specular highlights* are defined as the bright areas in your image that are caused by direct reflections of light on shiny objects, or when the light source is visible in the image. It's fine for these to be reproduced as solid white.

1. Adjust Exposure

The Exposure slider determines how bright the brightest area of your image will be. If you move the slider too far to the right, you'll end up losing highlight detail by forcing the brightest area of the image to solid white. To see which areas of your image are losing detail, hold the Option/Alt key while moving the Exposure slider. Areas that appear white contain no detail whatsoever (they've become solid white), while areas that appear in color indicate areas that have been ***clipped*** in the individual red, green or blue color channels and are close to becoming pure white in the image.

Start by moving the slider until you see large areas of white **A** and then back off until only small colored areas are visible **B**. Now let go of the Option/Alt key and adjust the Exposure slider until you like the look of the image, knowing that if you move it beyond the stage you were at when you released the Option/Alt key, that you'll lose highlight detail.

2. Adjust Shadows

The Shadows slider determines how dark the darkest areas of your image will be. Just as with the Exposure slider, you can hold Option/Alt when dragging this slider to see exactly which areas are becoming solid black. Areas that show up as color are getting close to losing all detail (being clipped in certain color channels), while areas that appear solid black have lost all detail. Hold the Option/Alt key and move the slider until you see a large area of solid black **A** and then back off until you see only small areas of color **B**. Now release the Option/Alt key and adjust the slider to taste **C** knowing that moving the slider beyond the point you were at when you released Option/Alt will cause detail to be lost in the darkest areas of the image.

3. Adjust Remaining Sliders

After adjusting the overall brightness range of your image, it's time to fine-tune the look of your image by adjusting the Brightness, Contrast and Saturation sliders. There are no cut-and-dried rules for where the next three sliders should be placed; it's a personal preference for how you'd like to manipulate the look of your image. And unlike the last two sliders, Brightness, Contrast and Saturation sliders do not offer any special features to alert you of lost highlight or shadow detail.

The Brightness slider will change the overall brightness of the midtones of your image. Move it until your image is to your liking **A**. Now move on to the Contrast slider. Moving this slider to the right will add some "pop" to your image by increasing its contrast **B**. Before you move on, adjust the Saturation slider to control how colorful your image will be. Most images will benefit from a boost in saturation by moving the slider to the right of center **C**.

CAUTION

Watch the Histogram. When adjusting the Brightness and Contrast sliders, keep on eye on the histogram at the top of the dialog box. If white spikes appear at either end of the histogram, then you're losing highlight detail (spike on right end) or shadow detail (spike on left end). When that's the case, readjust the Exposure or Shadow slider to regain the lost detail.

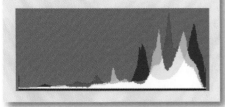

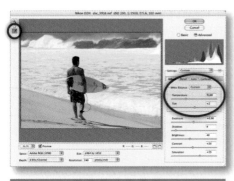

White Balance. The Temperature and Tint sliders allow you to shift the overall color of your image toward warm or cool colors. Moving the sliders to the left of center will make the image appear cooler (toward blue or green), while moving them to the right of center will make the image appear warmer (toward yellow or red).

4. Specify White Balance

The White Balance setting controls the overall color of your image, making it appear cool (blue-green), warm (yellow-red) or neutral (no color bias). There are three ways to adjust the White Balance: using the pop-up menu; moving the Temperature and Tint sliders; or using the Eyedropper that appears in the upper left of the dialog box. All three methods are just different ways of changing the Temperature and Tint sliders. If the image has an area that should obviously not contain any color (white, black or gray areas), then you can choose the Eyedropper tool and click around in that area to have Photoshop calculate the proper Temperature and Tint settings to render that area neutrally. If you don't have such an area, then cycle through the choices that are available from the White Balance pop-up menu until you find the one that delivers the most pleasing result and then fine-tune the adjustment by moving the Temperature and Tint sliders.

Sharpening Prefs. The default setting for Sharpening is 25, not 0, which means that every image will automatically be sharpened. If you'd prefer to wait to sharpen until after you've performed adjustments in Photoshop (but still *preview* sharpening here in Camera Raw), turn on the Advanced setting in the upper right of the Camera Raw dialog box, choose Preferences from the pop-up menu (right-pointing triangle located to the right of the Settings pop-up menu), and choose Preview Images Only from the bottom pop-up menu.

5. Adjust Detail Tab Settings

The sliders found under the Detail tab cause subtle changes, so before continuing double-click on the Zoom tool in the upper right of the dialog box to view your image at 100%. The Sharpness slider will increase the overall sharpness of your image. Jack prefers to use the default setting of 25 as a starting point for most images, while Ben prefers to set it to zero and perform all sharpening at the end of the production workflow. We find that the default setting of 25 for Color Noise Reduction is too high for most images; a setting between 3 and 5 is usually more than enough to soften any colorful noise into the image. Luminance Smoothing should be used sparingly to reduce noise caused by shooting with high ISO settings.

6. Adjust Lens Settings

The settings found under the Lens and Calibrate tabs are only available after choosing the Advanced option in the upper right of the dialog box. The Chromatic Aberration Red/Cyan and Blue/Yellow sliders can help reduce color fringing problems sometimes seen at the edges of images shot with wide angle lens. We sometimes use the Vignetting Amount and Midpoint sliders to darken the edges which help focus the viewer's attention toward the middle of the image.

7. Adjust Calibrate Settings

The settings found under the Calibrate tab allow you to change how Photoshop interprets the colors in your image. These sliders are often used to simulate the look of certain traditional film types. They were designed for advanced users, but that doesn't mean you have to be afraid of them. In this case we experimented with the sliders to see if we could get a more pleasing color in the water. For this image, all it took was to bump up the Blue Saturation setting.

TIP

Dimension in Inches. You can figure out how large your image will be by using the Size and Resolution setting you've specified in the Camera Raw dialog box. Just divide the two numbers you've chosen in the Size pop-up menu by the Resolution setting.
In our example:
2464 ÷ 240 = 10.27" wide
1632 ÷ 240 = 6.8" tall

Space: Adobe RGB (1998)
Depth: 16 Bits/Channel
Size: 2464 by 1632
Resolution: 240 pixels/inch

8. Specify Workflow Settings

In the lower left of the Camera Raw dialog box, set the Space menu to sRGB IEC61966-2.1 only if its primary use is to be displayed on a web page. Choose Adobe RGB (1998) for all other uses. Set the Depth pop-up menu to 16-Bits/Channel if you plan on making significant changes to the tonality of the image (pulling out additional shadow detail using Curves, for example). Finally, set the Resolution to what's required for your output device, and then click OK to open the image in Photoshop.

BEN WILLMORE

File Browsing with Raw Images

Work efficiently with the File Browser and RAW format images.

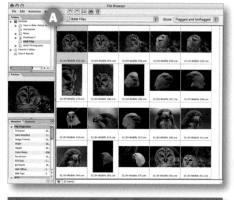

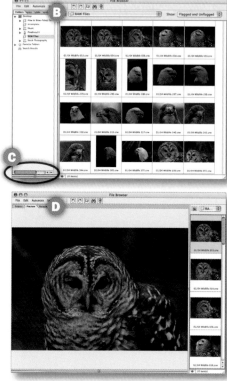

1. Review and Flag Images

After finishing a photo shoot you might have a large number of images, but only a small portion of them might be worth opening immediately in Photoshop. To find those images, choose File>Browse and then navigate to the folder of images using the hierarchal folder view that's available under the Folders tab **A**. Once you're viewing the correct folder, drag the Preview, Metadata and Keywords tabs onto the Folders tab area to place all the sections into one grouping **B** and then drag the two horizontal divider bars to the bottom of your screen **C**.

Now click on the Preview tab and drag the vertical divider bar that shows up between the preview and the thumbnail images to the right so you can only see one column of thumbnails **D**. Next, use the right arrow key on your keyboard to advance through large previews of each image. As you find the ones that have the best tonality and composition and are in sharp focus, type Command/Ctrl-' (apostrophe) to flag those images. Continue doing that until you've made it all the way through the folder.

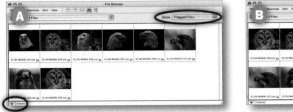

2. Arrange Into Groupings

Next, click on the double arrow icon that is found near the lower left of the File Browser to hide the preview area and choose Flagged Files from the Show pop-up menu in the upper right of the File Browser. That will make it so you are only looking at the thumbnails of the images you flagged **A**. Now drag each image to change their order and sort them into groupings that have similar brightness, contrast and color **B**.

> **TIP**
>
> **Hide the File Browser.** Holding down the Option/Alt key when double-clicking on an image in the File Browser will close the File Browser window and open the image.

3. Open One Image from Each Group

Hold the Command/Ctrl key and click on *the first image from each group* so that you end up with multiple images highlighted. Now, let go of the Command/Ctrl key and double-click on any one of the selected images to open it in the Camera Raw dialog box.

4. Adjust and Update Each Image

Adjust the first image to your liking, then hold the Option/Alt key and click the Update button (what used to be the OK button). Updating an image will attach the Camera Raw settings to it so they will be used the next time the image is opened. Once you've done that to the first image, the next image should open in the Camera Raw dialog box. Repeat this process until you've adjusted and updated each image.

> **TIP**
>
> **Bypass Camera Raw.** Hold Shift when opening a file in the browser to bypass Camera Raw and open the image using the updated settings.

5. Apply Raw Settings to Each Group

Now select the first set of images in the File Browser, Control/right-click on one of the selected images and choose Apply Camera Raw Settings. In the pop-up menu that appears, choose First Selected Image, and then click OK to apply the same settings to the rest of the images in the group. After doing that to each group, you can double-click to open an individual image and fine-tune the updated Camera Raw settings. █

2

PROCESSING & PRESENTING

Saving, Safeguarding &
Selling Yourself

EMBEDDING
INFORMATION &
COPYRIGHT *30*

WATERMARKING,
LABELING &
SIGNING *32*

USING LAYER
STYLES *34*

CREATING
FILL LAYERS *35*

USING PICTURE
PACKAGE *36*

MAKING PDF
SLIDE SHOW
PRESENTATIONS
38

CREATING INSTANT
WEB PHOTO
GALLERIES *40*

USING ACTIONS TO
OPTIMIZE IMAGES
FOR E-MAIL AND
THE WEB *43*

YOU'VE TOILED AWAY for hours preparing your digital feast. You've cooked up enormous quantities; every pixel is seasoned to perfection and you're ready to serve up your lovely creations to your waiting public. What now? For the time being, put aside all thoughts of printing and think electronic. When you think that way, the door of possibilities swings wide open in Photoshop. There are some wonderful tools designed to safeguard, catalog and present your images, and in this chapter we'll bring it all together and make it easy to understand and completely manageable.

You might be thinking, "Why isn't this chapter at the end of the book?" The reason it's here instead of at the end is that during the course of working through the projects, we expect that you'll become a veritable image-producing factory, and many of your images might need the kind of attention that we'll be covering in this chapter. For instance, you might wish to optimize some images for emailing to a friend or coworker, or get them all ready for a web gallery. Or, if you're security-conscious, you might find it useful to know how to embed copyright information, add a customized digital watermark, or simply add your company's name or logo to your images.

To Serve and Protect

Security has become such a buzzword these days, it's not surprising that Adobe has come up with a number of features in Photoshop that will help you safeguard your proprietary images from improper or illegal use by others. Once

you've sent your image out electronically (posted it on a website for instance), some people think it's fair game and wouldn't hesitate to use it for their own purposes. Of course, there are no guaranteed ways to stop this, but you can at least put up a fight.

There are a number of things you can do to foil those who might be ethically challenged. You can add a watermark to identify your image, which will make it easy to view the image, but difficult to reproduce without the mark. In addition, you can embed a digital profile of ownership and copyright information that will stay with the file wherever it might end up. This in itself won't stop anyone from illegally using your images, but if they ever get caught with them, there won't be any question about ownership.

Your Message in a Bottle

The benefits of the File Info dialog box go far beyond just security measures. It is also a wonderful tool for communicating essential information to potential customers and authorized users of your images. For instance, if you were a photographer looking to sell stock photos of river otters, you could use the File

Info dialog box to enter keywords like "otters, wildlife, river, stock photo," and so on. Then when your image is posted on a website, these keywords would be searchable on the Web, therefore leading potential customers to your site.

The Package Deal

Photoshop is a marvel when it comes to automating tasks that used to keep us up late at night while we slaved away over images, preparing them one-at-a-time for their final destination. You can now liberate yourself from much of this painstaking work because Photoshop can look at an entire folder of images, and almost instantly create picture packages, web photo galleries and slide presentations. We'll show you how to use some of Photoshop's most useful automation tools, including a fast way to prepare your images for emailing. And of course we'll be throwing in our own special twists that will make these features more valuable and time-saving than ever.

D01C02LO1-Info-After Cust.psd

Description

Description
AP Categories
Camera Data 1
Camera Data 2
Categories
History
Origin
Advanced

Document Title: Deco SD Convention Center

Author: Jack H. Davis

Description: ©JHDavis, How to Wow Inc.
All rights reserved
For educational use only – this image, or derivative
works, can not be used, published, distributed or

Description Writer:

Keywords: Davis; How to Wow; Wow; Architecture; San Diego;
Convention Center; Sepia; Abstract

⚠ Commas can be used to separate keywords

Copyright Status: Copyrighted

Copyright Notice: ©JHDavis, How to Wow Inc.

Copyright Info URL: www.software-cinema.com/wow

Go To URL...

Powered By
xmp™

Created: 5/11/04
Modified: 5/11/04

Application: Adobe...tosho
Format: appli...on/vnd

Cancel   OK

Embedding Information & Copyright

When moving images electronically, it's essential to maintain copyright, usage information and vital details needed to catalog your images.

TIP

Creating a ©. Use the Type tool to enter a copyright notice (or another custom text label) by typing Option-G (Mac) or Alt-0169 (Win, using the numeric keypad).

○ ○ ○
Actions

☑ ▶ Gradient Map
☑ ▶ assign profile, then close
☑ ▶ example
   ▼ Apply ©/Info

1. Create a New Action
Let's create an action so we can quickly apply copyright information to a group of images. With a file open, choose Window>Actions, click on the New Action icon at the bottom of the Actions palette and name it something like "Apply ©/Info".

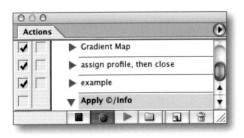

D01C02LO1-Info-After Gen.psd

2. Enter File Info for a Template
Choose File>File Info, enter any image use restrictions in the Description field, enter search terms for the author/creator in the Keywords field (we'll add keywords specific to the image in a moment), set the Copyright Status pop-up menu to Copyrighted (which will cause a copyright symbol (©) to appear in the image's title bar within Photoshop), place a copyright symbol (©) and your name in the Copyright Notice field, and enter your web address in the Copyright Info URL field.

Document Title:

Author: Jack H. Davis

Description: ©JHDavis, How to Wow Inc.
All rights reserved
For educational use only – this image, or derivative
works, can not be used, published, distributed or

Description Writer:

Keywords: Davis; How to Wow; Wow

⚠ Commas can be used to separate keywords

Copyright Status: Copyrighted

Copyright Notice: ©JHDavis, How to Wow Inc.

Copyright Info URL: www.software-cinema.com/wow

3. Save Metadata Template

Once you have your general information entered, choose Save Metadata Template from the upper-right menu of the File Info dialog box. By doing that you can easily apply the file information you just saved to any image by choosing File>File Info and then choosing the template from the same upper-right menu of the File Info dialog box.

4. Create Droplet

Now, click OK to exit the File Info dialog box, then click on the Stop button at the bottom of the Actions palette to complete your action. Then choose File>Automate>Create Droplet, pick the name of the action you just created from the Action pop-up menu, turn on the Suppress Color Profile Warnings checkbox and set the Destination pop-up menu to Save and Close. Finally, click the Choose button, specify a location and click OK.

5. Batch-Process Images

That last step created a small file on your hard drive that is known as a droplet. You can drag any number of files onto the droplet to quickly embed your copyright info. If you'd rather not use a droplet, you can apply the action to multiple files using the File>Automate>Batch command.

6. Process Individual Images

Now you can go back to individual files, choose File>File Info and add information that is specific to each individual file (like Document Title, Description information and Keywords).

Save Metadata Template

Template Name: ©JHDavis

Cancel　　Save

Actions

✔ ▶ assign profile, then close
✔ ▶ example
✔ ▼ Apply ©/Info
✔ ▶ Set File Info of current doc...

Create Droplet

Save Droplet In
Choose...　Pixelhead II:Users:ben:Desktop:Apply ©|Info

Play
Set: Default Actions.atn
Action: Apply ©/Info
☐ Override Action "Open" Commands
☐ Include All Subfolders
☐ Suppress File Open Options Dialogs
☑ Suppress Color Profile Warnings

Destination: Save and Close
Choose...

Document Title: Deco SD Convention Center
Author: Jack H. Davis
Description: ©JHDavis, How to Wow Inc. All rights reserved For educational use only – this image, or derivative works, can not be used, published, distributed or
Description Writer:
Keywords: Davis; How to Wow; Wow; Architecture; San Diego; Convention Center; Sepia; Abstract

⚠ Commas can be used to separate keywords

Copyright Status: Copyrighted
Copyright Notice: ©JHDavis, How to Wow Inc.

Copyright Info URL: www.software–cinema.com/wow

Watermarking, Labeling & Signing

Add a legal, aesthetic or defensive overlay to show ownership, sign, or to restrict the use of your images

1. Enter Type or Paste Art

You have a few options to get the copyright symbol, logos, or text labels into your image. Your first option is to use the Type tool to enter a copyright notice (or another custom text label) by typing Option-G (Mac) or Alt-0169 (Win, using the numeric keypad). Or, you could use the technique shown in Chapter 9, "Combining & Collaging" on page 229 to import a logo from Adobe Illustrator. Your last option is to choose the Custom Shape tool **A**, click on the custom shape preview in the Options bar **B**, choose Symbols from the side menu of the drop-down palette **C** and then choose the Copyright custom shape preset **D**. Then hold Shift and click and drag within your image to create a Shape Layer **E**.

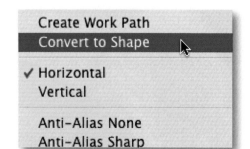

2. Convert Text to a Shape

We're going to end up saving our mark as a Custom Shape tool preset, so if you used the Type tool in the previous step (instead of the Custom Shape tool, or importing a logo from Adobe Illustrator), choose Layer>Type>Convert to Shape so you end up with a Shape layer.

3. Create or Apply Layer Style

Now let's stylize our text or logo. To allow most of the underlying image to show through, change the Fill setting at the top of the Layers palette to 15% and the Opacity to 50%. Next let's embed the color white into our layer style by choosing Color Overlay from the Layer Style pop-up menu at the bottom of the Layers palette, clicking on the color swatch and choosing white. Now click on Drop Shadow on the left side of the dialog box, set the Distance to zero, the Size to 15, the Opacity to 50%, turn on the Layer Knocks Out Drop Shadow checkbox and then click OK.

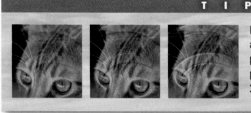

T I P

Preset Styles. Instead of creating a style from scratch, use one of the preset styles in the HTW Styles Sampler. Examples at left are: Wow Halo 21, Wow Halo 23 and Wow Halo 24.

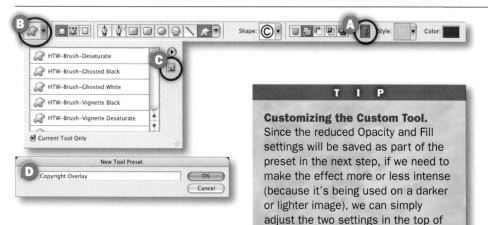

T I P

Customizing the Custom Tool. Since the reduced Opacity and Fill settings will be saved as part of the preset in the next step, if we need to make the effect more or less intense (because it's being used on a darker or lighter image), we can simply adjust the two settings in the top of the Layers palette, without needing to go into the Layer Styles dialog box.

4. Create Tool Preset

If you started by entering text in step 1, then choose Edit>Define Custom Shape before continuing. Now, with the styled Shape layer still active, and the Custom Shape tool active, click on the Link icon in the Options bar **A**, click on the tool icon on the far left of the Options bar **B**, click on the New Tool Preset icon on the right of the drop-down palette **C** and give this tool preset a name **D**. Now, anytime you'd like to mark an image, choose the Custom Shape tool, click on the tool icon in the Options bar, choose the preset you made and then click and drag across your image. 🔲

Using Layer Styles

A Layer Style is a collection of settings that are attached to a layer to create a visual effect (like a drop shadow). These styles can be easily modified, copied and saved as presets. Since they are only settings (or procedures) attached to a layer (instead of being made strictly of pixels), they do not degrade in quality when the image is scaled, rotated or transformed. Combining multiple styles lets you create sophisticated effects.

Creating a Layer Style

To create a Layer Style, either make a choice from the Layer Style pop-up menu at the bottom of the Layers palette or choose Layer>Layer Styles. The ***Opacity*** setting at the top of the Layers palette will affect both the layer contents and any Layer Styles applied to the layer. The ***Fill*** setting on the other hand will keep the edge elements of the Layer Styles at full strength while lowering opacity of the pixels that make up the layer.

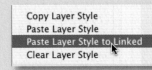

Hiding Layer Styles

Once you have a Layer Style applied to a layer, you can click on the arrow symbol that appears on the right side of that layer to expand or collapse the list of styles applied to the layer. Turning off the eyeball icon next to any of the Layer Styles will temporarily hide the style, while turning off the eyeball next to the word "Effects" will hide all the styles applied to that layer. You can also Control/right-click on the style icon that appears on the right side of a layer and choose Hide All Effects to hide the Layer Styles on all layers.

Copying Layer Styles

With the styles list expanded, drag one of the styles to the horizontal line that appears below any other layer to apply that style to the second layer. Drag the word "Effects" to apply all the styles from one layer to another. If you'd like to apply a style to multiple layers, Control/right-click on the Layer Style icon on the right of a layer that contains a style, choose Copy Layer Style, then after linking multiple layers together, Control/right-click on the Layer Style icon again and choose Paste Layer Style to Linked.

Saving Layer Styles

To use the same Layer Style multiple times do this: With a style-applied layer active, choose Window>Styles, click on the New Style icon at the bottom of the Styles palette and give the style a name. To apply the style, click on another layer and click on the style you'd like to apply within the Styles palette. You can also drag a style from the Styles palette and drop it onto any layer that is visible in the main image window.

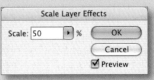

Scaling Layer Styles

Once you have applied a style to a layer, you can adjust the settings that make up the style by double-clicking on any of the styles in the styles list attached to that layer. To modify all the settings at once, try choosing Layer>Layer Style>Scale Effects.

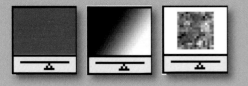

Creating Fill Layers

Fill layers are a special type of layer that is created by defining a series of settings that create the look of a layer. These layers produce results that look identical to filling an area with a solid color, pattern (using Edit>Fill) or using the Gradient tool. The main difference is that they are defined by simple settings (like angle, scale and color), so they can easily be changed, or transformed at any time with no quality loss.

Creating Fill Layers

You can create a Fill layer by choosing one of the top three options that are available in the Adjustment Layer pop-up menu at the bottom of the Layers palette, or by choosing Layer>New Fill Layer.

Solid Color Layers

A Solid Color layer is the simplest of the three Fill layer types. When you create one, you will be presented with a color picker that determines the color that will fill the new layer.

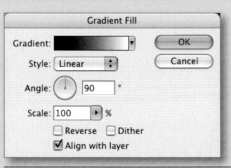

Gradient Fill Layers

A Gradient Fill layer offers many of the same controls that are available with the standard Gradient tool. But unlike the Gradient tool, the length of the transition from the beginning and ending color of the gradient is controlled with the Scale setting and the position of the gradient can be changed by dragging within the main image window. As you'll see below, a Layer Mask or Vector Mask can limit where a Fill layer appears. When that's the case, the Align with Layer checkbox will cause the start- and end-points of the gradient to be controlled by the boundaries of the visible layer as defined by the mask.

Pattern Fill Layers

A Pattern Fill layer is defined by a simple repeating pattern that is used to fill the entire layer. The Link with Layer checkbox will cause the pattern to be repositioned each time you use the Move tool with the Pattern Layer active. You also click and drag within the main image window to reposition the gradient when the Pattern Fill dialog box is open.

Masking Fill Layers

When you create a Fill layer, it will automatically have a Layer Mask attached to it. If a selection is active when creating the layer, then the mask will automatically be created in a way so as to limit the fill so it only shows up within the selected area. You can also use the Shape tools to mask a layer by first choosing Layer>Add Vector Mask>Reveal All.

Modifying Fill Content

You can modify the settings that make up a Fill layer by double-clicking on the Fill Thumbnail icon on the left side of the layer to access the Color, Gradient or Fill dialog box.

Using Picture Package

Transform one or more images into a collection of standard-sized prints conveniently arranged on a single page.

1. Choose Page Size & Layout

Start by choosing File>Automate> Picture Package and setting the Page Size and Layout pop-up menus to what you desire. Turn on the Flatten All Layers checkbox if you won't be editing the resulting image in Photoshop. Set the Mode pop-up menu to CMYK if you'll be printing your pages of photos on a commercial printing press; otherwise use RGB. Set the Resolution to what's appropriate for your images; if you're not sure, use these guidelines:

- If your images will include text or a copyright (see step 4), use a resolution of at least 300PPI.

- If your image doesn't contain text, set the resolution as low as 225PPI, which will make the resulting file about half the size of a 300PPI image.

Document

Page Size:	8.0 x 10.0 in
Layout:	(2)4x5 (2)2.5x3.5 (4)2x...
Resolution:	225 pixels/inch
Mode:	RGB Color

☑ Flatten All Layers

2. Edit Layout if Necessary

If the Page Size and Layout pop-up menus don't offer the specific settings you desire, then click the Edit Layout button in the lower right of the dialog box and specify a custom page size and layout to use. To add images to the layout, click the Add Zone button, then adjust its size with the Width and Height fields. Then drag within the preview area to reposition the image (we used a standard layout).

File
Folder
✓ Frontmost Document
Selected Images from File Browser

3. Load Images

Click on the Use pop-up menu and choose Frontmost Document if you'd like to use the active document, choose File if you'd like to use a specific file on your hard drive, or choose Folder if you'd like a separate document made for each image located in a folder. You don't have to use a single image for the entire layout; just click on any of the images to load a replacement. If you're using a folder, then any images that were manually replaced will be consistent in all layouts and the folder-derived images will be different for each page.

4. Add Copyright Watermark

You can overlay text onto your images to add a copyright notice or your web address by changing the setting found in the Label area. Here we've added some white text at 50% Opacity to credit the stock photo company this image is from. You can also include the file name, copyright, description, credit or title information that is found in the File Info dialog box which we mentioned at the beginning of this chapter.

Finally click on the OK button to create your picture package. If you used a folder of images to create your picture package, then you'll get one document for each image in the folder. 🎞

Making PDF Slide Show Presentations

Save a collection of images into a PDF file for easy distribution and presentation.

INSIGHT

Size Your Images. The size and resolution of the images you use will greatly influence the file size of your presentation and the quality of any images that are printed. So be sure to scale down images that are only to be viewed on-screen.

1. Sort Images in the File Browser

We'll start by selecting and sorting the images (the samples here are from a series of infrared photographs) to be used for our slide show presentation. Choose File>Browse, then navigate to the folder of images you plan to use. If you don't want to use all the images in the folder you're browsing, then hold Command/Ctrl-click on the images you want. With those images selected, click the Flag icon at the top of dialog box and then choose Flagged Files from the Show pop-up menu so you are only viewing the files that you selected. Now drag each image within the browser window to define the sorting order you'd like to use for your slide show. To create the slide show, type Command/Ctrl-A to select all the images and then choose PDF Presentation from the Automate menu in the File Browser.

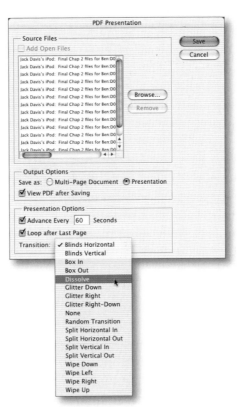

2. Choose Multi-Page or Presentation

There are two types of PDF presentations to choose from—Multi-Page Document, and Presentation. Since Mutli-Page PDFs are navigated manually in the Adobe Reader application, there are essentially no options when creating one in Photoshop. A PDF Presentation on the other hand offers a multitude of options to customize the result:

- The Advance Every setting determines how briefly each image will appear before the slide show advances.

- The Loop After Last Page option will cause your slide show to run continuously until the viewer manually pauses it or closes the file.

- The Transition pop-up menu controls the effect to be used when advancing each slide (we suggest you use simple ones for professional presentations and reserve the funky ones for your child's birthday party). These transitions will only be visible if the viewer is using Adobe Reader 6.0 or later.

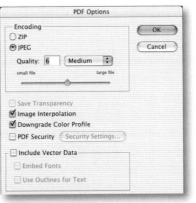

3. Choose PDF Options

Click the Save button in the PDF Presentation dialog box and you'll be prompted for saving options. Choose ZIP if you'll be printing the PDF and want to maintain the highest quality, or choose JPEG with a medium quality setting if you'll be viewing it on-screen. Turn on Downgrade Color Profile if your viewer might be using older versions of Acrobat Reader (Adobe Reader's former name).

4. View Presentation

Now that your PDF presentation is complete, you can open the file in the free Adobe Reader application and click through a multi-page presentation (using the on-screen arrow buttons), or view a slide show (mouse-click or arrow keys).

Creating Instant Web Photo Galleries

Quickly transform a folder full of images into an interactive Web photo gallery.

1. Sort & Rename in File Browser

Start by selecting and sorting your images just as we did in the previous project. Since the images are sorted into the order they will appear in the web gallery, you can choose Batch Rename from the Automate menu of the File Browser. This allows you to number the images using the serial number feature and to specify a consistent name, which is better than using the generic names (like DCS_256.jpg) that your digital camera creates.

2. Choose Template Style

Now choose Web Photo Gallery from the Automate menu in the File Browser, set the Use pop-up menu to **Selected Images from File Browser**, click the Destination button and choose where to save the gallery on your hard drive. Now choose a preset template at the top of the dialog box and enter an email address if "Feedback" is in its name.

3. Choose Banner Settings

Now change the Options pop-up menu to Banner and enter the photographer's name, the current date, and a name for the web photo gallery you're creating.

T I P

Tell a Story. If you've spent the time to enter titles and descriptions for each image in the File Info dialog box (see the beginning of this chapter), then why not use them as captions for your images and thus "tell a little story" as the pictures progress. You can do that by turning on the various checkboxes in the Titles Use area at the bottom of the dialog box.

4. Choose Large Image Settings

Choose Large Images from the Options pop-up menu. Turn on the Resize Images checkbox and enter a maximum dimension for your images (larger images will cause your site to load slower). The template you've chosen will determine the maximum image size you can use (800 for the Horizontal templates). Set the JPEG Quality setting to Medium unless you have a compelling reason for higher-quality images or faster load times.

5. Choose Thumbnails Settings

Switch to Thumbnails in the Options pop-up menu and specify how small the thumbnail images should be. Keep in mind that the smaller the thumbnails, the more of them will fit on-screen without having to scroll, but the harder it will be to see detail.

6. Choose Custom Colors

Choosing Custom Colors from the Options pop-up menu allows you to customize the colors used in your site to suit your personal taste.

7. Choose Security Settings

The Security settings allow you to overlay various text on top of each image. By setting the color to white or black and lowering the Opacity to 50%, you can add a subtle copyright warning to all your images. That's a nice safety measure just in case someone attempts to download an image from your gallery since the copyright is visually embedded into the image.

T I P

A Quick Way to Batch Process. The Web Photo Gallery feature is a great tool for batch-processing images. You can use the Security option to "watermark" or label each image (with control over rotation, positioning and the opacity of the text). After creating a gallery, just throw away everything in the resulting folder except for the Images folder and you'll end up with a series of scaled, watermarked and JPEG compressed images! Bingo!

8. Save Web Site

When you click the OK button in the upper-right of the Web Photo Gallery dialog box, Photoshop will start to create your web gallery. When it's complete. you'll end up with a folder **A** that includes a file called "index.htm", which is the home page for your gallery and can be opened in any web browser. Along with that will be three folders: the Pages folder contains an HTML file for each page of the site, the Thumbnails folder contains the small JPEG images that are used for navigation and the Images folder contains the larger-sized JPEG images.

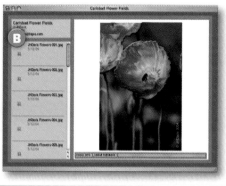

9. Relocating Files

You can move the location of the main folder on your hard drive as long as you keep its contents unaltered and together as a group. The files are linked by their filenames, so changing the name of a file or folder **A** will cause the gallery to no longer function properly **B**.

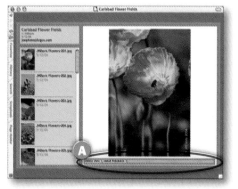

10. Gather Feedback

If you used one of the three templates that includes the word "Feedback" in its name, then you'll have Image Info and Image Feedback tabs available at the bottom of each large image **A**. Clicking on the Image Feedback Tab **B** will allow the viewer to enter comments about each image that will be received by the email address you specified when you created the web photo gallery. But since each image has its own feedback panel, it's not possible to receive a single email with comments about all the images; instead you'll get one email for each image that is commented on. ▥

Using Actions to Optimize Images for Email and the Web

We have provided some special actions that are designed for quickly preparing your images to be sent via email or displayed on the Internet. They can be used to almost instantly scale an image to the proper size and save it in a web-friendly format.

Image Interpolation: Bicubic Sharper

Setting Preferences

Most images need to be scaled down before being saved for use on the Internet. To obtain sharp, high-quality images when scaling (through an action or otherwise), choose Preferences>General and set the Image Interpolation pop-up menu to Bicubic Sharper. That setting will typically allow you to scale down an image without having to apply any sharpening afterward.

Loading & Using Actions

Actions
- Wow–JPEG duplicate – 800px max
- Wow–JPEG duplicate – 700px max
- Wow–JPEG duplicate – 600px max
- Wow–JPEG duplicate – 500px max
- Wow–JPEG duplicate – 400px max
- Wow–JPEG duplicate – 300px max

To access the actions used to prepare images for the Internet, choose Window>Actions, click on the side menu and choose HTW Actions Sampler (assuming you've copied the actions to your hard drive as discussed on page 19). Once the actions are loaded, scroll down the list of actions until you come to the section labeled Wow-Bonus Actions. That's where you'll find the Wow-JPEG Duplicate Actions that we'll be using on this page. Each action is designed to scale your image to a different predefined maximum size and save it in the JPEG file format. Just click on the action you'd like to use and then click the Play button at the bottom of the Actions palette.

Editing the Actions

Actions
- ▼ Wow–JPEG duplicate – 800px max
  - Duplicate first document
- **A** ▶ Stop
  - ▶ Stop
  - ▶ Stop
  - ▶ Flatten Image
- **B** ▶ Fit Image

The actions include a few safeguards to ensure that you've set your preferences properly. If you've chosen Bicubic Sharper as we mentioned above, then you can click on the arrow next to each action and turn off the Toggle Dialog icon **A** for the steps named "Stop" to suppress those warning dialog boxes. If you'd like to modify the actions so that they create specific sized images, click on the arrow next to the action name to expand the action and then double-click on the step called Fit Image **B** and enter a new setting.

Batch-Processing Images

TIP

Saving a Copy. The actions mentioned on this page use the Image>Duplicate command, which automatically adds the word "Copy" to the end of the filename. That's a quick way to differentiate between JPEGs that are originally from the camera and those that have been scaled for the Web.

To modify dozens of images using the actions mentioned on this page, use the choices available in the File>Automate menu. If this will be a one-time operation, then choose File>Automate>Batch, choose the proper action from the top of the dialog box, turn on the Suppress Color Profile Warnings checkbox and then click OK. If on the other hand, you plan to apply these actions on a regular basis, then choose File>Automate>Create Droplet, click the Choose button to specify a name and location for the droplet, choose the desired action, turn on the Suppress Color Profile Warnings checkbox and then click OK. Finally drag any number of images onto the resulting droplet to apply the action. 🖳

3

ADJUSTING & OPTIMIZING

Balancing the Ingredients and Sweetening to Taste

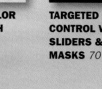

HAVE YOU EVER WATCHED one of those behind-the-scenes documentaries that shows you a day-in-the-life of a starlet getting ready to attend her first awards show? It's amazing the amount of preparations these actresses go through before they even think about applying their makeup or stepping into their couture designer dresses and made-to-torture stiletto heels. There are mud baths and seaweed facials, pedicures and manicures, facial-hair plucking and all sorts of other strange and exotic treatments that we'd rather not know about. The point we're trying to make is that these women, who end up looking so incredible by the time they step onto the red carpet, go to a lot of effort to get their "base layer" in tip-top condition before they start piling on the paint, gowns and other adornments.

Getting your photos ready for enhancement is not much different. Before you even *think* about embellishing, you want your original image to be at its best. You wouldn't want to spend hours putting together a gorgeous collage using images that are grainy or blurry or have unsightly color casts, would you?

Of course not! That's why, before you go charging off to the juicy chapters, you're going to take the time to work through *this* one. At the end of it, you should have the skills necessary to whip all your photos into shape, whether they need just a little tweaking or major surgery.

Going Straight

Before you tamper with even one pixel in your image, you want to make sure that your photograph is sitting straight and pretty. You might need to fix a crooked horizon, change the perspective of a building, or simply crop your image. We'll walk you through the tools that will do all of these things quickly and easily. And for those of you who cringe when you think about scanning all those old family photos in shoe boxes under the bed, you'll love Photoshop CS's Crop and Straighten Photos command.

The Surgeon's Tools

You can't do the work of a digital surgeon without knowing how to use your instruments. We'll show you how to get the most out of some of Photoshop's most essential selection tools, and you'll

learn some surprising new twists to the old way of doing things. Pay close attention to this section, because knowing how to make a good selection is key to your success in Photoshop.

Lifting the Veil

You might be surprised to see what's hiding beneath the façade of a seemingly bad or mediocre photo. Once you've given it a chance to show itself, you might have a real gem on your hands. To help you find the diamond in the rough, we'll give you the mini-grand tour of adjustments: color correction, tonal adjustments, fixing contrast and color balance.

We'll also show you a clever way to compensate for changing lighting conditions by taking two opposing exposures with your camera, and later combining them in Photoshop.

To polish it all off we'll show you our noise taming technique—an incredibly quick way to reduce the appearance of noise and specks in your photos, and how to professionally sharpen them so that they will pop right off the page.

Cropping, Straightening & Adjusting Perspective

Before you start exploring the color and tonal adjustment techniques in this chapter, let's make sure we're starting with a straight, true original image. In this section are three techniques for straightening and correcting perspective.

Perspective Crop

The Perspective Crop feature in the Crop tool can be a lifesaver whenever you have a photo of a rectangular object that was photographed off center. Photographing off center will cause an image to be in perspective. Sometimes that's done simply because the photographer is going for an interesting angle, but it can also happen when the lens being used isn't wide enough to cover the entire object, or because it's a piece of art framed behind glass where a straight-on shot using a flash would produce tremendous glare (as would have been the case with this shot of an antique Hawaiian poster).

To correct an off-square object, start by choosing the Crop tool and clicking the Clear button in the Options bar at the top of your screen **A** to make sure you don't scale or constrain the image. Next, click and drag across the entire image to create a cropping rectangle, release the mouse button and then turn on the Perspective checkbox in the Options bar at the top of your screen **B** (there are two states to the Crop tool's settings depending on if a cropping rectangle is active or not). Now, drag each corner handle on the cropping rectangle and position them so they match the four corners of the rectangular object **C**. Then press Enter to crop and straighten the image.

> **TIP**
>
> **Straighten Only.** If you'd rather not crop out the surrounding image but you still want to fix the perspective, first get the corners of the cropping rectangle to align with the object. Next, drag the **side** handles away from the object until the entire image is within the cropping rectangle. The angles of the sides will still match the angle of the rectangular object, and when you press Return/Enter to crop the image, it will be straightened.

> **TIP**
>
> **No Snap.** If you need to position one of the corner handles of the cropping rectangle near the edge of your image, it may snap to the edge of the document. To temporarily turn off snapping, hold the Control key while you drag one of the corner handles.

Crop And Straighten Photos

If you find it tedious to scan lots of photos and then have to crop and straighten each and every one of them, you'll be happy to learn about a little gem buried under the File menu. Choosing File>Automate>Crop And Straighten Photos will automatically rotate, crop and copy/paste a bunch of images that were scanned together. There are no options for this feature; just choose the menu and Photoshop will do the rest. To make this feature work its best, keep the following in mind:

- Make sure none of the images touch the edge of the scanner glass.

- Make sure none of the images overlap or touch each other.

- The cleaner you keep the scanner's glass and lid, the better Photoshop will be able to separate the images from the white background.

Keystone Correction

Keystoning is a common problem when shooting tall buildings. Since the top of the building is farther away from the camera than the bottom, the top of the building appears smaller. The traditional method for avoiding keystoning is to use a camera that allows you to tilt and shift the lens separately from the film, leaving them both parallel to the building. Since those cameras and lens are expensive and we have Photoshop at our command, let's explore how to digitally correct keystoning.

Start by typing Command/Ctrl-J to place a copy of the original image onto a new layer. Next, choose View>Show>Grid to make the default grid visible, then, if necessary, modify the grid settings by choosing Preferences>Guides, Grid & Slices from the Photoshop menu (Mac), or Edit menu (Win). Now type F to enter Full Screen mode, and then type Com-

mand/Ctrl-T to begin transforming the image. Hold the Command/Ctrl key and drag the upper left and right handles until any vertical lines in the image line up with the grid lines **A**. Then to correct for any foreshortening in the image, drag the top middle handle straight up until any square objects are square **B**. ⌨

Mastering Selections: Lasso Tool

Many people dread the Lasso tool because we tend to fall back on it when an automated selection process doesn't work. Using the Lasso by itself is often a painstaking and time-consuming process, requiring you to manually trace around the edges of an object to isolate it from its background. But, after learning our nifty Lasso tricks, you'll begin to see this tool in an entirely new light.

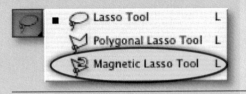

Start with the Magnetic Lasso Tool

You might not be aware that there are actually three different Lasso tools: the Lasso tool, the Polygonal Lasso tool and the Magnetic Lasso tool. When using the Magnetic Lasso tool, you have at your disposal the capabilities of all three Lasso tools.

Option/Alt Gives You the Other Tools

When using the Magnetic Lasso tool, hold the Option/Alt key while the mouse button is pressed to access the normal Lasso and Polygonal Lasso tools. When Option/Alt is held, *dragging* will produce a free form shape just like the normal Lasso tool; clicking *point to point* (without dragging) will produce straight line segments like the Polygonal Lasso tool.

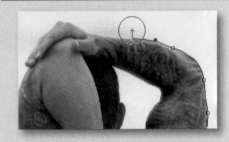

Drag to Auto-Cling to Objects

The Magnetic Lasso tool makes selecting an object easy. Just press the Caps Lock key to transform your cursor into a circle with crosshair, then place the crosshair on the edge of the object you'd like to select, click the mouse button once to start (no need to keep the button held down) and "float" your cursor around the object. The Magnetic Lasso will constantly search within its circular cursor trying to find an edge to cling to (it clings to the edge that is closest to the crosshair), so you just need to keep the edge within the circle.

Width: 10 px

Width Determines Cling Zone

The Width setting in the Options bar determines the size of the circle and therefore the cling zone. You can change the Width setting *while* dragging around the edge of an object by pressing the square bracket keys (][). If you have a well-defined edge you can use a higher width setting and move faster; for a less distinct edge, use a smaller "brush" and carefully follow the contours.

Edge Contrast: 10%

Edge Contrast Determines What's An Edge

The Edge Contrast setting determines how much contrast there must be between subject and background in order for it to be considered a clingable edge. The higher the setting, the more contrast is needed to get the tool to cling to an object.

Other Magnetic Lasso Tricks

Double-click to finish a selection, or press Esc to abort the selection. Click to manually add points and press Delete to remove points which enables you to back up. ⌨

Mastering Selections: Quick Mask Mode

Quick Mask mode liberates you from the crude marching ants that represent typical selections and replaces them with what they really are—grayscale images that isolate an area with soft or hard edges. If you've never experienced Quick Mask mode, you're in for a treat. Just think—you'll no longer have to speculate about those mysterious feathered edges (where do they really start and end?).

Q is for Quick Mask

The marching ants that indicate a normal selection are not always useful when editing a selection. Their wiggly edges can be distracting, they don't show you exactly which areas of the selection are feathered (soft edged), and it's just too easy to accidentally lose the selection by clicking in the wrong place. *When you have an active selection* and you'd like to get a more accurate view, type Q to enter Quick Mask mode.

Quick Mask Is a Quick Channel

Typing Q will transform your selection into a grayscale image that will temporarily be stored at the bottom of the Channels palette. It will also overlay the black areas of that channel onto your image as a semitransparent red overlay, causing selected areas to appear normal and nonselected areas (also known as masked areas) to appear red. That's ideal since feathered areas of a selection will appear as a soft transition from red to clear. Once you're done viewing and editing your selection in Quick Mask mode, type Q again to transform the selection back into the marching ants you're accustomed to.

Paint to Change Selection

In Quick Mask mode, you don't need to use selection tools (Lasso, etc.) to modify a selection. Instead, you can use any feature that will produce black, white or a shade of gray! Just paint with black to add to the red overlay and mask more of the image, or paint with white to expand the selected area (soft brushes create feathered edges).

Filters Replace Selection Commands

If you're used to visiting the Select menu to modify a selection using choices such as Feather, Expand and Contract, you'll be glad to know that you can get the same results by applying filters while in Quick Mask mode. The advantage of using filters is that unlike the Select commands, the filters offer a visual preview which doesn't force you to think numerically. Replace the commands found in the Select menu with the following filters:

- Feather = Filter>Blur>Gaussian Blur
- Contract = Filter>Other>Minimum
- Expand = Filter>Other>Maximum
- Smooth = Filter>Noise>Median
- Border = Filter>Stylize>Glowing Edges ▥

Mastering Selections: Background Eraser

The Background Eraser is not officially a selection tool, but it can be used to isolate an object from its background and if you know a few tricks you can transform it into a precision selection tool. It is especially good for images that contain crisp or soft-edged objects that contrast with their surroundings. It takes a bit of effort to master the Background Eraser tool, but your investment of time will be well worth it.

The Crosshair Is the Key

The Background Eraser deletes the color that appears under the crosshair from within the circular cursor. Use it to trace objects while keeping the crosshair on the colors that you want to be deleted—never let the crosshair touch the object you want to keep.

Tolerance Controls Range

The Tolerance setting in the Options bar determines how much Photoshop will stray from the color that appears under the crosshair. Low settings will limit the range of colors deleted, while higher settings will cause Photoshop to delete colors that are much brighter or darker than what's under the crosshair.

Protect Foreground

If the Background Eraser deletes too wide a range of colors (even after adjusting the Tolerance setting), then Option/Alt-click **on the color that you want to prevent it from deleting** (which will become the foreground color), and turn on the Protect Foreground checkbox.

Sampling

The Sampling pop-up menu sets how Photoshop will determine the color which is to be erased. Our recommendation is to use the **Once** setting, because for each stroke, it resamples the color under the crosshair, allowing for constant fine-tuning of the erasure.

Set Your Limits

Choosing Discontiguous from the Limits pop-up menu will allow the Background Eraser to delete a color from inside the entire circular cursor, even if it has to jump across an area that should be kept (like deleting the center of an "O").

Use a Contrasting Background to Reveal Problem Areas

The checkerboard that appears in areas that you've deleted can hide many defects in your image. Placing a layer full of a contrasting color under the extracted layer will often reveal problem areas.

Convert to a Selection

If you work on a duplicate layer, you can convert the resulting hole into a selection by Command/Ctrl-clicking on the name of the extracted layer and then dragging the duplicate layer to the trash. ▥

Mastering Selections: Color Range

The Color Range dialog box is useful when you need to isolate a particular color in an image. Selections that are created using Color Range are not usually great for isolating an object in such a way that you can copy and paste it into another document. That's because it usually delivers many partially selected areas that are more useful when performing color or tonal adjustments to the image.

Click to Define a Color

When you choose Select>Color Range, you'll be presented with a grayscale image that represents the selection you have created thus far (white indicates selected areas and black indicates nonselected areas). Since you haven't told it what colors you want to select yet, the preview won't be displaying anything useful. Click within your document to define the general color you'd like to select and get an updated preview.

Expand and Contract Selection with Eyedroppers

Click the Plus Eyedropper tool and then click on additional areas of your image to expand the range of colors that will be selected. If you accidentally click on a color you don't want selected, then click on it with the Minus Eyedropper tool to remove it from the selection.

Adjust Fuzziness to Control Range

The Fuzziness slider determines how far Photoshop will stray from the colors you've clicked on. We suggest that you start with the Fuzziness slider all the way to the left and try to define the color as much as possible using the Eyedropper tools. Then, once you can no longer improve the selection preview with the eyedroppers, move the Fuzziness slider to the right until you start to see areas that you don't want selected showing up, and then back off until you find the highest setting that will deliver what you want without extending into the surrounding image.

Preview Selection

For a larger preview choose one of the options available in the Selection Preview pop-up menu. That will enable you to see the selection preview overlaid on the main image.

Refine Color Range Results

Once Color Range delivers a selection, you are free to use features such as Quick Mask mode and/or a saved Alpha Channel to refine the results. ▦

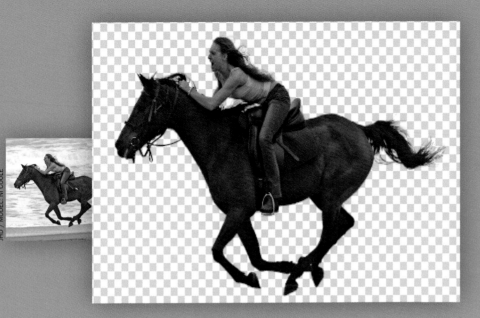

JHD / MODEL: NI COOLE

Extracting Complex Objects

Use Extract to quickly isolate complex objects from their backgrounds.

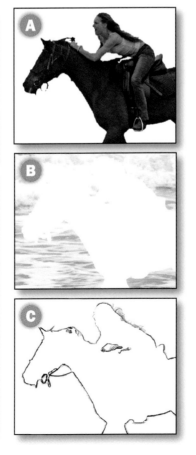

1. Evaluate the Image

To understand how the Filter>Extract command works to separate an object from its background, it helps to imagine that your image is divided into three regions: areas you are absolutely sure you'd like to *keep* **A**, areas you're sure you'd like to *trash* **B**, and the *transition* between those last two areas **C**. The *keep* region will be defined with a blue overlay (known as the fill); the *transition* region will be defined with a green overlay (known as highlighting); the *trash* region will not be covered with any color. The key to using Extract is to define these three areas accurately:

- The *keep* region shouldn't contain a single speck of the background.
- The *trash* region shouldn't contain a single speck of the subject.
- The *transition* region should overlap both the subject and background and include any soft-edged transitions or partially transparent areas since they contain a combination of subject and background.

2. Highlight Transition

Define the transition region by using the Edge Highlighter tool and tracing around the edge of the object you'd like to keep. For soft-edged or partially transparent areas, choose a brush large enough to cover the entire transition **A**. Use a very thin highlight in areas that have crisp edges (or turn on the Smart Highlighting checkbox so Photoshop will search for a crisp edge within your brush area and automatically apply minimal highlighting) **B**.

INSIGHT

Unbroken Highlight. The green highlighting is the only thing that prevents the blue fill from covering the entire image. The highlighting must be a continuous unbroken line; otherwise the fill will seep through any breaks in the highlighting and spill onto the background of the image.

3. Fill Keep Region

Once you've traced around the entire subject and created a continuous, unbroken outline, Photoshop doesn't know which side of the outline you'd like to keep. To define the **keep** region, choose the Fill tool and click within the subject of the image. If that causes the fill color to cover your entire image, then Command/Ctrl-Z to undo, inspect the highlighting and patch any holes.

4. Preview Extraction

Click the Preview button to see the results of your efforts. The checkerboard pattern that appears behind your image **A** represents a transparent (or empty) area, but makes it difficult to see the bits you might have missed. To see how your image will look on a different background, choose Other from the Display pop-up menu and choose a color that contrasts with the image **B**.

5. Fix Problem Areas

Next, double-click on the Zoom tool to view the image at 100% magnification, then choose the Hand tool and drag around your image looking for problem areas. Choose the Cleanup Tool and paint over any remnants of the background that are still visible, or hold Option/Alt and paint over any translucent areas that should be opaque.

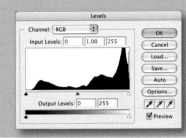

Understanding Levels

The Levels dialog box is one of the most versatile inventions in Photoshop's history. With it you can adjust your images to optimize contrast and brightness, transform scanned images into effective masks and perform quick and easy color correction. But unlike Brightness & Contrast, Levels requires a bit more knowledge to master. Below is a jump start that should get you off on the right foot with Levels.

The Gradient Is Your Guide

The key to understanding how Levels works is to know the relationship between the five sliders and the gradient at the bottom of the dialog box. That gradient represents all the brightness levels that could possibly be in your image.

The Histogram Shows What You Have

The bar chart in Levels (also known as the histogram) indicates which brightness levels are present in your image. Just look directly below each bar to see which brightness level it represents. The height of the bars indicates how prevalent each shade is compared to the others in the image. A gap in the histogram (no bar) indicates that the shade directly below the gap is nowhere to be found in the image.

Black Point Slider

The **upper left** slider in Levels is known as the Black Point slider because it forces areas to black. Specifically, it forces the shade that appears directly below it and all shades darker than that to solid black.

White Point Slider

The **upper right** slider in Levels is known as the White Point slider because it forces areas to white. Specifically, it forces the shade that appears directly below it and all shades brighter than that to solid white.

Midpoint Slider

The **middle** slider controls the overall brightness of the image by brightening or darkening all the shades between black and white, without changing the extremes (black/white). In reality, it changes the shade that appears directly below it to a brightness of 50%.

Black Level Slider

The **lower left** slider is called the Black Level slider because it controls how dark black will become. Moving the slider forces black areas to the shade the slider points at.

White Level Slider

The **lower right** slider is called the White Level slider because it controls how bright white will become. Moving the slider forces white areas to the shade the slider points at. The bottom sliders **lower** contrast in your image, while the top sliders **increase** contrast.

Understanding Curves

Curves is one of the most powerful yet misunderstood features in Photoshop. Unlike other adjustments that limit you to choosing between adjusting the Highlights, Midtones and Shadows of your image, Curves takes it to another level by allowing you to target and adjust specific brightness levels. That one feature makes Curves the preferred choice of professionals who want ultimate control over their images.

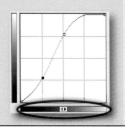

Bottom Gradient Is Where You're Starting

As with Levels, the gradient at the bottom of the Curves dialog box represents all the brightness levels you could possibly have in your image. The "curve" above (which starts out as a straight diagonal line) indicates how much light or ink would be needed to create the shades that appear in the gradient. Click on the dual arrow symbol in the middle of the gradient to switch between visualizing the graph as values of light and as ink density.

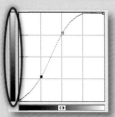

Side Gradient Is Where You're Headed

The gradient on the left side indicates how bright or dark an area will become if the curve is moved to a particular height. If white appears at the top of the gradient, then moving part of the curve to the top will force an area to solid white by adding as much light as possible to that area. If black appears at the top, then moving the curve to the top will force an area to solid black by adding as much ink as possible to the area.

Height Determines Brightness

The height of the curve at any particular point determines how bright the shade directly below that area will become. With light, moving the curve above its original position will brighten, and moving it down will darken. When thinking about ink, it's the opposite.

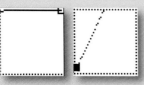

Angle Determines Contrast

The angle of the curve determines what kind of a contrast change will be applied to the image. Making the curve steeper than the original will increase contrast, while making it flatter will decrease contrast.

Working with Points

You can control the shape of the curve by adding and repositioning points. To add a point, click anywhere along the curve and then drag the point (or use the arrow keys) to the desired location. The arrow keys will move the active (solid black) point leaving any inactive points (hollow squares) untouched. Command/Ctrl-clicking within an image will cause Photoshop to add a point directly above the brightness level you clicked on, effectively targeting your adjusting to that brightness level. To remove a point, either Command/Ctrl-click on it, or simply drag it off the grid area. ▥

JHD / MODEL: JENNA

Dodging & Burning with Layers

Try these fast and flexible methods for pulling out detail, accentuating shapes and toning down distractions.

1. Create Dodge & Burn Layer

Photoshop's Dodge and Burn tools don't deliver the quality, flexibility and speed that are the How to Wow mantras. They force you to think about your image as being made out of isolated highlights, midtones **or** shadows and are nowhere near as forgiving or flexible as the technique presented here.

To achieve the ultimate in versatility, we'll place our dodging and burning on a separate layer above the background image. That way we will never damage the original. Start by Option/Alt-clicking on the New Layer icon at the bottom of the Layers palette, set the Mode pop-up menu to Overlay, turn on the **Fill with Overlay-neutral color (50% gray)** checkbox, name it "Dodge & Burn" and then click OK.

2. Dodge with White

To get ready to brighten areas of the image (also known as dodging), type D to reset the Foreground/Background colors to Black/White, type X to exchange the Foreground/Background colors to paint with white, set the Brush tool Opacity to between 5 and 15% and choose a large, soft-edged brush. Paint over any areas you'd like to brighten. In this case, we painted over her shoulder, cheeks and eyes to pull out detail. Since we're using such a low opacity setting, you might need to paint over areas more than once to get a noticeable change.

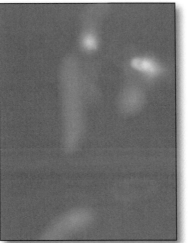

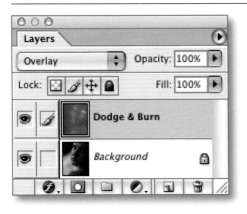

3. Burn with Black

Now let's start to darken areas of the image (also known as burning). If you've just finished dodging your image, then type X to exchange the Foreground/Background colors so that you'll end up painting with black. Now paint over the edge of her jaw to accentuate the shape of her chin and jaw line. Next, paint over any bright areas that you find to be distracting (like the bright area on the edge of her nose). Remember you can interactively change the size of your brush on the fly by tapping on the square bracket keys (][).

4. Fine-Tune Result

Since we've finished dodging and burning the image, click on the word Opacity at the top of the Layers palette and drag left and right to adjust the Opacity to control the strength of our adjustments (we left ours at 100%). For a more subtle effect (without the chance of increasing color saturation along with contrast), try switching the Blend Mode of the layer to Soft Light. If you don't like a fix you have made, you can select a 50% gray from the Swatches palette and "neutralize" your Dodge & Burn layer to its original state. 🔲

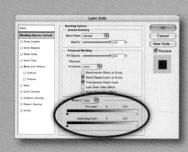

Blend If Sliders

The Blend If sliders allow you to hide or show parts of a layer based on their brightness. When applied to an Adjustment Layer, the sliders think of the content of the layer as being the result of the adjustment that is being applied. The sliders only hide or show areas of the active layer; they do not permanently delete anything. We'll be using the Blend If sliders for quite a few projects throughout this book.

Accessing the Blend If Sliders

The Blend If sliders are located in the Blending Options section of the Layer Style dialog box. To access the sliders, do one of the following: Double-click in the area to the right of the layer's name; Control/right-click on the layer and choose Blending Options; select it from the Layer Style pop-out at the bottom of the Layers palette; or choose Layer>Layer Styles>Blending Options.

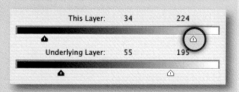

This Layer Black Slider

The upper-left slider causes the areas of the active layer to disappear if they are as dark as the shades shown to the left of this slider. This is useful when you need to remove a background that is darker than the subject (like fireworks or lightning).

This Layer White Slider

The upper-right slider causes the areas of the active layer to disappear if they are as bright as the shades shown to the right of this slider. This is useful when you need to remove a background that is brighter than the subject of the image (like text or a logo).

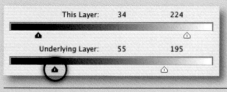

Underlying Layer Black Slider

The lower-left slider causes areas of the active layer to disappear where the underlying image is as dark as the shades that appear to the left of this slider. This is useful for allowing the texture of the underlying image to show through.

Underlying Layer White Slider

The lower-right slider causes areas of the active layer to disappear where the underlying image is as bright as the shades that appear to the right of this slider. Like the Black Slider, this, too, is useful for allowing the texture of the underlying image to show through.

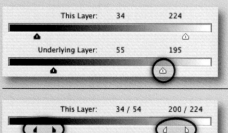

Splitting Sliders to Smooth Transitions

Each of the sliders can be split into two parts by Option/Alt-dragging either edge of the slider. Splitting the slider creates a smooth transition between the visible and hidden areas. The wider the two halves of a slider are spread apart, the softer the transition will be. The brightness levels that appear between the two halves of the slider are the ones that will be partially transparent. ▦

Blend Modes

Blend modes are found in over a dozen areas of Photoshop, the most popular of which is at the top of the Layers palette. Blend modes allow you to control how the information on one layer interacts with the content of the underlying layers. The modes are organized into multiple groupings based on similarities between the modes. Let's take a look at how they are organized.

Basic Modes

The Basic modes include Normal and Dissolve. They are grouped together because they don't depend on the content of the underlying image. Normal is the default mode, while Dissolve transforms partially transparent areas into a noisy pattern of solid dots.

Darken Modes

The Darken modes include Darken, Multiply, Color Burn and Linear Burn. They are grouped together because all those modes cause white to disappear (also known as being neutral), and anything darker than white has the potential to darken the underlying image. These modes are useful when you want to add density to an image.

Lighten Modes

The Lighten modes include Lighten, Screen, Color Dodge and Linear Dodge. They are grouped together because all those modes cause black to disappear, and anything brighter than black has the potential to lighten the underlying image.

Contrast Modes

The Contrast modes include Overlay, Soft Light, Hard Light, Vivid Light, Linear Light, Pin Light and Hard Mix. They are grouped together because with all those modes, 50% gray will disappear, anything brighter has the potential to brighten the underlying image while any areas darker have the potential to darken the underlying image. These modes are ideal for adding contrast and exaggerating the detail contained in an image.

Comparative Modes

The Comparative modes include Difference and Exclusion. They are grouped together because with both of them, layering two identical images on top of each other produces solid black while any areas that don't match will appear as a color or shade of gray. These modes are very useful when attempting to align two objects.

Color Modes

The Color modes include Hue, Saturation, Color and Luminosity. They are grouped together because all of them work by dividing the colors that make up your image into three components: Hue (meaning basic color), Saturation (meaning how colorful or intense), and Luminosity (meaning how bright). These modes are great when you want to change the color of an object or to control how adjustments are applied to an image.

Shadow & Highlight Resuscitations

Coax out highlight and shadow detail to rescue "tonally challenged" originals.

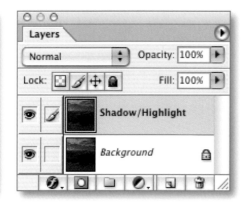

1. Duplicate Original Layer

To keep the original image safe and intact, type Option-Command-J/ Alt-Ctrl-J to copy the original image onto a new layer. Name the layer "Shadow/Highlight."

2. Adjust Shadows Settings

To pull out detail in the darkest areas of the image, choose Image> Adjustments>Shadow/Highlight and adjust the Amount slider under the Shadows area. Since our original was significantly backlit and quite dark, we need to move the slider all the way to the right before we'll start to see enough detail.

3. Adjust Advanced Shadow Settings

Turn on the Show More Options checkbox to access an extended range of settings. The Tonal Width setting determines how far the brightening effect will make its way into the midtones of the image. Lower settings will limit the change to the darkest areas of the image while higher settings will cause the brightening effect to change more of the image (we used 40%). Once you have the Amount and Radius settings where you'd like them, adjust the Radius setting to control how the darkest areas of the image blend into the surrounding areas (we used 80px).

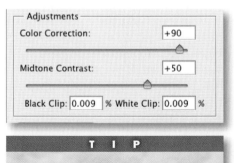

4. Adjust Color & Contrast

Now let's control how colorful the image is by adjusting the Color Correction slider (we used +90 to make the tropical water quite intense). Next, adjust the Midtone Contrast slider until the image has the desired amount of contrast (we used +50). If after adjusting the image you find you've lost detail in the brightest highlights or darkest shadows, then adjust the Black and White Clip settings. Just click on one of those numbers and then use the up and down arrow keys while you watch your image to figure out which setting delivers sufficient detail (we used .009% for both).

TIP

Keep an Eye on the Histogram.
Remember to keep your histogram palette open when making tonal corrections in your image, so you can make sure you are not clipping shadow or highlight detail.

Combining Multiple Exposures

Quickly combine a highlight exposure with a shadow exposure to create an image with tremendous dynamic range.

1. Take Two Exposures

Both digital and film cameras can only capture a limited brightness range (both of which are more limited than the range of the human eye). When the scene you're attempting to photograph is beyond the range your camera is capable of capturing, you're going to end up with either blown-out highlights, or plugged-up shadows. When that's the case, consider placing your camera on a tripod and making two exposures—one to maintain shadow detail **A**, and the other to maintain highlight detail **B**. Once you've loaded both images into Photoshop, drag the darker of the two images into the lighter one using the Move tool (while holding down the Shift key to help the files line up) so both images are in a single document.

2. Align Images

With both images now in one document, let's fine-tune their alignment. With the top layer active, change the Blend Mode pop-up menu at the top of the Layers palette to Difference mode and then take a look at the result. In Difference mode, areas that appear as solid black indicate where the active and underlying layers are identical. Areas that appear as shades of gray and color indicate areas that are different than what's below. Use the Move tool to reposition the top layer until the image becomes as dark as you can get it (use the arrow keys to nudge the image one pixel at a time).

3. Adjust Blending Options

Now let's blend our two exposures together. Change the Blend Mode pop-up menu at the top of the Layers palette back to Normal and then choose Layer>Layer Styles>Blending Options. Since the shadows on the top layer don't contain any detail, let's hide those areas to reveal the underlying image (which has properly exposed shadows). Move the upper left Blend If slider to the right until you see sufficient shadow detail appearing (we used 200), then hold Option/Alt and drag the left edge of that slider toward the right until you create a smooth transition between the shadows and midtones of your image (we used 20). Then, before you leave the Blending Options dialog box, change the Blend Mode pop-up menu near the top of the dialog box to Darken, which should help improve the image in any areas where there is a slight misalignment of the two images (created by blowing trees for example). ▥

Neutralizing Color Casts

Photoshop, not surprisingly, provides an overwhelming number of methods for performing color correction. They range from the á la carte approach (do it yourself step-by-step) to the package deal (where Photoshop does most of the work for you). Your line of attack will depend on your knowledge level and comfort with the technology used.

In this section you will find five well-tested methods to choose from. Try each one and decide for yourself which one you'd like to use for a specific image and then refer back to this page anytime you need a refresher on color correction or when you know there must be a better way.

© DEAN COLLINS

Auto Color

To access the Auto Color Correction options, create either a Levels or a Curves Adjustment Layer and click on the Options button near the lower right of the dialog box. There are two general approaches to using this dialog box: you can either use the Enhance Per Channel Contrast setting **A** or the Find Dark & Light Colors setting **B**. Each will produce a slightly different result. In either case, turn on the Snap Neutral Midtones checkbox and then adjust the two Clip settings to control how much shadow and highlight detail you get.

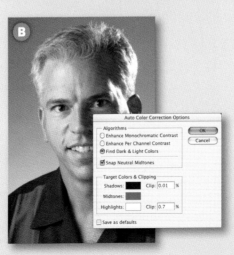

Gray Point Eyedropper

Another method for color correcting an image is to choose Levels from the Adjustment Layer pop-up menu at the bottom of the Layers palette and click on the middle Eyedropper in the lower right of the dialog box (the same tool is also available in Curves). After choosing that tool, click on any object that **should not** contain color within your image. You can use any shade of gray from white to black as long as it doesn't have the slightest hint of color in it.

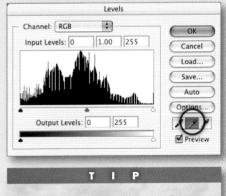

T I P

White Balance. The Camera Raw dialog box offers a similar eyedropper that will usually produce a better result than the one used above.

Average Blur

Now let's explore how to use a seldom-used filter in an unusual way. Start by typing Command/Ctrl-J to duplicate the active layer, then choose Filter>Blur>Average. That will show you the overall color that makes up your image. Next, type Command/Ctrl-I to invert the color, which should provide you with the opposite color as the one that is creating the color cast infecting your image. Now set the Blend Mode pop-up menu at the top of the Layers palette to Color and experiment with the Opacity until you find the setting that produces the most balanced looking image (we used 25% for the image above).

Color Balance

You can shift the color of the Shadows, Midtones and Highlights separately by choosing Color Balance from the Adjustment Layer pop-up menu at the bottom of the Layers palette. To adjust an image, start with the area that has the most dramatic color cast (the Highlights in our example), then adjust the three sliders by adding the opposite colors from the ones you have too much of (hence the increase of blue and cyan here) until you've rid that area of the color cast, then move on to the other choices (Midtones and Shadows) and adjust them as well.

Variations

By choosing Image>Adjustments>Variations, you'll be presented with your original image in the center of a dialog box with different color variations surrounding it. Clicking on any of the surrounding images will move that variation to the middle and re-populate the surrounding images. Then, just click on the image that looks the best and repeat until the one in the center is the best of them all.

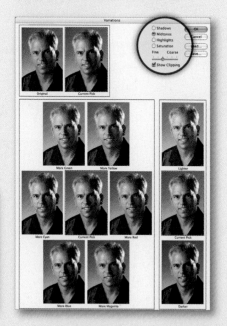

Adjustment Layers

The choices available in the Image>Adjustments menu affect a ***single*** layer and make permanent changes to your images. Adjustment *Layers* on the other hand usually affect ***all*** underlying layers, are not permanent and allow you to fine-tune the adjustment even years after the image has been saved and closed. Adjustment Layers are a key ingredient to upholding our boyscout oath of quality, versatility and speed.

Creating an Adjustment Layer

To apply an Adjustment Layer to your image, choose one of the adjustments available from either the Layer>New Adjustment Layer menu or the Adjustment Layer pop-up menu at the bottom of the Layers palette.

Stacking Order

By default, an Adjustment Layer affects all the layers that appear below it in the Layers palette, but none of the layers above. You can drag an Adjustment Layer up or down in the Layers palette to change the stacking order of the layers and therefore control which layers are affected. The stacking order of the layers also determine the order in which adjustments are applied. The bottommost Adjustment Layer is thought of as being applied first while the topmost Adjustment Layer is applied last.

Editing Adjustment Layers

A large icon appears near the far left of each Adjustment Layer and reflects the type of adjustment that the layer contains. Double-clicking on that icon will open the adjustment dialog box that was used when creating the Adjustment Layer, and allow you to fine-tune the settings being used. Click on the eyeball icon for the layer to toggle its visibility.

Limiting Adjustments

To make an Adjustment Layer apply to a single layer, hold Option/Alt when choosing the adjustment type from the Adjustment Layer pop-up menu at the bottom of the Layers palette and turn on the ***Use Previous Layer to Create Clipping Mask checkbox.*** Or if you're working with a preexisting Adjustment Layer, you can Option/Alt-click on the horizontal dividing line between an Adjustment Layer and the underlying layer. You can also have an Adjustment Layer apply to multiple layers by placing the desired layers in a Layer Set (which looks like a folder). Once you've got the layers in a set, place the Adjustment Layer into the same set, click on the name of the set and then change the Blend Mode menu at the top of the Layers palette to Normal.

> **T I P**
>
> **Layer Masks.** You can also limit where an adjustment is applied by painting on the Layer Mask that is attached to each Adjustment Layer.

Making It Permanent

To permanently apply an adjustment that comes from using an Adjustment Layer, click on the Adjustment Layer to make it active, and choose Layer>Merge Down.

Layer Masks

A Layer Mask is a grayscale image attached to a layer that, based on the shades of gray that appear in the mask, cause areas of the layer to become temporarily hidden or visible. Black areas in the mask will cause the corresponding part of the layer to become hidden, while white areas cause them to remain visible. Shades of gray in a Layer Mask cause areas of the attached layer to become partially transparent.

Adding a Layer Mask

To add a Layer Mask to the active layer, do one of the following: Select one of the options available in the Layer>Add Layer Mask menu or click on the Layer Mask icon at the bottom of the Layers palette. You cannot add a Layer Mask to the Background Layer. All Adjustment Layers start with Layer Masks attached. If a selection is active when you create a Layer Mask, the mask will automatically be filled in such a way to cause the areas that are not selected to become hidden. Hold Option/Alt when creating a Layer Mask to either start it out filled with black, or to hide any areas that are selected.

Switching Between Layer and Layer Mask

When a Layer Mask is attached to an image layer, a double border will appear around either the Image Preview Thumbnail or the Layer Mask Thumbnail in the Layers palette to indicate which is active for editing. You can also tell which thumbnail is active if you look to the right of the eyeball icon for the active layer. If a Paintbrush icon appears, then the layer is active, or if the Layer Mask icon appears in that area, then the mask is active.

Editing Layer Masks

Any tool that is available when working on the Background Layer of a grayscale document can be used to edit the Layer Mask. That includes, but is not limited to: painting and retouching tools, adjustment dialog boxes, and filters.

Viewing a Layer Mask

To toggle the visibility of the mask within the main image window, Option/Alt-click directly on the Layer Mask Thumbnail image attached to the active layer. You can also type \ to view the contents of the Layer Mask as a color overlay over the main image window.

Disabling & Deleting a Layer Mask

Shift-clicking directly on the Layer Mask Thumbnail image attached to the active layer will temporarily disable the mask and cause any hidden areas of the layer to become visible once again. Shift-click on the Layer Mask a second time to reenable the mask. If you'd like to permanently remove the Layer Mask, then drag the Layer Mask Thumbnail to the Trash icon at the bottom of the Layers palette. You'll have the choice of applying the mask (which will permanently erase any hidden areas), or discarding it (which will bring hidden areas back into view).

Targeted Color Control with Sliders

Use Hue/Saturation to isolate and then shift the basic color of an area.

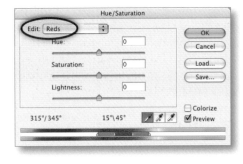

1. Apply Hue/Saturation

Start by choosing Hue/Saturation from the Adjustment Layer pop-up menu at the bottom of the Layers palette. When the Hue/Saturation dialog box appears, click on the Edit pop-up menu and choose the color that is closest to the shade you want to change.

2. Make an Exaggerated Change

Choosing a color from the Edit pop-up menu causes the Hue/Saturation dialog box to isolate a range of colors. To easily see the area that has been isolated, move the Hue slider all the way to the right and move the Saturation slider to +100.

INSIGHT

Subtle Changes. If you'd like to use the same general color technique to make more subtle changes to an image, then check out the Unifying Skintones technique found in Chapter 5, "People & Portraits."

3. Narrow Color Range

Just choosing a color from the Edit pop-up menu is not usually enough to isolate a single color. To narrow the range of colors that are being adjusted, drag one of the small triangular sliders that appears between the two color bars at the bottom of the dialog box toward the others so they end up in one tight mass. Then click on your image to center the sliders on the color you're clicking on.

4. Isolate Exact Color Range

Let's make sure the range of colors we're working on is wide enough to encompass the entire area we are attempting to shift. Choose the Plus Eyedropper tool from the lower right of the dialog box and then click on multiple areas of the image that you want to shift until the entire area changes color. If you accidentally click on an area you didn't mean to or if an area that shouldn't change shifts in color, just click on that area with the Minus Eyedropper tool.

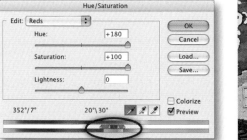

5. Fine-Tune Color Range

Now that you have the general range of colors isolated, drag the small triangular sliders between the two colors bars to make the color shift blend into the surrounding image. This will create a less abrupt transition between the area that is changing color and what surrounds it, and will often prevent pixelated edges.

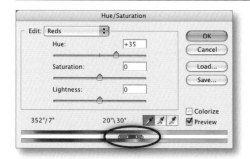

6. Adjust Hue and Saturation

Now that we've precisely isolated a range of color, move the Hue and Saturation sliders back to the middle to revert back to the original colors. Then, adjust the Hue to shift the basic color and the Saturation to control how colorful the area is. Be careful changing the Lightness setting–this sometimes causes the adjustment to look unnatural. ▥

Targeted Color Control with Sliders & Masks

Using a Hue/Saturation adjustment with Layer Masks to isolate similar colors and make subtle adjustments.

1. Choose Hue/Saturation

For this color treatment, we'll expand on the technique used for the last project and shift three colors using a single Adjustment Layer, but this time in a more subtle fashion. Start by choosing Hue/Saturation from the Adjustment Layer pop-up menu at the bottom of the Layers palette.

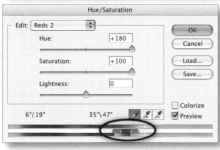

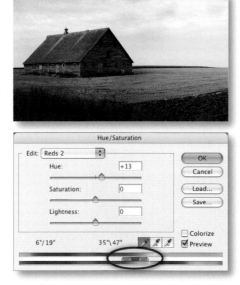

2. Isolate & Adjust Reds

Now let's shift the overall color of the field from its reddish-yellow to a purer yellow color. Choose Reds from the Edit pop-up menu at the top of the Hue/Saturation dialog box, and then move the Hue and Saturation sliders all the way to the right to make an exaggerated change to the image. Now move your mouse onto the image and click within the field to have Photoshop concentrate on that area, and then either use the eyedroppers (as we did in the previous technique) or manually adjust the sliders at the bottom of the Hue/Saturation dialog box to limit the change to the field (don't worry if the barn shifts; we'll mask it out later). To shift the field to more of a yellow color, we set the Saturation slider back to zero and then moved the Hue slider to +13.

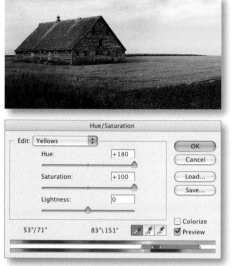

3. Isolate & Adjust Yellows

While still in the Hue/Saturation dialog box, choose Yellows from the Edit pop-up menu (you can adjust up to six different ranges of colors in a single Hue/Saturation Adjustment Layer). Using the same technique mentioned in step two, isolate the yellow/green area that appears in the lower portion of the image while not worrying if the barn is included in the color range that will be shifted. Then to make that lower area less colorful, move the Saturation slider toward the left and adjust the Hue slider until you obtain a more pleasing contrast between the dark area at the bottom of the image and the bright field.

4. Isolate & Adjust Blues

Now let's fine-tune the sky. While you're still in the Hue/Saturation dialog box, choose Cyans from the Edit pop-up menu, move the Hue slider to +180, move the Saturation slider to +100 to exaggerate the selection and then adjust the tiny sliders that appear between the two color bars until you've isolated the colors within the sky. Once you have the sky isolated, move the Hue and Saturation sliders back to the middle to get back to the original sky color. Then to darken the sky overall, move the Lightness slider to −26. Anytime the Lightness slider is adjusted, the colors within the image will become less colorful, so move the Saturation slider to +43 and move the Hue to +19 to shift the sky to a deeper blue, and finally, click OK.

5. Paint on Layer Mask

You'll notice that the barn color shifted the reds and yellows in the image. To bring the barn back to its original state, type D to reset the Foreground color to black, choose the Brush tool and with the Adjustment Layer still active, paint over the barn. ▥

Targeted Color Control with Colorize & Masks

Use custom shapes along with the Hue/Saturation dialog box to add a cool custom-colored flame job (or corporate logo?) to a classic car.

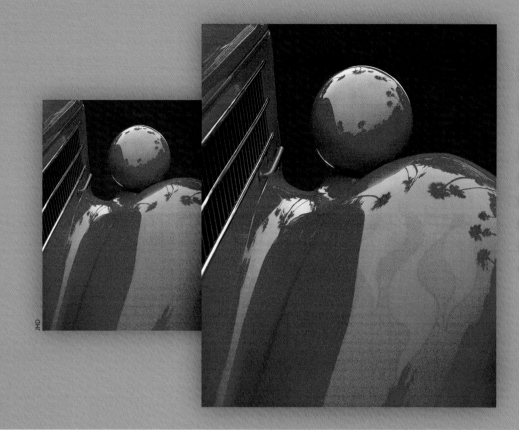

1. Prepare Shape Tool

Choose the Custom Shape tool in the Tools palette **A**, click on the Custom Shape preview **B** and choose the Nature library from the side menu of the pop-up palette **C** (it's one of the libraries of Custom Shapes that ship with Photoshop) and then choose the Custom Shape called Fire **D**. In this instance, we used the Custom Shape tool to define the area we want to colorize, but you can use any selection method you can think of to create your design. See page 48 for tips on selecting.

2. Draw Flame

Click and drag to create a flame shape (hold Shift if you want to constrain the shape). Don't worry about the color at this point because we'll define that later. In this case, just make the flame large enough to cover a good portion of the fender.

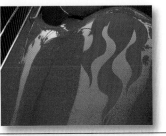

3. Rotate Flame

With the newly created Shape Layer active, type Command/Ctrl-T, move your mouse *beyond* one of the corner handles and drag to rotate the flame shape so that it matches the angle of the fender.

4. Load Shape as a Selection

Hold down the Command/Ctrl key and click on the Shape Thumbnail for the flame layer to load its shape as a selection. Then before moving on, drag the Shape Layer to the Trash icon at the bottom of the Layers palette. You'll be left with just the active selection.

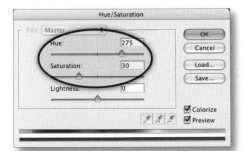

5. Adjust with Hue/Saturation

Now choose Hue/Saturation from the Adjustment Layer pop-up menu at the bottom of the Layers palette, turn on the Colorize checkbox to replace all the color in the selected area and then set the Hue and the Saturation to taste (we set the Hue to 275 and the Saturation to 30 to create a purple flame).

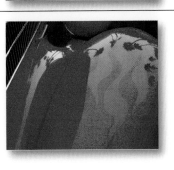

6. Blur & Refine Mask

To give the edge of the flame an airbrushed appearance, we'll soften the edge by choosing Filter>Blur>Gaussian Blur and setting the Radius to 2. Then to make the flame fade out as it gets near the front of the fender, choose the Brush tool, set the Foreground Color to black and paint using a large, soft-edged brush. ▥

Noise Reduction

Reduce the appearance of both color and luminance noise with a simple one-two punch.

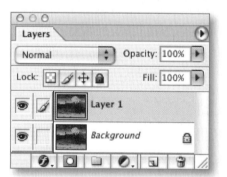

1. Color Noise Reduction

Digital cameras are notorious for introducing specks and grain (referred to as noise) into dark images. We'll launch a two-pronged attack against the little pests. Start by typing Option-Command-J/Alt-Ctrl-J to copy the original image onto a new layer and name it "Color Noise Reduction."

2. Apply Gaussian Blur Filter

Our first strike will be to tackle the color specks that are commonly found in digital photographs. Choose Filter>Blur>Gaussian Blur and experiment with the Radius setting until you find the lowest setting that blends the colorful specks into the surrounding image (we used 3 for this image). Don't worry if the rest of the image is looking blurry; just concentrate on what's happening to the colorful specks (we'll fix the detail in a moment).

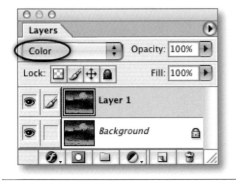

3. Change Blend Mode to Color

Now let's use our blurred copy of the image to make the colorful specks blend in while bringing back the overall detail of the image. Change the Blend Mode menu at the top of the Layers palette to Color so that the blur effect does not affect the brightness of the image (which contains most of the detail).

4. Luminance Noise Reduction

Since filters only affect one layer at a time and our image is currently made from two layers, we'll need to create a layer that combines the two layers before continuing. With the top layer active, hold down Shift-Option-Command/Shift-Alt-Ctrl and type N to create a new layer and then E to merge what's visible into that empty layer.

5. Apply Median Filter

Now let's try to reduce the grain without making the image look blurry. Choose Filter>Noise>Median and experiment with the Radius setting until you find the lowest setting that blends the noise (we used 2), while maintaining edge detail.

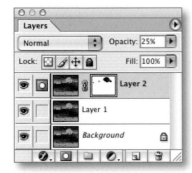

6. Adjust Opacity & Mask Layer

Now let's try to obtain a good balance between detail and grain by adjusting the Opacity of the newly filtered layer until you find the best compromise between noise removal and fine image detail (we used 25%). Then to control where the effect is applied, click on the Layer Mask icon at the bottom of the Layers palette and paint with black to bring back fine detail or texture in areas where noise wasn't a problem (like the white area of the wave). ▥

Scaling, Sharpening & Resolution

We have one last stop before we head into the world of Wow. To properly equip ourselves for the journey, we need to spend some time with the often overlooked but critical issues of resolution, scaling and sharpening. Pay close attention to what we have to say here and you should be forever liberated from pixelated or soft images. From this point on, you should end up with images that pop off the page with a sharpness and detail you can be proud of.

TIP

How to Cheat. If you need to make a huge enlargement, consider having your image printed on a continuous tone output device at a photo lab and rescanning the print at the desired resolution on a flatbed scanner..

Resolution Tips

The resolution setting attached to your document determines how large the pixels that make up your image will be when the image is printed. Image resolution is measured in Pixels Per Inch (although many people refer to it by a similar term called Dots Per Inch). The higher the resolution of your image, the smaller the pixels will be when the image is printed (more of them crammed into each linear inch). The key to getting a detailed image is to make sure the resolution setting isn't too low for your particular output device.

Keep the following in mind when choosing the resolution for your image:

- When printing to an ink jet printer, you can get away with a resolution as low as 150PPI, although 225-300PPI would be ideal.

- When printing on a commercial printing press, ask your printer which Halftone Screen setting they will use to output your images (measured in Lines Per Inch, or LPI) and multiply it by 1.5 (for average images) or 2 (for images with minute detail or that might be enlarged slightly once they are placed in a page layout program). Therefore, a typical resolution for printing with a 150LPI screen would be 225PPI.

Scaling Tips

Use the following tips when scaling an image up or down in Photoshop:

- We recommend as a general default setting that you choose Preferences>General from the Photoshop menu (Mac), or Edit menu (Win) and set the Image Interpolation pop-up menu to **Bicubic Sharper.**

- When **scaling an image down** using the *Bicubic Sharper* method, there is usually no need to resharpen the image.

- If you need to **enlarge an image,** choose Image>**Image Size**, turn on the Resample Image checkbox and set its pop-up menu to **Bicubic Smoother** before entering the desired width, height and resolution settings. This will override your Preferences setting of *Bicubic Sharper* for those times you need to enlarge a file.

- You may have read about a technique for enlarging images that involves scaling the image up in small increments to achieve high quality. That technique was invented before the Bicubic Smoother feature was available and for most situations, is no longer necessary.

Unsharp Mask Tips

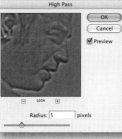

Keep the following tips in mind when applying the Unsharp Mask filter (Filter>Sharpen>Unsharp Mask):

- To eliminate visible haloing, keep the Radius between .5 and .8 pixels for small images that will be viewed on-screen.

- You can get away with Radius settings above 1 for larger images that will be printed and viewed from a distance.

- Lower Amount settings allow you to use high Radius settings, while high Amount settings will require low Radius settings.

- If sharpening the image exaggerates the noise in areas that used to look smooth, then increase the Threshold setting until the area smooths out (usually between 1 and 5).

- If you notice color fringing after sharpening an image, select Fade>Unsharp Mask from the Edit menu and change the Blend Mode to Luminosity.

Scaling & High Pass Technique

When it's necessary to enlarge an image, consider using the following steps to get additional apparent detail (the above image was blown up from a 2 megapixel file to a 10x12 inch print):

Choose Image>Image Size, turn on the Resample Image checkbox and set the pop-up menu to Bicubic Smoother. After specifying those settings, enter the width, height and resolution you desire.

Next, duplicate the original image onto a new layer by typing Command/Ctrl-J. Or if your image is made from multiple layers, click on the top layer, hold Shift-Option-Command/Shift-Alt-Ctrl and type N and then E.

Now choose Filter>Other>High Pass and adjust the Radius (for images with a lot of fine detail use a setting between 2 and 10, and for images with less detail use a setting between 10 and 50).

With the High Pass filtered layer active, change the Blend Mode at the top of the Layers palette to either Soft Light (more

subtle) or Overlay (more dramatic) and then adjust the Opacity setting to control the strength of the effect.

If applying the High Pass filter exaggerated the noise in your image, then choose Filter>Noise>Median and experiment with the Radius setting until you find what's needed to reduce the noise (usually 1-3).

Finally, for additional punch, click on the underlying layer (original image layer) and apply the Unsharp Mask filter.

A similar technique is used in the Popping Images with High Pass technique in Chapter 6, "Enhancing & Exaggerating."

4

RETOUCHING & REPAIRING

Refining Images by Reversing Aging and Removing Distractions

THE SKILLS YOU GAIN by working through the next two chapters will serve you for a lifetime. Wherever you are headed in your quest to excel in photography, you will never regret taking the time to master the art of precision retouching. Yes, we said, "art." Some people consider retouching to be its own art form, and indeed there are some world-class masters out there who are paid oodles of money to discreetly alter reality without the public ever knowing. The best retouchers are not only expert at using the tools of the trade, they have developed a discriminating eye for the subtlest detail and know how to stay true to their subject.

When in Doubt, Restrain Yourself

Before we get into what you can expect to learn in this chapter (and especially the following Chapter 5, "People & Portraits"), we feel it's important to make an argument for aesthetics. Hands down, the arsenal of retouching tools in Photoshop is state-of-the-art and phenomenally effective. But sometimes there can be a little too much of a good thing, and the results can range from just a bit unnatural to downright scary.

You've got the same challenge as any cosmetic surgeon, and I'm sure you've seen enough overdone, overstretched face lifts to know exactly what we're talking about. If your goal is for out-and-out transformation, just ignore our preaching. But if your goal is to improve and enhance your subject without detection, then we urge you to use these tools with a little restraint.

Turning Back the Clock

Most people don't exactly keep their photos in museum-like condition. Ever since the day that the first sepia print made its way into an album, our photos have taken a beating. They get torn, scuffed, stained, wrinkled and faded. If your goal is to return a photograph to its former glory, you'll take pleasure in the first part of this chapter that shows you how to remove the signs of age and wear-and-tear from your photos. You'll learn how to use the Healing Brush and Patch tool in combination with filters and Layer Masks to get rid of dust and scratches and remove color casts.

And for those super challenging jobs, like a photo torn completely in half, we'll show you how to take advantage of the complete arsenal of retouching tools that will result in the original damage being imperceptible. You'll learn how to rebuild missing elements of your photo by borrowing bits and pieces from other parts of your image and combining them in clever ways that realistically simulate the missing components.

Blue Skies on a Dreary Day

Anytime you've got a photo that includes the sky, you'll notice that it has a tremendous impact on the appeal of the overall image. There will be times that you have a shot that is great in every way, except that it has a drab and dreary sky. In this chapter we'll walk you through two easy techniques to dramatically improve the skies in your images. The first way is to borrow a better one from another photo and integrate it into your image's less appealing background. And if you don't have a good "blue yonder" to steal, we'll show you how to punch up or replace the existing one using Gradient Fill layers.

Dust & Scratch Removal

Use the Healing Brush, Dust & Scratches filter and Levels command to rid an image of unwanted problems and artifacts.

1. Duplicate Background Layer

Since we have a thousand or so pieces of dust, let's see if we can stay away from the Healing Brush for a while and concentrate on using the Dust & Scratches filter to do the majority of the work. Since filters have to work directly on an image layer and we want to make sure we have access to the original version of the image, type Option-Command-J/Alt-Ctrl-J to copy the original image onto a new layer and call it "Dust & Scratches."

2. Apply Dust & Scratches

Now to start blending the specks and other defects into the surrounding image, choose Filter>Noise>Dust & Scratches. Start with both the Radius and Threshold settings as low as they can go, then bring up the Radius setting until the specks, scratches, noise and dust disappear (we used 5). The only problem with this result is all the original texture and film grain is gone, and so is all the fine detail. Both of these are a dead giveaway of a bad retouching job. First, let's bring back the inherent grain in the image by increasing the Threshold setting until you find the highest setting that doesn't bring back the artifacts we are trying to remove (we used 15).

TIP

Paint It In. If there are only a few problems with an image and it's rather sharp to begin with, then consider Option/Alt-clicking on the Layer Mask icon and painting with white to paint **IN** the fixes, rather than painting with black on a white mask to paint **OUT** the fixes to reveal the original detail below.

3. Mask Filter's Result

Next, to bring back some of the detail lost in some areas of the face and hair, click on the Layer Mask icon at the bottom of the Layers palette, choose a soft-edged brush and paint with black over the areas that used to have fine detail (eyes, mouth, hair strands, etc.). Don't worry if you re-expose small problem areas; you're going for speed at this point. If you remove too much of the filtered result, then type X to switch your foreground color to white and paint back the filtered layer.

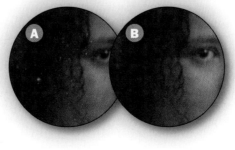

4. Fine-Tune Mask

At this stage, we've fixed 3/4 of the problems in the image **A**, but in doing so, we may have revealed some of the smaller specks. Get a much smaller brush, choose white to paint with, zoom in and paint over any remaining specks until they are all gone **B**. Use a brush tip that's a tiny bit larger than the problem specks; don't worry about areas of the image that couldn't be repaired with the Dust & Scratches filter (we will address them next).

5. Create a Repair Layer

The Dust & Scratches filter can't fix all the problems in this photograph, so let's start to work on the more complex areas of the image. But before we continue, let's create a new layer to contain these more elaborate corrections. Right now our image is made from two layers, so click on the top layer, hold down Shift-Option-Command/Shift-Alt-Ctrl, type N to create a new layer and then E to merge a copy of the visible layers into that new layer. Now double-click on the name of the layer and call it "Repair."

TIP

Oval Brushes. Click on the Brush Preview in the Options bar, set Hardness to 75%, Angle to 60, and the Roundness to 60. That brush will produce an irregular edge which will help blend retouching into the image.

Angle: 60°
Roundness: 60%

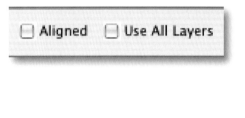

6. Set Up Healing Brush

Choose the Healing Brush and then change the following settings in the Options bar: turn off the Use All Layers checkbox because we've already copied our image onto a fresh layer and therefore won't have to copy from the rest of the layers (that option is processor intensive, so having it off will cause the tool to be more responsive). Next, turn off the Aligned checkbox so we only have to switch sources when we move to an area of differing texture.

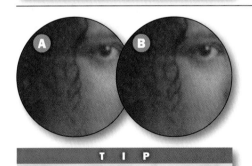

TIP

Short Strokes. Paint with very short brush strokes so that you don't have to worry about your source area being large enough to completely cover the problem you are retouching. By doing that, you'll only need to change the source when you move to areas that have different texture.

7. Heal Remaining Problems

Now look for any remaining problem areas (the cheeks, tips of the fingers, etc). When you find an area that needs additional repair, set your sample, or source point by Option/Alt-clicking in a nearby area that is similarly textured (but doesn't have any defects). Now, release the Option/Alt key and then paint over the offending area. If you run into a high-contrast line that needs repair, center your cursor on a clean portion of the line and Option/Alt-click to set the source. Then center your cursor over the line where it needs to be repaired before clicking the mouse button to heal the area.

8. Neutralize Color Cast

Now that we're done cleaning up the defects in the image, let's work on the color cast. Let's create a layer that contains a solid color that is representative of the general color cast of our image by typing Command/Ctrl-J to duplicate the Repair layer, and then choosing Filter>Blur>Average. Now type Command/Ctrl-I to invert that color, then change the Blend Mode at the top of the Layers palette to Color **A**. You now have the ***opposite*** of the color cast controlling the color of the image. That is what we need, but it's overwhelming the colors of the original, so lower the Opacity at the top of the Layers palette until the old color cast has been neutralized, somewhere between 5% and 50% (we used 50) **B**. See page 64 for more ways to remove a color cast.

9. Increase Contrast

Now let's make the image pop off the page by reviving the original dynamic range of our heirloom photograph. Choose Levels from the Adjustment Layer pop-up menu at the bottom of the Layers palette and move the upper left and right sliders toward the middle (we used 28 and 184). If you'd like, you could add a Hue/Saturation Adjustment Layer at this point to bump up the saturation to your taste. 🏛

Using the Healing Brush

Before the Healing Brush came along in Photoshop 7, convincing retouching was a laborious task. More primitive retouching tools such as the Clone Stamp (which we occasionally still need to use) require you to choose an area to copy or clone from that has the same brightness, texture *and* color as the area you plan to retouch. Not so with the awesome Healing Brush! It automatically preserves those attributes, which gives you much more flexibility when retouching.

Choosing a Source

When using the Healing Brush, you should look for a clean-textured area that is similar to the texture in the area that needs retouching. Option/Alt-clicking within that area will set it as the source point to clone from. Now move to the problem area, release the Option/Alt key, and paint over it with the Healing Brush. As you paint, Photoshop will copy from the area you designated as the source and paste it over the area you are repairing. You'll see two cursors on-screen: a crosshair which represents where you are **copying from** and a normal brush cursor for the area you are **copying to**. Each cursor will move in unison, so you have to watch the crosshair closely to make sure it doesn't bump into an area that has detail you don't want to copy.

Blending Texture with Color and Brightness

When you release the mouse button after cloning, the Healing Brush does its magic. It copies the texture from the area you were cloning from and then it looks around the entire edge of the area you've retouched and blends the resulting texture into the surrounding brightness and color. That means you only have to look for proper texture in the area you clone from—it could be a completely different color or brightness than what you need to retouch. That makes the Healing Brush essential when retouching faces and other areas of relatively consistent texture.

Use Hard, Irregular Brushes

The Healing Brush is most effective when applied with a relatively hard-edged brush (we like the Hardness set to 75%). Since the tool itself blends the retouching into the surrounding area, your brush tip doesn't have to. We prefer to use an oval-shaped brush tip to further disguise the corrected areas, since it creates a more irregular edge by automatically rotating its angle while you stroke the brush.

No Alignment to Save Time

Turning the Aligned checkbox off in the Options bar and painting with short brush strokes can make your retouching a lot easier. With the Aligned checkbox turned off, Photoshop will reset the sampling source back to the areas you last Option/Alt-clicked on each time you release the mouse button. That ensures you'll always have defect-free areas of clean texture to clone from and you only have to define a new source when you start retouching an area that needs a different type of texture than your current source area.

Using the Patch Tool

Think of the Patch tool and Healing Brush like identical twins—at first glance they are almost indistinguishable, but upon closer inspection you'll identify the differences. The Patch tool uses a unique method to choose both the source and destination for retouching. As you'll see below, the Patch tool has come into its own for retouching large areas, while the Healing Brush shines when correcting smaller areas.

Selecting a Source

If you've ever attempted to use the Healing Brush to cover a large area, you've most likely run into the problem that your source area just didn't offer a large enough piece of clean texture to completely cover the area you were attempting to retouch. The Patch tool makes it much easier to ensure the source area is large enough. It initially works just like Photoshop's Lasso tool, allowing you to trace around the area that needs to be retouched. Since the Patch tool has the same blending capabilities as the Healing Brush, the edge of the selection will define the colors that will be used to blend the resulting retouching into the surrounding image.

Drag Selection to Clone

Once you've defined the area to be retouched, in its default Source mode you can click anywhere within that selected area and drag it to a part of the image that has clean texture. While you drag, Photoshop copies the information that is currently within the selected area and "pastes it" into the original selection previewing what you'd end up copying if you released the mouse button. Just drag the selection to an area of appropriate texture that is large enough to fill the selection. When you release the mouse button, Photoshop applies the texture to the originally selected area and blends it with the color and brightness that surrounds it. You might be tempted to use the Patch tool to retouch the majority of images, but we'd try to talk you into using it sparingly. You see, the larger the area you end up patching in one chunk, the more unnatural the blended result may appear. It's better to spend twice as much time cloning small areas with the Healing Brush than try to save time by working on large chunks and getting unnatural results.

Use Opacity or Fade to Lessen Effect

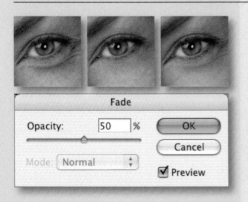

Using the Patch Tool (or Healing Brush) to remove every wrinkle, age spot and crease from an otherwise normal-looking person will transform your subject into something a little less than human (as you can see every day on the covers of fashion magazines). The solution is to either place the retouching on a duplicate layer above the original image and lessen its effect by lowering the Opacity of the layer, or by using the Edit>Fade command immediately after applying a patch directly to the original image. By lowering the opacity either way, you will blend the result of your retouching with the original image, effectively reducing, but not eliminating problem areas. ▥

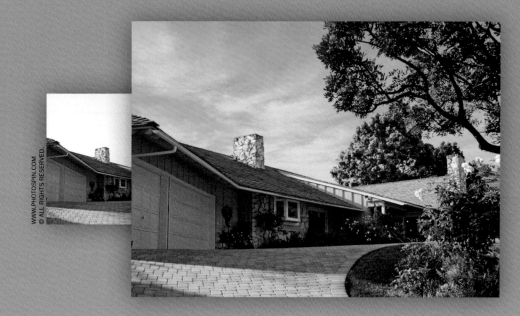

Sky Replacing

Use Channels to help isolate and replace the sky and add life to an otherwise dull image.

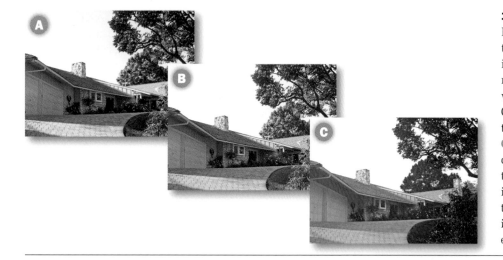

1. Copy Contrasty Channel

First we need to select the sky. Since this image has intricate objects bordering the sky, we'll let Photoshop do most of the work so we don't have to waste time manually tracing any edges. Choose Window>Channels and click on the Red **A**, Green **B**, and Blue channels **C** to inspect their contents. Look for the channel that contains the greatest contrast between the sky and its surroundings (typically the blue channel). Drag the Blue channel to the New Channel icon at the bottom of the Channels palette to create a duplicate channel.

2. Adjust the Channel

Now we need to refine that channel so the sky is white and everything else is black. Choose Image>Adjustments>Levels, and click on the Black Eyedropper icon in the lower right. Then click on the trees to force them to black, choose the White Eyedropper and click on the sky to force it to white. That should leave us with a few shades of gray in between to ensure a smooth edge.

3. Clean Up the Channel

Next, choose the Brush tool and paint with black or white to touch up the channel. You'll want to use a hard-edged brush since the architecture has a crisp edge.

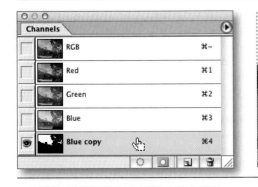

4. Load Channel as a Selection

Let's load our channel as a selection by holding the Command/Ctrl key and clicking on its name. Next, click on the topmost channel to get back to the full color image. Then to make sure the edge isn't too crisp, choose Select>Feather, set the Radius to .5 and click OK (you might have to go as high as 1 or 2 for high-resolution files).

5. Paste In New Sky

Now switch to a replacement sky image, choose Select>All and then choose Edit>Copy. Then switch back to the original image and choose Edit>Paste Into, which will place the sky on a new layer that has a Layer Mask based on the selection that was active. Since the Layer Mask and image are not linked, you can drag with the Move tool to reposition the sky.

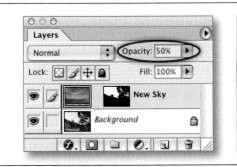

6. Transform the New Sky

If necessary, choose Edit>Free Transform, then scale, distort, or flip the sky so it matches the perspective and lighting direction of the image. Double-click to finish the transformation. For this nondescript overcast sky, we can reduce the Opacity of the layer to make it less intense and more natural looking.

7. Tweak the Mask

With the Sky layer's mask active, fine-tune the edge transition by choosing Image>Adjustments>Levels. Moving the upper-right slider will push the sky into the background **A**, while moving the upper-left slider will pull it away **B**. 🖮

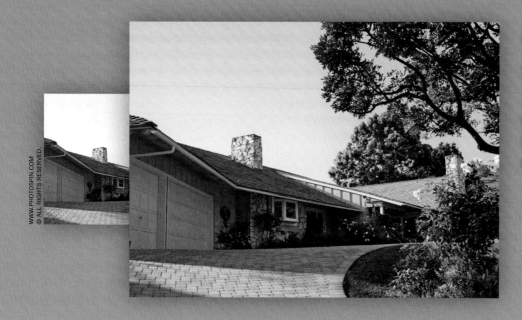

Sky Manufacturing

Use Gradient Fill Layers to create your own skies from scratch.

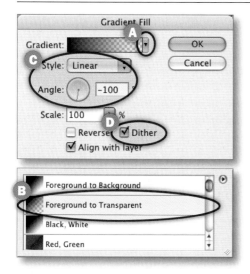

Feather Selection

Feather Radius: .5 pixels   OK   Cancel

1. Load & Feather Selection

Here's a quick variation on the last technique. Use this one when you don't have an appropriate replacement sky to use and would rather make one from scratch. Start by Command/Ctrl-clicking on the name of the alpha channel you created in the previous technique (there's no reason to repeat ourselves here). Now soften the selection by choosing Select>Feather and using .5.

Gradient Fill

Gradient: A   OK
C Style: Linear   Cancel
Angle: ◯ -100
Scale: 100 %
D Reverse ☑ Dither
☑ Align with layer

B Foreground to Background
Foreground to Transparent
Black, White
Red, Green

2. Create Gradient Fill Layer

Next choose Gradient from the Adjustment Layer pop-up menu at the bottom of the Layers palette. Click on the down-pointing arrow next to the Gradient preview **A** and choose the Foreground to Transparent gradient **B**. Now set the Style to Linear and then experiment with the angle setting **C** until the angle of the new "sky" looks appropriate for your image (we used −100°). Then before moving on to the next step, turn on the Dither checkbox **D**, which will help to prevent visible banding in the gradient.

Channels

RGB   ⌘~
Red   ⌘1
Green   ⌘2
Blue   ⌘3
Blue copy   ⌘4

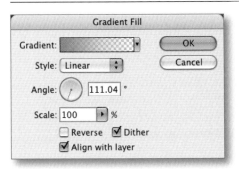

3. Customize Gradient

While still in the Gradient Fill dialog box, click directly on the Gradient Preview to access the Gradient Editor. To change the color used in the darkest area of the gradient, double-click on the lower-left color swatch **A** and choose a light shade of blue (we used H: 220, S: 45, B: 100). Next, double-click on the color swatch on the opposite end of the gradient **B** and choose the same color. Once you've done that, adjust the midpoint **C** to determine how quickly or slowly the gradient fades out.

4. Fine-Tune Gradient Settings

After clicking OK in the Gradient Editor, you'll be back in the Gradient Fill dialog box where you can click and drag within your image to position the gradient. Once you've finalized the position of the gradient, click the OK button in the Gradient Fill dialog box. Now that the gradient is in place, if your new gradient sky is being *layered on top of* an overcast sky (instead of being used to *replace* a cloudy sky), then adjust the Opacity setting at the top of the Layers palette (we used 50% so that it looks more believable). You can also tweak the mask as we did in the previous technique.

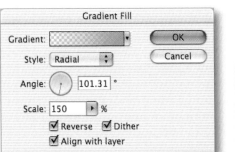

5. Variation: Use a Radial Gradient

If you'd prefer a sky that appears a little more natural by having a slight curve to it, then double-click on the Gradient icon for the Gradient layer you just created and change the Style pop-up menu to Radial, turn on the Reverse checkbox and bring the scale up as high as it will go (150%). You can also move the center of the gradient by clicking and dragging in the document window.

6. Rasterize a Gradient Fill

You'll see that the maximum Scale setting doesn't produce a subtle enough transition in the gradient, nor does it allow for non-uniform scaling of the gradient. To remedy the situation, click OK in the Gradient Fill dialog box and then Control/right-click on the right side of the gradient layer and choose Rasterize Layer **A**. That will convert the gradient from a bunch of *settings* that produce a result into a layer full of *real pixels*. Now turn off the link symbol that appears next to the Layer Mask **B** so transformations will affect the image and not the mask. Then click on the Layer Preview Thumbnail so the layer is active **C** and not the Layer Mask.

7. Scale Your Gradient

Finally, type Command/Ctrl-T and scale the Gradient layer to better fit your image. Then "squish" the gradient vertically to turn it into a flattened oval and reposition the center toward where the horizon line in your image should be. It may be necessary to zoom out on the image to be able to drag the Free Transform handles out far enough.

8. Add a Touch of Noise

If you notice any banding, or would like to add a subtle "digital camera noise" to your newly manufactured sky (to make it blend more with the film grain or noise in the original image), select Filter>Noise>Add Noise and choose the Gaussian and Monochromatic options, with a setting of 1 or 2.

Tonal Rescue

Bring a one-of-a-kind photo back from the dead using Levels, the Channel Mixer, Filters and Blend modes.

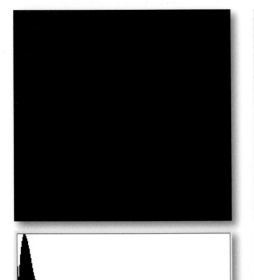

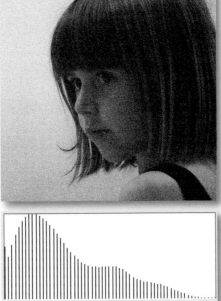

1. Extend Range with Levels

Sometimes you're shooting a once-in-a-lifetime event (like your daughter's first ballet recital), but it's dark, you're across the room, and out of flash range. Even adjusting your in-camera settings can't save it (like setting the ISO sensitivity to a zillion!)—what can you do?

At first glance, it looks like there is next to no information in the image. To see just how much detail *is* there, choose Levels from the Adjustment Layer pop-up menu, click on the Options button and choose Enhance Monochromatic Contrast (using any of the other two options would bring in way too much of the noise that's in the Blue channel). Then increase the contrast by moving the upper left and right sliders (we used 26 and 151) to get it as close to a full tonal range as you can.

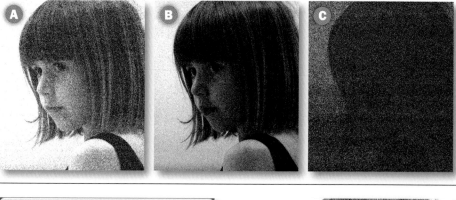

2. Inspect the Channels

Since there really isn't much color information in this image, let's convert it to monochrome. Choose Window>Channels and click on the individual channels to see the raw material we have. The Red channel **A** looks OK, the Green channel **B** looks even better and the Blue channel **C** is absolutely useless. Now let's mix those channels together to create the best monochrome image we can get.

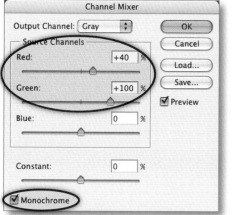

3. Convert to Monochrome

Choose Channel Mixer from the Adjustment Layer pop-up menu at the bottom of the Layers palette. Turn on the Monochrome checkbox and zoom in on the image to either 50% or 100% to get an accurate view of what we have to work with. Start with the Red and Blue sliders set to 0 and the Green slider at 100% (since it looked the best in the Channels palette). Now bring up the Red slider to brighten the image and balance the contrast (we used +40).

INSIGHT

Green Is Best. Most digital cameras have twice as many green sensors as they do for red and blue. Therefore, the Green channel has significantly less noise and often the most detail.

4. Add a Soft Glow

Now let's soften the noise in the image (while imitating an edgy film grain look) by adding a soft glow effect. To accomplish that, we're going to use the Gaussian Blur filter. Since filters can only work on a single layer at a time and our image is made out of three layers, hold Shift-Option-Command/Shift-Alt-Ctrl and type N to create a new layer and then E to merge a copy of the underlying layers into the new layer. Now choose Filter>Blur>Gaussian Blur and use a setting of 10 (just make sure you can still see the major body contours without seeing any noise). Now to transform the result into a soft glow effect, change the Blend Mode menu at the top of the Layers palette to Soft Light. Finally adjust the Opacity to control the strength of the effect (we used 80%). ▥

Color Resuscitation

Achieve the best possible mix of corrected color and contrast—in a severely compromised photograph—using *Curves* and the *Channel Mixer* dialog box.

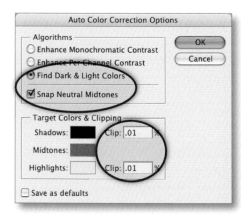

1. Try Automatic Color Correction

Let's start by finding out if Photoshop is capable of automatically color correcting our image. To access the Auto Color Correction dialog box, choose Curves from the Adjustment Layer pop-up menu at the bottom of the Layers palette and then click on the Options button in the lower right of the Curves dialog box. To perform automatic color correction, choose Find Dark & Light Colors, turn on the Snap Neutral Midtones checkbox, and set both Clip values to .01%. That didn't do much for the color, but it did give us the tonal range we need. Before moving on, click the OK button in the Auto Color Correction dialog box, which will send you back into Curves.

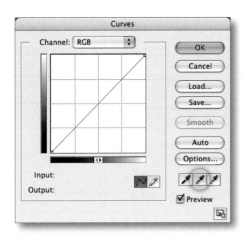

2. Manually Correct Color

Since Photoshop wasn't capable of automatically correcting the color, let's do it ourselves. Click on the middle eyedropper in the lower right of the Curves dialog box and then click on something within the image that should be a neutral gray (like the road). Experiment by clicking on different areas of the image until you find the spot that delivers the best color (we used the white toy that's dangling from the child's leg). We'll use this version of the image for the basis of our *color*, and make a custom black-and-white version to achieve the best possible *tonal* range.

T I P

Shadow Detail. If you want to bring out shadow detail when using Curves, Command/Ctrl-click on part of the image (just make sure none of the eyedroppers are chosen) to lock in something you don't want to change (like the white shirt shown here), then Command/Ctrl-click on another area and use the up and down arrow keys to brighten the second area without losing detail in the first area.

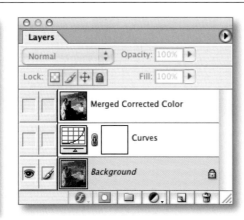

3. Merge a Copy Into a New Layer

Since we're going to be mixing the colors of the current image with an optimized grayscale version of the same image, we'll need to create a combined layer that contains the color version of the image. With the top layer active, hold Shift-Option-Command/Shift-Alt-Ctrl and type N to create a new layer, and then E to merge a copy of the underlying image into that new layer. Then to prepare the image for the next step, click on the bottom layer and then click on the eyeball icons for all the other layers to hide them.

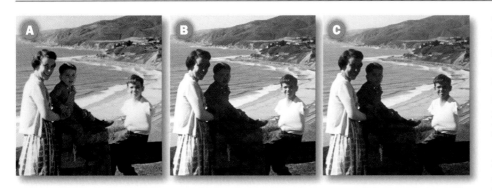

4. Inspect the Channels

Now let's get ready to create the ideal grayscale image that we'll use to blend with the color version. Choose Window> Channels and click on the individual channels to inspect the raw material that makes up the image. The Red channel **A** has good shadow detail, while the Green **B** and Blue **C** channels look almost identical. But, as usual, the Blue channel contains the most noise. Now that we know what we have to work with, let's mix those channels together to create a "black-and-white" image.

5. Convert to Black-and-White

To create a monochromatic version of the image, choose Channel Mixer from the Adjustment Layer pop-up menu at the bottom of the Layers palette and then turn on the Monochromatic checkbox at the bottom of the Channel Mixer dialog box. The default setting starts out with 100% of what was in the Red channel. Since both the Red and the Green channels contained usable raw material, bring the Red slider down to 75% and then bring the Green slider up to 60% to obtain good midtone and shadow detail.

6. Check Histogram

Before leaving the Channel Mixer dialog box, choose Window>Histogram. If the histogram is weighted toward the right side and has a tall spike on the end, the image has blown out highlights (no detail) and doesn't constrain dark shades. When that's the case, lower the Constant slider to introduce darker shades and reduce or eliminate the spike.

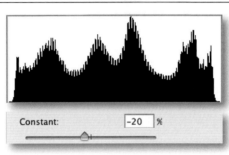

7. Mix Color with Grayscale

Now let's blend the optimized color version of the image with the optimized monochromatic version we just finished making. Turn on the eyeball icon on the topmost layer to make the color correct-ed version of the image visible again (but **not** the Curves layer) and with that top layer active, set the Blend Mode at the top of the Layers palette to Color. That will cause Photoshop to use the **color** of the top layer with the tonality of the black-and-white version.

8. Reduce Color Noise

Because we're using the top layer only for its color, we can also use it to get rid of some of the color noise by choosing Filter>Blur>Gaussian Blur. Setting the Radius to 3 looks to be enough to soften the color noise and any color fringing. ▦

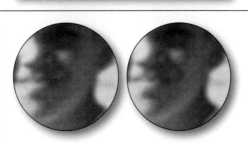

Photo Repair & Restoration

Use the full arsenal of Photoshop tools to repair and restore an abused antique photograph.

1. Crop & Add Canvas

Let's begin by cropping, straightening and adding canvas space to the image. Choose the Crop tool, type D to set the Background color to white (which will be used when adding space to the image) and type F to enter Full Screen mode. Next, click and drag to create a cropping rectangle, release the mouse button and then move beyond one of the corner handles and drag to rotate the rectangle until it matches the angle of the image. Now, drag the left side handle over until the person's face is centered in the rectangle and then double-click to finish cropping the image.

2. Select General Tonality

Now let's improve the contrast of the image, which should help to reveal all the problems inherent in the file. We'll use the Auto feature in Levels, but we don't want the white edge and scratches to influence the adjustment. Let's target the areas the adjustment will analyze by choosing the Rectangular Marquee tool and selecting important areas of the face, then hold Shift and select additional areas (like the lace at the bottom).

3. Adjust Tonality

Choose Levels from the Adjustment Layer pop-up menu at the bottom of the Layers palette. Look at the histogram to see the brightness range used within the image. Now click the Auto button and watch what happens to the Histogram—it automatically extended the range of the image. Now click the Options button, and make sure Enhance Per Channel Contrast is chosen so Photoshop will extend the contrast range for each of the color channels, which will produce the greatest dynamic range. Next, adjust both Clip settings to .01 to avoid losing detail in the highlights and shadows and then click OK.

4. Edit Mask & Set Blend Mode

Since the adjustment we just performed affected both the color and tonality of the image (and we wanted to retain the sepia toned look of the original), change the Blend Mode at the top of the Layers palette to Luminosity, which will prevent the adjustment from affecting the colors in the image. Now let's get the adjustment we just made to apply to the entire image by dragging the Layer *Mask* attached to the Levels Adjustment Layer to the trash icon at the bottom of the Layers palette.

5. Create a *Rough* Repair Layer

Before we fix the major damage to the photograph, let's create a layer to hold our retouching. Click on the bottom layer to make it active and then type Option-Command-J/Alt-Ctrl-J to duplicate the layer (name it "Repair-Rough Global"). By placing this layer below the Levels Adjustment Layer, we'll be able to later fine-tune the adjustment and it will apply to both the original image and our repair layer.

6. Choose Healing Brush Options

Choose the Healing Brush, and click on the Brush Preview in the Options bar to access the brush settings drop-down palette. Now, set the Angle and Roundness of the brush to 60% so you have an oval-shaped brush and set the Hardness to 75%. Before continuing, turn off both the Aligned and Use All Layers checkboxes in the Options bar.

TIP

High-Contrast Edges. When you come across a defect that is in an area of contrast (like the edge of an object) you have to be careful; otherwise you'll end up blending your retouching into the surroundings. An easy way to prevent that from happening is to use a corresponding edge with the same contrast as your healing source. Option/Alt-click on the "clean" edge to set it as the source, with the Option/Alt key still held down (so you can see the crosshairs), move the brush over the problematic edge, release the Option/Alt key (so you don't set a new sample source) and heal away.

7. Remove Obvious Defects

With the Repair-Rough Global layer active, and a large brush chosen (30 pixels in our case), Option/Alt-click in an area that has clean texture, then release the Option/Alt key and paint over any nearby defects (scratches, dust, lint, folds, etc.). At this stage, concentrate on the largest problem areas that have no inherent detail and work fast. We'll deal with the smaller details later. Also, remove any distracting elements (like the secondary long chain necklace in this image, for instance). Use very short brush strokes so you don't have to change the source very often. If you mess up when retouching, type Command/Ctrl-Z to undo the last step (add Option/Alt if you need to go back multiple steps).

8. Create a *Detail* Repair Layer

We're about to start working with the smaller but critical details in the image, but to make sure that we can easily get back to the last stage if we need to, let's create a new layer to hold the detail work. Drag the Repair-Rough Global layer to the New Layer icon at the bottom of the Layers palette. Then double-click on the duplicate layer's name and call it "Repair-Details".

9. Detailed Repair

Now let's fix any remaining defects, but ignore areas that have to be completely reconstructed. We'll be working in tight quarters around important areas of detail, so you'll need to be much more careful with the source that you use (being extra careful with contrasty edges and so on). For this phase of the job, you'll need to work with a much smaller brush. For areas like the nose, just blend away artifacts, but don't try to paint in new detail with the Healing Brush because we'll do that next.

10. Reconstruct with the Clone Stamp

Now we can focus on recognizable areas that have fine detail but may not blend into their surroundings (the eyes, hair and clothing). The old-fashioned Clone Stamp tool is perfect for this because it uses the texture, color *and* tone of the source (not *just* the texture, like the Healing Brush). It can be used to *re-create* areas, not just blend out defects. For example, you can set the Opacity of the Clone Stamp tool to 50%, choose a brush the size of the inner nostril, and then Option/Alt-click on a dark area near one of her eyes. Then move to the nostril and paint within the shadow area to darken it.

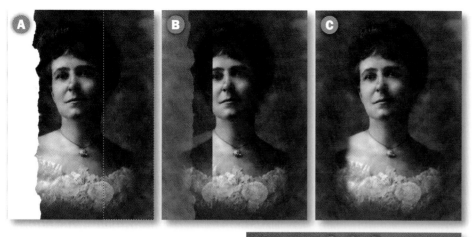

TIP

Look Out for Symmetry. After blending in the flipped piece of the background, you might want to consider modifying the background so the two sides aren't identical. Use the Healing Brush to alter the details in the background so it is no longer a mirror copy of what's on the right.

11. Reconstruct Background

We're ready to start reconstructing areas that are missing from the original image. Click on the Repair-Detail layer, use the Marquee tool to select the right 1/3 of the image **A** and then type Command/Ctrl-J to copy that area to its own layer. Now type Command/Ctrl-T, click near the middle of the transformation rectangle (but not on the crosshair), and drag it to the right side of the image. Control/right-click within the image, choose Flip Horizontal, then double-click to finish the transformation. To see how this new piece lines up with the underlying image, lower the Opacity setting at the top of the Layers palette to 80% **B**. Now let's blend that piece into the surrounding image by clicking on the Layer Mask icon at the bottom of the Layers palette, choosing a soft-edged brush, and painting with black to hide the sharp edge and any area that is covering up our subject. Now bring the Opacity back to 100% **C**.

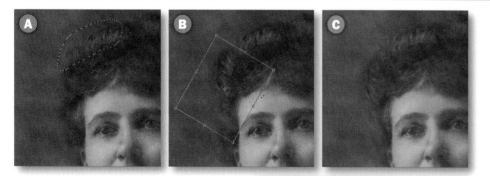

TIP

Simplify with Sets. You'll end up with five or six patch layers after you finish reconstructing all the damaged areas of this image. To organize those patch layers, click in the empty space next to the eyeball icons for each of those layers (to link them together) and then choose New Set from Linked from the side menu of the Layers palette.

12. Reconstruct Remaining Details

For recognizable details in the image, it's best to reconstruct the area by copying elements from the surrounding image rather than trying to smooth out a defect with the Healing Brush. That's how her right shoulder, left eye, and parts of the hair were fixed.

To fix the hair, we used the Lasso tool, to select a clean portion of the top edge of her hair **A**, feathered it by 5 pixels, turned off the Eyeball icon for the Levels Adjustment Layer, and chose Edit>Copy Merged. Then we chose Edit>Paste to place the patch onto its own layer, typed Command/Ctrl-T and rotated and repositioned it into place **B**. Finally, we clicked on the Layer Mask icon at the bottom of the Layers palette, chose a soft-edged brush and painted with black to further blend the hair patch layer into the surrounding image **C**.

13. Create a Vignette

Now that we've completed the restoration, let's think about the presentation of the image. Adding a vignette effect will take your attention away from the background and edges of the shoulders and dress, allowing us to further disguise any problem areas. Type F to enter full screen mode, and type Command/Ctrl-minus a few times to zoom out on the image. Now choose the Elliptical Marquee tool and drag over the image to create an oval. (If you need to reposition the oval as you're drawing it, hold the spacebar and drag.)

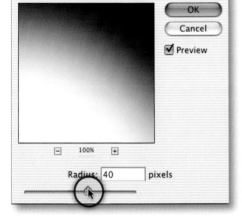

14. Feather Selection with Quick Mask

Now type Q to enter Quick Mask Mode so you see the selection as a color overlay. Next, choose Filter>Blur>Gaussian Blur and experiment with the Radius setting to figure out how much of a fade-out you'll need to make the edge look good (we used 40 pixels). Now type Q again to exit Quick Mask Mode and return to your selection, then choose Select>Inverse so that the edge of the photo is selected instead of the central portion of the image.

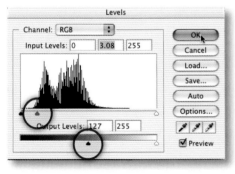

15. Lighten Edge with Levels

Now let's lighten the edges of the image while leaving the central portion unchanged. Click on the topmost layer to make it active, choose Levels from the Adjustment Layer pop-up menu at the bottom of the Layers palette and move the lower left slider to lighten the darkest areas (we used 128) of the image and then adjust the middle slider to fine-tune the effect (we used 3.0).

5

PEOPLE & PORTRAITS

The Fine Art of Fixing People (or How to Make Someone Look the Way They THINK They Look!)

I T'S AN UNAVOIDABLE TRUTH. Most of us wish we could change something about our appearance. The list of desires is sometimes a long one. We want to look younger, healthier, thinner, prettier, handsomer, stronger and sexier. Some folks resort to drastic measures that cost barrels of money and usually involve doctors and nurses, needles and scalpels. Ouch! Here in our own little world of Photoshop, we prefer to take the easier, less painful route. We offer you this chapter as the ultimate beauty treatment. Spend an hour with us, and it will be like you just spent a month being pampered at a Beverly Hills health spa. So, get your mouse ready, throw out your wrinkle creams, toupees, teeth whiteners and diet books, and let Photoshop give you the makeover of your dreams.

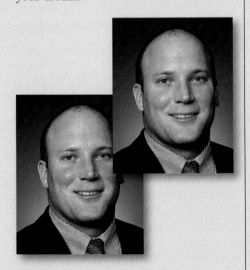

Prepare Your Instruments

As you don your surgical gown to prepare for the procedures in this chapter, you'll want to get your instruments ready. As with many chapters in this book, we'll be working with a number of tool presets, so if you haven't already loaded them up, go back to page 19 and follow the instructions for loading the presets which we have provided on this book's companion CD.

In many cases throughout this book, you can substitute your own photos for our practice images, but in this case we will be zooming in and working on very fine details, so, to fully take advantage of each technique, we strongly recommend that you start by using the sample images provided on the CD.

Avoiding Frankenstein

One of the greatest pitfalls for the inexperienced retoucher is to give in to the temptation to overdo it. Whether you're a hobbyist working on a snapshot of your dear granny, or a professional working on the cover of a posh fashion magazine, your objective should be one and the same: You should be aiming to enhance the features that make the subject "who they are," while minimizing the elements that might distract from expressing that personal uniqueness.

You've probably noticed this in some magazines, where a celebrity photo looks ridiculously blemish-and-wrinkle-free, sometimes to the extent that the person's skin looks almost plastic, and their face and expression no longer look like their own! This is the result of a retoucher (or client!) run amok. Truly professional retouching goes undetected. While you might spend hours in Photoshop giving someone a face lift, your efforts should never be obvious.

So, as you go about the business of performing eye-lifts, teeth bleaching, laser peels, and hair transplants (a definite exception to our "undetectable" rule), we encourage you to set your goals high, be true to your subject and when in doubt, always err on the side of subtle.

Controlling Blemishes & Wrinkles

Reduce and eliminate wrinkles, blemishes and other age-related features to help someone look like they were having a terrific day—where good lighting, make-up and even a good night's sleep combined to make them look their best.

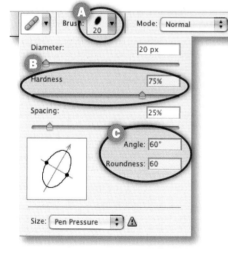

INSIGHT

Use All Layers? The Use All Layers checkbox in the Healing Brush was introduced in Photoshop CS. It allows you to have all your retouching work appear on an empty layer above your image. The concept sounds great, but it's computationally intensive, which means that Photoshop might not be able to keep up with your painting. We prefer to duplicate the main image layer and work with the Use All Layers checkbox turned *off* because Photoshop will be more responsive.

1. Set Up Healing Brush

Choose the Healing Brush, and click on the Brush Preview in the Options bar **A** to access the Brushes drop-down palette. Since the Healing Brush does most of the blending that is needed, use a high Hardness setting (we used 75%) **B**. Next, create an oval brush by setting both the Angle and Roundness settings to 60 **C**. Using an oval brush will deliver a more random and irregular edge than a round brush, making it more difficult to see the edges of areas that have been retouched. Since we want to use the same source area to heal different areas, turn off the Aligned checkbox in the Options bar **D**. By doing that, the only time you'll have to change your source is when you start retouching a different type of skin texture.

2. *Remove* Obvious Defects

We'll be performing our retouching in two stages. In the first stage we'll completely *remove* undesirable features, then we'll go back and *reduce* the impact of any areas that we don't want to completely eliminate.

Type Command-J/Ctrl-J to duplicate the active layer, then rename it "Remove." Use the Healing Brush (see Chapter 4, "Retouching and Repairing") to remove any details that you want to completely get rid of: frown lines across foreheads, age spots on a neck, dark circles under eyes, unkempt hair, dust and lint. Here are a few tips to keep in mind:

- Use a small brush and small strokes so the Healing Brush doesn't have to do extensive blending; it'll look more realistic that way.

- Each time you work on an area of different texture (forehead, nose, head, neck, etc.), just choose a different matching source from which to paint.

- At this stage, it's better to do too little rather than too much since we'll be performing another step to reduce artifacts. Extreme retouching jobs can make your subject unrecognizable; you never want your client to hear, "Is that your daughter?"

TIP

Working at the Edge. When using the Healing Brush in an area that contains a high-contrast edge, center the brush on the edge before Option/Alt-clicking to set the sample point **A**. Then center your brush again on a different part of the same line before clicking the mouse button to retouch the image **B**. That way the line will remain continuous and won't blend into the surrounding image **C**.

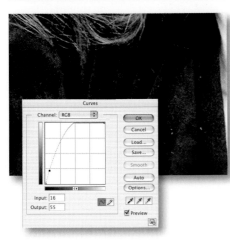

3. Use Curves to Reveal Defects

If you're not sure what to retouch because you can't see enough detail in an area, choose Curves from the Adjustment Layer pop-up menu at the bottom of the Layers palette, hold down Command/Ctrl, click in the area of your image that is dark, and use the up arrow key to brighten and add contrast to that area. Then, with the Remove layer active, perform your retouching and when done, drag the Adjustment Layer to the trash.

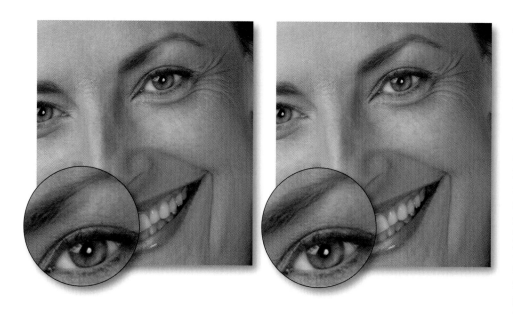

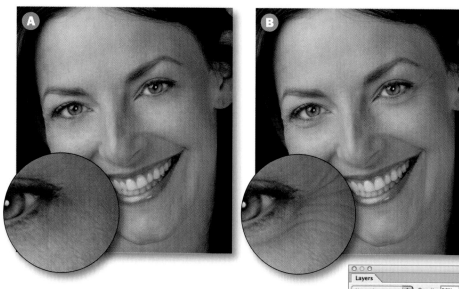

4. Manual Patching

Since it's different for the Healing Brush to rotate or scale areas, we'll manually "heal" her left eyebrow (right side of the photo). Start by selecting a small portion of the right eyebrow, then choose Select>Feather, set the Amount to 2 and then click OK. Then copy the selected area onto its own layer by typing Command/Ctrl-J. Now use the Move tool to reposition the layer so that it is over the other eyebrow. Type Command/Ctrl-T, then Control/right-click and choose Flip Horizontal, then move your mouse beyond one of the corner handles and drag to rotate the image until it matches the underlying image. Now set the blend mode of this Patch layer to Darken so the copied hairs blend into the surrounding ones and lower the opacity if necessary to soften the result.

5. *Reduce* Distracting "Features"

Now it's time to start working on those features that you'd rather reduce than remove. These might be recognizable (but less desirable) features that would make your retouching obvious to anyone who knows the subject of the photograph. With the top layer active, make a Merged Visible layer by holding down Shift-Command-Option/Shift-Ctrl-Alt and typing N to create a new layer, then E to merge what's visible into that new layer. Now go to town and get rid of every wrinkle, blemish, and crease until you have achieved perfectly smooth (though alien-like) skin **A**. Now lower the Opacity at the top of the Layers palette to control how much the retouching will affect the underlying image (we used 50%) **B**.

As a final (and optional) step, click on the Add Layer Mask icon at the bottom of the Layers palette and paint with black at a reduced Opacity to bring back any detail that was reduced too much, such as the corners of the eyes. ▥

Manual Patching Examples

In the previous technique, we *manually* patched a portion of a woman's eyebrow (as opposed to having the Patch tool or Healing Brush *automatically* blend areas).

Let's look at a few more examples of the manual technique so you can see just how versatile it is, and why sometimes it's just better to do things "the old-fashioned way."

Hair Patching

Skin Patching

The groom in this wedding photo needs the careful attention of a hair stylist. To make sure nobody is distracted by his flyaway hair, we'll manually patch it so that the viewer's attention goes directly to the bride. We started by selecting an area of hair to the right and above the area that needs to be retouched. Next we chose Select>Feather, set the Amount to 3, clicked OK, and then typed Command/Ctrl-J to place the selected area on its own layer. We next typed Command/Ctrl-T, dragged the patch into place over the flyaway hair, moved beyond a corner handle and dragged to rotate the patch and then double-clicked to finish the transformation. Finally the blend mode of the layer was set to Darken and the Opacity was lowered to 80%.

This image was retouched in a similar fashion to the previous one. A source area of the neck was selected, the selection was feathered 3 pixels, the area was copied to its own layer and then transformed to cover the problem areas of the neck. Then to blend the retouching into the image, the Blend Mode of the retouching layer was set to Lighten so it could only brighten the shadows of the underlying image and the Opacity was adjusted at the top of the Layers palette. ▥

JHD / MODEL BREEZEE REIFLER

Pore & Skin Softening

Make subtle changes to smooth out skin and reduce the appearance of pores.

Noise Removal Filters. There are three primary filters found under the Filter>Noise menu that are used for removing noise, grain and texture from an image:

- **Despeckle** removes tiny specks.
- **Median** smooths subtleties in an image while trying to maintain any sharp edges.
- **Dust & Scratches** is a more sophisticated version of the Median filter, which adds a Threshold setting that determines how different pixels must be from the surrounding area before the filter takes effect. (This allows for subtleties like grain to be maintained.)

1. Duplicate Layer

Let's start by copying the original image onto a new layer so we can easily control which areas are softened and which areas are to remain unchanged. Type Option-Command-J/Alt-Ctrl-J to duplicate the original image onto a separate layer. (Holding the Option/Alt key will cause Photoshop to prompt you for a layer name [we used "Dust & Scratches"].)

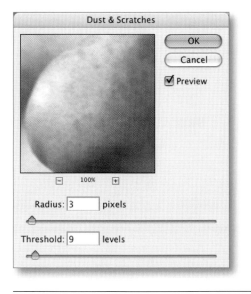

2. Apply Dust & Scratches Filter

Now let's smooth out the skin by choosing Filter>Noise>Dust & Scratches. Start by setting the Threshold to zero so the filter affects the entire image. Now set the Radius to 1 (the lowest setting possible) and then raise it until you discover the lowest setting that is capable of smoothing out the skin. In our case a Radius of 3 was enough to rid the image of noticeable pores, wrinkles, etc. Then to avoid unnecessarily softening textured areas (such as noise or film grain), raise the Threshold setting until you find the highest setting that still smooths the skin without bringing back artifacts (we used 9).

3. Paint on Layer Mask

To ensure that the softening effect doesn't affect important details such as the eyelashes and hair, hold the Option/Alt key and click on the Layer Mask icon at the bottom of the Layers palette. That will create a Layer Mask that is filled with black, which will hide the filtered layer. Now, choose the Brush tool, set the Opacity to 100%, select a large, soft-edged brush and paint with white to *paint **in** the softening effect.* Then to further blend portions of the filtered image with the original, reduce the Opacity of the Brush tool to somewhere around 80% and paint over additional areas. Finally, to compare the original image with the filtered result, click on the eyeball icon for the filtered layer multiple times to toggle its visibility.

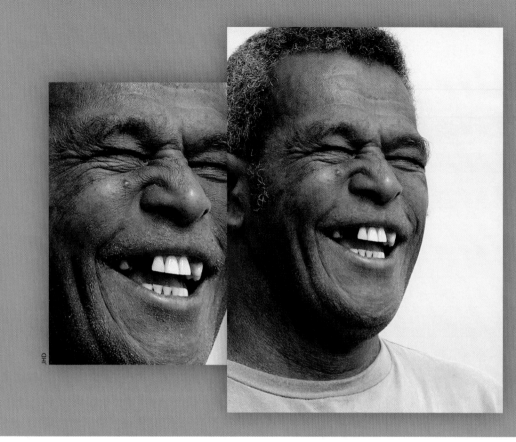

Skin Conditioning & Shaving

Quickly "condition" weathered or aged skin, and shave away 5 o'clock shadow.

1. Duplicate Layer

As with the previous technique, we'll need to start by duplicating the original image onto a new layer. To try a variation on the method used previously, hold Option/Alt and drag the Background layer to the New Layer icon at the bottom of the Layers palette and set the name of the layer to "Dust & Scratches."

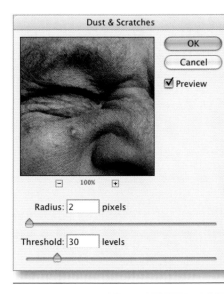

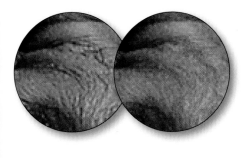

2. Apply Dust & Scratches Filter

Then to smooth the skin, choose Filter>Noise>Dust & Scratches. Start by setting the Threshold to zero so the filter affects the entire image. Now adjust the Radius setting to find the lowest setting that is capable of smoothing out the wrinkles in the skin (for this 1000-pixel-wide photo, we used 2). To avoid losing detail in other areas of the image, (and to retain the image's inherent film grain) while continuing to hide the fine lines and wrinkles and whiskers, raise the Threshold setting until you find the highest setting that still smooths the skin (we used 30).

3. Create a Negative Layer Mask

Now let's hide the filtered layer completely by holding the Option/Alt key and clicking on the Layer Mask icon at the bottom of the Layers palette. Choose a large, soft-edged brush, and *paint with white to apply the softening effect* in the areas that need it the most. Now for a more subtle change, reduce the Opacity setting of the Brush tool to somewhere around 80% and paint over his 5 o'clock shadow and some of the neck wrinkles.

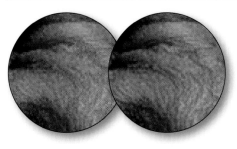

4. Reduce Opacity of Filtered Layer

Now that we're done masking the filtered layer, let's control how strong the effect is applied to the image. You can do that by clicking on the word "Opacity" at the top of the Layers palette and then dragging to the right or left. This is a new feature introduced in Photoshop CS known as **scrubby sliders,** which allows you to quickly change a setting without having to type numbers (we ended up with 75%).

Skin Smoothing for a Porcelain Glow

Focus attention and remove distracting details with blend modes, the Blend If sliders and the Lens Blur filter.

1. Repair Image

The first step in this technique is to use what you learned from Chapter 4 to clean up any defects in the image on a duplicated repair layer. That means getting rid of stray hairs, removing blemishes, evening out the highlights on the lips and fixing any rips or unwanted wrinkles in the clothing. In our example, we've already done that for you.

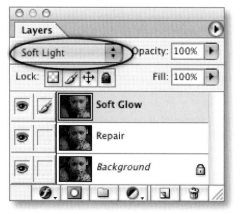

2. Duplicate Using Soft Light

Before moving on, click on the top layer and type Command-J/Ctrl-J to make a duplicate—we renamed the layer "Soft Glow." Change the Blend Mode menu at the top of the Layers palette to Soft Light, which will add contrast to the image. Choose Filter>Blur>Gaussian Blur, adjust the Radius to achieve the desired amount of softening, and click OK. You want to use an amount that smooths the skin and softens distracting detail, but doesn't overwhelm the features of the face (you might try a setting between 5 and 50, depending on the resolution of the image). We used 10.

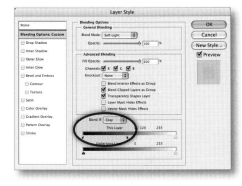

3. Bring Back Shadow Detail

Now let's bring back the shadow detail we lost when we added contrast to the image. Double-click to the right of the name of the Soft Glow layer to access the Blending Options dialog box. Move the upper-left slider toward the right to bring back the shadow detail in the image (we used 120), then hold Option/Alt and drag the left edge of that slider to split it into two pieces to create a smooth transition (we ended up with the sliders at 0 and 120).

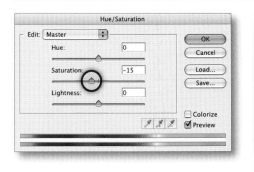

4. Adjust Saturation

When we increased the contrast, the saturation of all the colors in the image also increased. If you'd like to tone that down a little, choose Hue/Saturation from the Adjustment Layer pop-up menu at the bottom of the Layers palette and lower the saturation (we used –15).

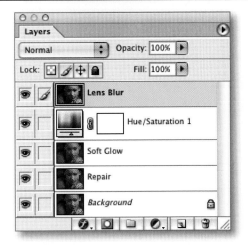

5. Create a Merged Visible Layer

We're almost ready to apply a filter that will selectively blur the image, but since filters only apply to a single layer, we'll need to create a new layer that contains the result of merging all the visible layers together. But since we don't want to lose the capability of getting back to previous versions of this image, we'll merge a *copy* of those layers. With the top layer active, type Command/Ctrl-Shift N to create a new empty layer and name it "Lens Blur." Then to merge a copy of the other layers into our new layer, hold Command-Option-Shift/Ctrl-Alt-Shift and type E.

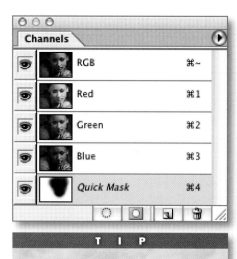

Depth Maps. A Depth Map is a grayscale image that is usually stored in the Channels palette and used when blurring an image using the Lens Blur filter. In a Depth Map, black represents an area that should remain in focus, white represents areas that should be blurred and shades of gray represent areas that will be partially blurred.

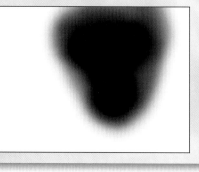

T I P

Reset Tools. If you ever try to paint with the Brush tool only to find that it doesn't deliver what you expect, then try the following:

- Type Command/Ctrl-D (Deselect) to make sure a selection isn't limiting where you can affect the image.
- Check the foreground color to see if it's identical to the image you are attempting to change.
- Make sure the proper layer is active.
- If all else fails, Control/right-click on the Tool icon on the left side of the Options bar and choose Reset Tool.

6. Create a Depth Map

Let's define the areas of the image we'd like to keep in crisp focus (the main features of eyes, nose and mouth), the areas that we want to have a soft focus (chin and ears), and areas we want to be out of focus (the distractions of the wrinkled hands, textured sweater, and background). We'll do this by creating a **Depth Map**. Choose Window>Channels to view the Channels palette, type Q to enter **Quick Mask mode,** choose a soft-edged brush and then paint with black over the areas you'd like to keep in focus. Even though your foreground color is set to black, your paint will show up as a red overlay. That's because what you're really doing is adding black to a temporary channel (the one at the bottom of the Channels palette) and the black areas of that channel are being displayed as a red overlay on your image. Before you move on, lower the brush's Opacity setting to 50% and paint over the areas that you'd like to have semi-sharp, leaving the background untouched.

7. Save Depth Map as a Channel

Now that we have our Depth Map defined, we need to make sure it stays at the bottom of the Channels palette. Since we're in Quick Mask mode our current channel is only temporary (typing Q would make it disappear and become a selection). So, once you're done painting, drag the bottom channel (the one called Quick Mask) to the New Channel icon to duplicate it. Then type Q to exit Quick Mask mode and type Command/Ctrl-D to get rid of the resulting selection.

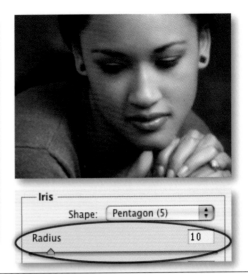

8. Apply Lens Blur Filter

We're ready to blur the image, so choose Filter>Blur>Lens Blur. There are numerous settings in the Lens Blur dialog box, but there's only one designed for setting the amount of blurring in your image. Experiment with the Radius setting until you find the setting that produces the result you desire (we used 10 for this 1000-pixel-wide image). You can toggle the Preview checkbox near the top of the dialog box if you'd like to get a quick before and after comparison.

9. Load Depth Map

To blur the areas we defined earlier and leave the rest of the image sharp, change the Source pop-up menu to the name of the Depth Map you saved in the previous step (called Quick Mask copy in our example). If Photoshop happens to blur the face and keep the background in focus, then you can easily turn on the Invert checkbox that appears near the Source pop-up menu.

10. Fine-Tune Settings

The only problem with blurring the image is that the blurred areas will have no grain or noise and therefore won't match the general feeling of the rest of the image. To re-introduce a subtle texture into the blurred areas, bring up the Noise Amount setting to 5, choose Gaussian and turn on the Monochromatic checkbox.

Using Hue/ Saturation Adjustments

The Hue/Saturation dialog box offers much more than is apparent at first glance—you can change the basic color (known as the hue) of specific objects, make the color in your image more vivid (known as saturation), create monochromatic effects, and much more.

Let's take a look at what's available so you can get the most out of this invaluable tool. The Hue/Saturation dialog box performs four main tasks: It can adjust the Hue, Saturation and Lightness of an image and is able to isolate a range of colors within an image.

Hue

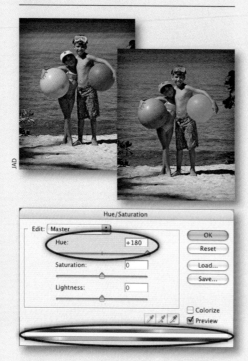

The Hue slider changes the basic color of every color in your image (when the Edit pop-up menu is set to Master, that is). To get a better understanding of how the Hue slider affects your images, open any colorful image and then move the Hue slider. Keep an eye on what is happening at the bottom of the Hue/Saturation dialog box. The top color bar indicates all the hues (or basic colors) that might be in your image. The bottom bar indicates what will happen to each of those hues. Just pick any hue from the top bar and then look directly below it to the bottom bar to see what it will become. Now compare the colors that appear at each end of the bars—they're identical because each bar represents the traditional color wheel that has simply been straightened into a horizontal line. Therefore, the Hue settings are measured from –180° to +180°, which forms the full 360° of a circle!

Saturation

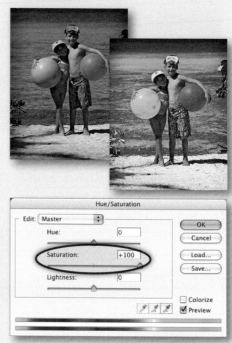

The Saturation slider determines how colorful your image will be. Moving the slider to the left of center will make the image less colorful, and moving it all the way to the left will remove all hint of color from the image. That might seem like a simple way to create a grayscale image, but there are better methods as you'll see in Chapter 7, "Color and Tone Treatments." Moving the Saturation slider to the right of center will make your image more colorful. Many images will benefit from a slight boost of saturation, but you have to be careful; otherwise you'll end up with artificial-looking colors or ones that are outside the range of colors your output device is capable or reproducing (also known as colors that are *out of gamut*).

Lightness

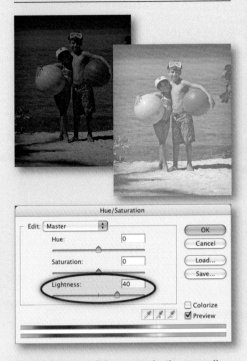

The Lightness slider controls the overall brightness of your image. Moving this slider all the way to the left will darken the entire image until it becomes solid black. Moving the slider all the way to the right will produce solid white. This slider is a poor substitute for the alternative methods of adjusting brightness (such as Levels and Curves), but can be useful when you fine-tune a particular range of colors by using the Edit pop-up menu at the top of the Hue/Saturation dialog box. See the next project "Unifying Skin Color & Tone" for more on practical uses for the Lightness slider.

Isolating a Range of Color

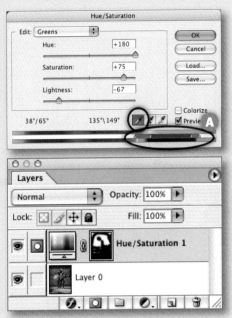

All the sliders available in the Hue/Saturation dialog box become much more useful once you've learned how to isolate a range of colors.

When the Edit pop-up menu at the top of the Hue/Saturation dialog box is set to Master, the sliders will affect every color in your image (that is unless you have a selection active). When you choose a color from the Edit pop-up menu, Photoshop will attempt to limit the changes to the general color you've specified. The problem is that there are only six colors listed in the menu: Reds, Yellows, Greens, Cyans, Blues and Magentas. When you choose a color, small sliders will appear between the two bars **A**. Those sliders indicate the range of colors that will be affected by the adjustment: The colors between the vertical bar sliders will change completely, while the colors between the vertical bars and the triangular sliders will be affected less (which makes the adjustment fade out into the surrounding colors).

Clicking within your image after choosing the left Eyedropper tool within the Hue/Saturation dialog box will cause the sliders to become centered on the color

you click on, effectively concentrating the adjustment on that particular color. Clicking on your image with the minus Eyedropper tool will cause the space between the vertical bar sliders to narrow and eliminate the color you clicked on from being within their range. Clicking with the plus Eyedropper tool will expand the area between the two vertical sliders to include the color you clicked on. You can also manually click and drag on the sliders to reposition them. We'll use the Hue/Saturation dialog box in many techniques throughout this book. We just wanted to make sure you had a general idea of how it works before moving on.

You can further isolate colors after leaving the Hue/Saturation dialog box by painting with black on the Layer Mask attached to the Adjustment Layer.

MODEL: TOM

Unifying Skin Color & Tone

Use Hue/Saturation and the power of its Edit menu to quickly unify skin tone– whether freckles, acne, or the occasional sunburn.

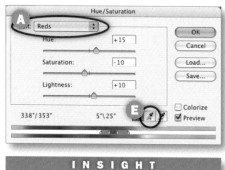

1. Determine the Colors to Be Adjusted
Choose Hue/Saturation from the Adjustment Layer pop-up menu at the bottom of the Layers palette. Choose Red from the Edit pop-up menu at the top of the Hue/Saturation dialog box **A** to get the color isolation sliders to appear **B**. Next, drag one of the outer sliders toward the others to slam them together into a single mass **C**. Now click within the image in the sunburnt area to center those sliders on the color you've clicked on and then move the hue slider until you see a radical change in the image **D** (not that we really want him to look this way). Click on the plus Eyedropper in the lower right of the Hue/Saturation dialog box and then click on additional areas of the sunburn until the color change covers the entire sunburn area **E**. Then to avoid an abrupt transition, drag the two triangular sliders away from the vertical ones to let the color shift blend into the surrounding image **F**.

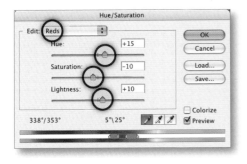

2. Adjust Reds

It's time to make the precise adjustment this image needs. Move the Hue slider toward the right of center to shift the color towards yellow and away from red. Even after doing that, the area we're adjusting is a bit too colorful and dark. So, move the Saturation slider to the left a little (we used −10) to make the area less colorful and then adjust the Lightness slider to balance the tone (we used +10). Once you have the color right, you're welcome to adjust the small sliders to fine-tune the transition.

3. Adjust Yellows

Now that we have the red areas in control, you can see an area of skin near the cheeks that appear yellowish. So, before leaving Hue/Saturation, change the Edit pop-up menu to Yellows and repeat the general technique that we used for step one to, in this case, isolate the yellows. Once you have the area isolated **A**, shift the Hue setting to −10 to make the yellow more red and blend with the surrounding image.

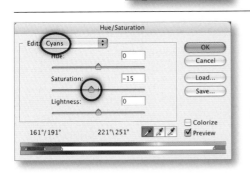

4. Adjust Blues

Tone down the background by choosing Cyans from the Edit pop-up menu and moving the Saturation slider to −15. We're almost done, but the overall color in the image is still a little too vivid, so set the Edit pop-up menu back to Master and lower the Saturation to −20 and then click OK to apply the adjustment.

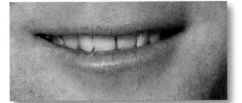

5. Paint on Layer Mask

When we shifted the reds and desaturated the overall colors, it made the lips look a little dull. To bring the lips closer to their previous state, choose a small, soft-edged black brush, set the Opacity of the Brush tool to 50% and paint across the lips to lessen the adjustment in that area.

Eye & Teeth Tweaking

Use Blend Modes and Brushes to neutralize and brighten eyes and teeth.

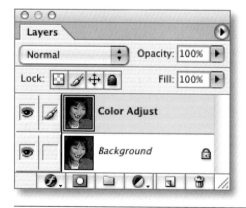

1. Duplicate Layer & Load Presets

Start by typing Option-Command-J/ Alt-Ctrl-J to duplicate the background layer and name it "Color Adjust." Then choose the Brush tool, click the tool icon on the far left of the Options bar **A** (*not* the Brush preview to its right), choose HTW-Tool Sampler.tpl from the side menu in the upper-right of the drop-down palette **B** and then click on the Wow-White Teeth-Neutralize preset **C**.

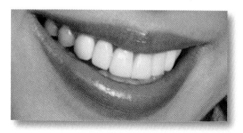 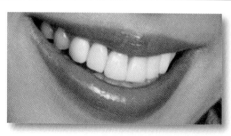

2. Reduce Stain on Teeth

Now choose a soft-edged brush that is about the same size as one of the smaller teeth and paint across the stains to reduce the yellow color. You might need to paint specific areas more than once depending on how strong the stain is.

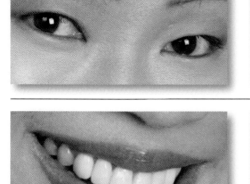

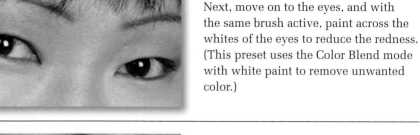

3. Eliminate Bloodshot Eyes

Next, move on to the eyes, and with the same brush active, paint across the whites of the eyes to reduce the redness. (This preset uses the Color Blend mode with white paint to remove unwanted color.)

4. Brighten Teeth

Now it's time to go back and *brighten* the eyes and teeth. Click on the Wow-White Teeth-Brighten preset, which will set the Blend mode to Soft Light, the Opacity to 15%, and the foreground color to white. Now paint across the stained portions of the teeth. Painting across specific spots multiple times to strengthen the brightening effect.

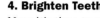

5. Brighten Eyes

Once you've got the teeth under control, use the same technique and tool preset to brighten the whites of the eyes.

6. Enhance Eye Color & Contrast

To finish this image off, let's brighten the colored area of the eyes. Choose the *Wow-Dodge&Burn-Extreme-use B&W* preset, choose white to paint with (black would darken) and paint around the iris. To add to the effect, try lightening the area of the iris that is opposite the main light source. (In this case, we lightened the lower right portions.) ▦

Red-Eye Removal

When time is of the essence, use tool presets to quickly remove red-eye and enhance eyes, skin and teeth.

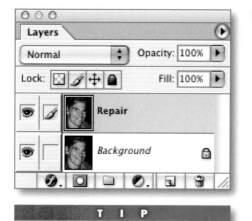

TIP

Tool Presets. The *Tool Presets* can also be accessed in a stand-alone palette by choosing Window>Tool Presets.

1. Duplicate Layer & Load Presets

Let's add a couple more tricks to the techniques we learned from the previous project. As we did in that project, start by typing Option-Command-J/Alt-Ctrl-J to duplicate the Background layer, but this time name it "Repair." Then choose the Brush tool, click on the Tool Presets icon on the far left of the Options bar **A**, choose HTW-Tool Sampler.tpl from the side menu in the upper right of the drop-down palette **B** and then click on the Wow–White Teeth–Neutralize preset **C**.

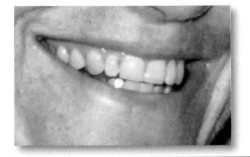

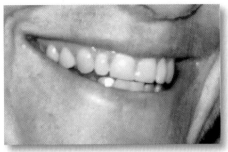

2. Reduce Stains on Teeth

Choose a soft-edged brush that is about the same size as one of the teeth and paint across the teeth to reduce the yellow color. Depending on how strong the stain is, you might need to paint across the stubborn spots more than once. Be very careful not to paint over the gums; otherwise they'll start looking gray.

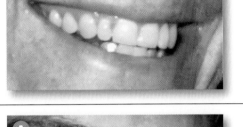

3. Brighten Teeth

Now to brighten the teeth, click on the Wow-White Teeth-Brighten preset, and then paint across the stained portions of the teeth. Painting across the teeth multiple times will strengthen the brightening effect.

4. Eliminate Red Eye

Now choose the Wow-Red Eye-Neutralize preset and paint across the pupil to take the red out **A**. After doing that, you'll still have a little red left since the red-eye extends beyond the pupil and into the iris. Choose the Wow-Red Eye-Blue Replace preset, hold Option/Alt and click on the iris color **B** and then paint across any red areas to get them to blend into the rest of the eye **C**.

5. Darken Pupil

Since red-eye affects not only color but tone, choose Wow-Red Eye-Darken and paint across the dark areas of the eye to darken that area. You don't have to worry about the specular highlight because the settings of this brush won't allow it to darken overly bright areas.

6. Reduce Red Skin Color

Her cheeks look slightly red, so choose the Red Skin Neutralize preset, Option/Alt-click to sample the normal area of skin and then paint across her rosy cheeks to reduce the red cast.

Body Reshaping

Use the Liquify Filter to tame those trouble spots that plague not only models, but also the best of us.

1. Select and Copy Area

Sometimes it's the little adjustments that can make the biggest impact in a photo, whether that photo is of a super model, a client, or one's self. (Hey, it was after a long book project, cut me some slack!) Start by using the Rectangular Marquee tool to select the general area you'd like to work on and typing Command/Ctrl-J to copy that area onto its own layer. Working on a duplicate of a small portion of the image will speed up the liquifying process and ensure that we always have the original untouched image as part of the Photoshop file.

2. Apply Liquify Filter to Left Side

Next, choose Filter>Liquify and choose the Push Left tool **A** by typing O (that's an Oh, not a zero). This tool shifts the pixels in your image based on the direction you drag the mouse. Dragging down pushes areas to the right; dragging up pushes them to the left; dragging right pushes up; and dragging left pushes down.

To slim the right side of the waist (left side of the photo), choose a large brush (we used a 100-pixel brush for this low-resolution image), reduce the Brush Pressure to 25, then click and drag down with the brush just barely touching the waist, so most of the brush is over the background **B**. If it's a little too obvious, then type Command/Ctrl-Z to undo it and try again. Whenever possible, use one continuous smooth stroke for a fix, rather than several shorter ones.

TIP

Quick Thaw. When using the Liquify Filters' Freeze Mask tool, you can hold the Option/Alt key to temporarily access the Thaw Mask tool to erase some of the freezing you've applied.

3. Freeze Areas That Shouldn't Shift

Let's move to the right side of the image where we're in much tighter quarters. If we use a large brush and shift the area surrounding the waist, we'll end up distorting the hand. To prevent an unnecessary shifting, choose the Freeze Mask tool **A** and paint over the hand and arm **B** so they won't be affected.

4. Apply Liquify Filter to Right Side

After we've frozen the areas we don't want to shift, let's start working on the left side of the body (right side of the photo). If we drag down with the Push Left tool, we'll end up exaggerating the "love handle" instead of minimizing it. So, choose a brush slightly smaller than what you used for the other side of the body, move your cursor so it partially overlaps the waist and drag up to push the body outline to the left **A**. You might need to take a second pass in such tight quarters **B**. 🖐

JHD / MODEL: JILL

Body Part Swapping

Cover distracting elements by creatively combining multiple images—in an attempt to turn a snapshot into a portrait.

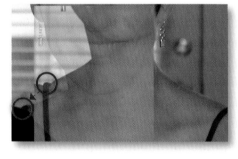

1. Add and Position Second Image

In our original photograph, someone is blocking the view of our model's shoulder. Use the Move tool to drag a replacement shoulder image (taken during the same session) into the main file, lower the Opacity at the top of the Layers palette and position it so it lines up with her shoulder and neck. Once they align, bring the Opacity back to 100%.

2. Blend Image with Layer Mask

Now that we have the replacement shoulder in place, let's blend it into the underlying image. Click on the Layer Mask icon at the bottom of the Layers palette, choose the Brush tool, set the Foreground Color to black and paint with a soft-edged brush to hide the chin, neck and background of the replacement shoulder—without revealing any of the "unwanted guest" that is under the shoulder layer.

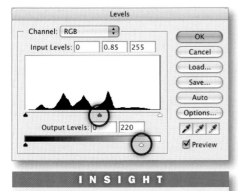

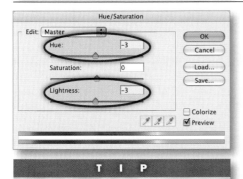

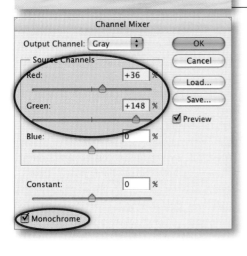

3. Match Tonality with Levels

Hold Option/Alt and choose Levels from the Adjustment Layer pop-up menu at the bottom of the Layers palette. Turn on the **Use Previous Layer to Create Clipping Mask** check box so the adjustment will only affect the Shoulder layer in Levels. Move the lower-right slider to darken the shoulder, then adjust the upper-middle slider to fine-tune both the brightness and contrast until the shoulder matches the rest of the image. Next paint on the Layer Mask with black at a reduced opacity over any areas that have become too dark to lessen the change.

4. Match Color with Hue/Saturation

Now let's get the color to match. Hold Option/Alt and choose Hue/Saturation from the Adjustment Layer pop-up menu at the bottom of the Layers palette, and turn on the **Use Previous Layer to Create Clipping Mask** checkbox. Now adjust the Hue slider to control the overall color, the Saturation slider to control how colorful the image is and the Lightness slider to fine-tune the shoulder's brightness (we used Hue: –3, Saturation: 0, and Lightness: –3). When finished, paint with black on the Layer Mask over areas that appear too red.

5. Convert to Grayscale

To convert the photo to "black-and-white," choose Window>Channels and click through the Red, Green and Blue channels to get a sense of their content. In this case, the Red channel is somewhat soft, the Green channel has good contrast and the Blue channel contains a bit of noise. Select the RGB channel again, then choose Channel Mixer from the Adjustment Layer pop-up menu. It starts off using 100% of what was in the Red channel. Let's lower that to +36 and then compensate by emphasizing the green (+148) to achieve good contrast.

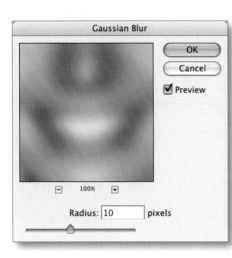

6. Add a Diffused Glow

With the top layer active, hold Shift-Option-Command/Shift-Alt-Ctrl and type N and then E to create a Merged Visible Layer that contains all elements that are currently visible. To soften the image and add additional contrast, choose Filter>Blur>Gaussian Blur, set the Radius between 5 and 30 (depending on the size of your file), click OK, and then change the Blend Mode menu at the top of the Layers palette to Overlay. If the result is too extreme, change the Blend Mode to Soft Light, or Lower the opacity of the layer (we used 75%).

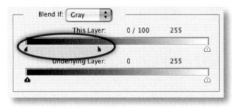

7. Bring Back Shadow Detail

Now let's bring back the shadow detail that was lost in the previous step. Double-click to the right of the layer's name to access the Blending Options dialog box. Move the upper-left Blend If slider to 100 to reveal the shadow detail in the underlying image. Then to create a smooth transition, hold Option/Alt and drag the left edge of the slider to 0.

8. Add Vignette

Finally, let's darken the edges of the image to draw the viewer's attention toward the center of the image. With the top layer active, choose Inner Shadow from the Layer Style pop-up menu at the bottom of the Layers palette, set the Distance to 0, the Size to 100 and set the Blend Mode to Overlay. Then adjust the Opacity setting to control how dark the edges appear (we used 75%). The effect can be subtle (as shown here) or extreme, depending on the Blend Mode you choose for the Inner Shadow effect. Try Soft Light, Hard Light, or even multiply (with reduced opacity).

Hair Replacement

Perform an instant hair transplant by borrowing hair from one photo and integrating it into another.

JHD / MODEL: GERSON

JHD / MODEL: ALEXANDRE KEESE

1. Import & Position Hair

By shooting two subjects with the same camera and flash setup, they will have very similar lighting, which will help to make the result look more realistic. Start by dragging the hair image **A** into the main document **B** using the Move tool. Then to align the shots, change the Blend Mode at the top of the Layers palette to Darken, which will cause the bright areas of the hair photo to disappear and allow some of the underlying image to show through **C**. Next, type Command/Ctrl-T, hold Shift and drag the corner handles to scale, or move your mouse beyond one of the corner handles and drag to rotate the hair image until it matches up with the underlying image. Before moving on, set the layer's Blend Mode back to Normal.

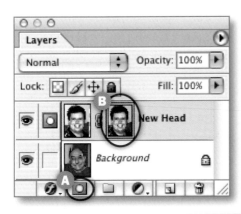

2. Create Hair Mask

Now let's use a Layer Mask to isolate the hair. Hold down Option-Command/Alt-Ctrl and type ~ (that's known as a *tilde* and is located in the upper left of most keyboards) to load the luminosity of the image as a selection and then click on the Layer Mask icon at the bottom of the Layers palette **A**. To see what this unusual step did, Option/Alt-click on the Layer Mask thumbnail in the Layers palette **B** to view the mask **C**.

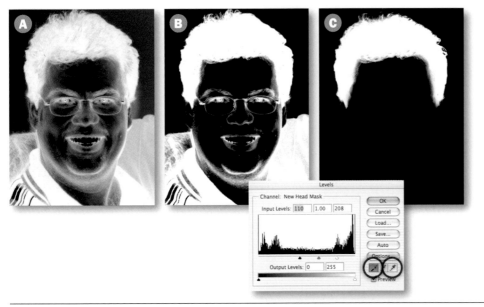

3. Refine Hair Mask

Let's refine the mask so that just the hair is visible (white in the mask) and the background is hidden (black in the mask). Type Command/Ctrl-I to invert the mask **A** and then choose Image>Adjustments>Levels. When the Levels dialog box appears, click on the White Eyedropper tool in the lower-right of the dialog box and then click on the darkest area of the hair to force it to white. Next, click on the Black Eyedropper and then click on the brightest area of the skin that surrounds the hair to force anything that is that shade or darker to black **B**. Then paint with black and white to touch up the result **C**. Now Option/Alt-click on the Layer Mask to view the image.

4. Blend the Hair with a Shadow

To make the hair seem more "at home" in its new surroundings, let's add a drop shadow to the forehead. Hold the Command/Ctrl key and click on the *Layer Mask Thumbnail* image in the Layers palette to load it as a selection. With the Lasso tool active, press the down arrow key five times to reposition the selection, then click on the bottom layer to make it active and choose Levels from the Adjustment Layer pop-up menu at the bottom of the Layers palette. Now move the lower-right Output slider in Levels to darken the forehead (we used 171).

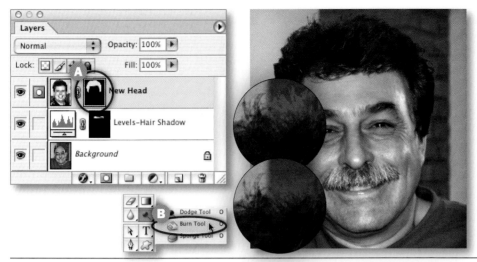

5. Darken Edge of Hair

Our mask has caused most of the background of the hair photograph to disappear, but there is still a slight light fringe around the top edge. To get rid of that fringe, click on the Layer Mask Thumbnail that is attached to the hair layer **A**, choose the Burn tool (it's hidden under the Dodge tool in the Tools palette) **B**, and paint over the edge of the hair using a soft-edged brush. This is one of the most practical uses for this tool; its ability to clean up a soft-edged mask by selectively darkening straggling perimeter pixels (and thus hiding them).

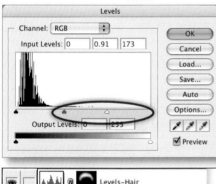

6. Adjust Tonality of Hair

With the hair layer active, use the Lasso tool to select the central portion of the hair, choose Select Feather and enter 30. Next, choose Levels from the Adjustment Layer pop-up menu at the bottom of the Layers palette, move the upper-right slider to brighten the highlights in the hair (we used 173), then to maintain the original darkness, drag the middle slider to the right to darken the hair overall (we used 0.91). Now choose the Brush tool and fine-tune where this highlighting is visible by painting with White or Black on the Layer Mask.

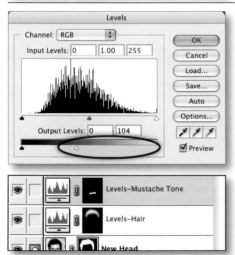

7. Match Moustache to Hair

Now that he's got this great new mane of hair, let's adjust his moustache to match the tone of the hair. Choose Levels from the Adjustment Layer pop-up menu at the bottom of the Layers palette, move the lower-right slider to the middle to darken the highlights, while maintaining shadow detail (don't worry if the rest of the image gets overly dark; just pay attention to his mustache) and then click OK. Next, type Command/Ctrl-I to invert the Adjustment Layer's mask and paint with white over the mustache to reveal the darkening adjustment. 🖳

6

ADDING DENSITY WITH BLEND MODES 134

DIFFUSED GLOWS 136

HIGHLIGHT GLOWS 138

SATURATED GLOWS 138

CONTRAST GLOWS 139

HIGH KEY GLOWS 139

POPPING IMAGES WITH HIGH PASS 140

SELECTIVE HIGH PASS 142

ENHANCING & EXAGGERATING

Go Beyond What Was Captured to What Was Experienced–or Even Better–to What You Want Your Audience to Experience

DENSITY GRADIENT "STYLE FILTERS" 144

COLOR GRADIENT "STYLE FILTERS" 146

CUSTOMIZING GRADIENT "STYLE FILTERS" 149

CREATIVE FOCUS CONTROL 151

DREAMLIKE FOCUS 153

ROMANTIC AURA FOCUS 153

DEPTH OF FIELD ALTERING 154

MOTION BLURRING & VARIATIONS 156

THE CRAFT OF PHOTOGRAPHY is much more than just good composition with flattering lighting. It is about finding and revealing the very essence of a moment. Your challenge is like that of a film director's—you must interpret the piece and determine what you want to communicate to your audience. Once you've made that decision, we can help you build up an arsenal of techniques that will assist you in guiding the viewer's attention to what you feel is most important about your image. Perhaps you'd like to emphasize something particularly compelling within a portrait, or the surreal colors of a coastal sunset, or a contrasting composition of antique architectural details set against soft wispy clouds.

Here you'll learn how to remove distracting detail, effectively alter contrast and creatively use color to enhance the subject of a photograph. You'll also learn how to exaggerate depth of field and add a sense of motion to your image. And throughout, we're going to concentrate on maintaining quality, keeping things as flexible as possible and doing things quickly.

Set the Mood by Altering Contrast

The overall mood of your image is key to conveying the story you want to tell. Are you looking for your image to pop off the page or do you want a softer, more delicate presence? To significantly change the mood of your image, you may accomplish it by selectively:

- Adding density
- Exaggerating contrast
- Applying glows

Focus Attention by Changing Depth of Field or Adding Motion

You can use depth of field and motion effects to dramatically alter the feel of your story and deftly guide your viewer's attention to the most important parts of your image. These techniques are ideal for those times when you've got a great subject but a less than perfect (or overly busy) background. Cleverly applied motion effects can distract your viewer from the background and put the focus directly on your subject.

In this chapter you will learn about:

- Selective blurring
- Altering depth of field
- Simulating motion

Transform Atmosphere by Changing Density and Color

Perhaps you've got an image that is generally good, but something is missing—there is a lack of excitement that you can't quite identify. Maybe the sky needs a shift in color or perhaps the composition needs to be emphasized by adding contrast. Working with color and density combined, you will be able to breathe new life into your photo and create some much needed drama for otherwise lifeless images. Following are projects that help with:

- Overlaying density
- Overlaying color
- Reshaping tone

Adding Density with Blend Modes

Make your images "pop" by adding subtle saturation and contrast while retaining shadow detail.

Empty Adjustment Layers: Duplicating the original image layer will double your file size. ***You can get the same result without increasing the file size by using an "empty" adjustment layer.*** Just create a new adjustment layer, don't make any changes (no adjustment) and then click OK. When using Blend Modes, Photoshop looks at the "empty" adjustment layer as if it contained the result of an adjustment. Since there is no adjustment, the adjustment layer is, in effect, an exact duplicate of the underlying image.

1. Duplicate the Original Layer

To copy the original image onto a new layer, either drag the name of the layer to the New Layer button at the bottom of the Layers palette, or type Command/Ctrl-J. If the image you're working with contains multiple layers, you'll need to merge all the layers in the image onto a new layer (a "merged visible" layer). You can do that by holding down the Shift-Option-Command/Shift-Alt-Ctrl keys and typing N and then E.

2. Change Blend Mode of Layer

With the layer you just created active, experiment with the Blending Mode menu at the top of the Layers palette.

- Multiply mode will darken the underlying image based on the brightness values found in the active layer. It's similar to sandwiching two 35mm slides together.

- Screen mode is the opposite of Multiply. It will brighten the image using the brightness levels in the active layer. (Imagine aiming two slide projectors onto the same screen.)

- Soft Light and Overlay and all the blending modes in their grouping will add contrast and saturation to your image. These two modes darken the dark areas while lightening the light areas, and are the ones you will typically use.

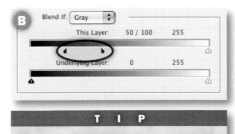

3. Apply Advanced Blending

To fine-tune the results (in this case maintaining control of shadow detail), we're going to use the Blend If sliders. To get to those options, do one of the following: Double-click on the thumbnail preview on the layer, Option/Alt-double-click on the layer's name, or choose Blending Options from the Layer Style pop-up menu at the bottom of the Layers palette. The Blend If sliders are located at the bottom of the Layer Style dialog box **A**.

Moving the left slider under the heading of This Layer will hide the darkest areas of the active layer, which will prevent the darkest areas of the active layer from effecting the underlying image. In order to get a smooth transition between the areas you have hidden and the areas that are visible, hold the Option/Alt key and drag the right edge of the slider (we used 50/100) **B**. 🔲

> **T I P**
>
> **Visualizing Changes.** If you're having trouble figuring out exactly what the Blend If sliders are doing to your image, then hide the underlying image by Option/Alt-clicking on the active layer's eyeball icon. With the underlying image hidden, you'll be able to see exactly which areas are being hidden, and you can also see the effect of splitting the sliders to create a gradual transition between visible and hidden areas.

JHD / MODELS: GENO AND DAKOTA

Diffused Glows

Add richness and soften distractions while maintaining detail with this quick "Make it Better" technique.

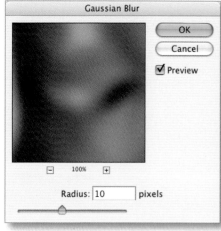

1. Duplicate and Blur Image

Start by duplicating the image onto its own layer by typing Command/Ctrl-J. Next, soften the image by choosing Filter>Blur>Gaussian Blur. Use a setting high enough to soften the image, but not so high that you can no longer make out image features (settings between 5 and 50 are typical; we used 10 for this 1000-pixel-high image).

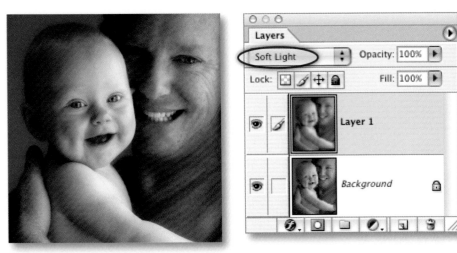

2. Choose Layer's Blend Mode

Just as stories thrive on conflict, photographs thrive on contrast, and for that reason, we'll use one of the contrast blending modes (usually Soft Light or Overlay). In this case, we'll go with the Soft Light blend mode, which will enhance the contrast without overly saturating the photograph.

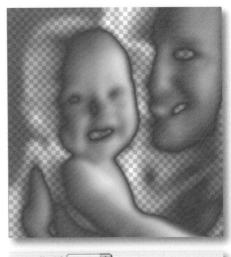

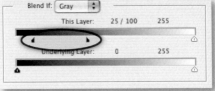

3. Apply Advanced Blending

In the process of adding contrast to the image, we lost a little shadow detail. We can bring back the shadow detail by "punching a hole" in the top layer which will reveal the shadow detail in the underlying image. We'll do that by choosing Blending Options from the Layer Style pop-up menu at the bottom of the Layers palette (it looks like a black circle with an "f" inside it).

To reveal the underlying shadow detail, move the left slider under the *This Layer* heading. Once you have sufficient shadow detail, Option/Alt-drag the right edge of the slider to create a soft transition (we used 25/100 for this image).

When you use the Blend If sliders, Photoshop hides areas of the active layer without deleting them. That means that you can always return to the Blending Options dialog box and fine-tune the results. If you'd like to see exactly what you've hidden in the active layer, Option/Alt-click its eyeball icon in the Layers palette to toggle between what is currently visible and the layer by itself. ▥

TIP

Final File Size. Each time you duplicate a layer, the file size of your image increases significantly. You can "guesstimate" how large those additional layers are making your image by choosing Document Sizes from the pop-up menu on the bottom edge of your image (Mac) or screen (Win). The right number is an approximation of our current file size, while the left number is roughly the file size of a flattened version of the image.

Diffuse Glow Variations

In the examples shown at right, we'll follow the same steps that we established in the last technique (duplicate layer, apply Gaussian Blur, set blend mode, apply Blend If sliders) but this time we will achieve different effects by varying the blending mode and Blend If settings used.

Highlight Glows

In this case we wanted to add a glow only to the highlights of the image. To accomplish that, we experimented with the different Lighten blending modes (Lighten, Screen, Color Dodge and Linear Dodge) since these modes can only brighten an image and primarily affect just the highlights of the image. Then, after choosing **Screen** mode, we needed to limit the brightness range that was being effected. The Blend If sliders were used to hide the darkest areas of the active layer and create a very soft fade-out as it moved into the brighter areas of the image (we used 50/200).

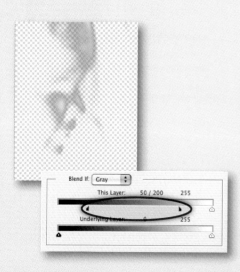

Saturated Glows

These techniques work equally well on landscapes, still lifes, or product shots. The dramatic personality change in the image above was created using the standard technique: duplicate layer, Gaussian Blur, change blend mode, apply Blend If sliders.

To give this image its unique look we used the **Overlay** blend mode, which caused the colors to become more saturated. And like the other examples, we had to take steps to ensure that we maintained shadow detail, so settings of 25/100 were used with the Blend If sliders.

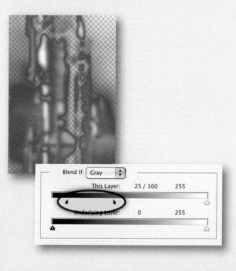

Contrast Glows

As with all these Diffuse Glow examples, this 1000-pixel-high image was blurred using the Gaussian Blur filter with a setting of 10. The resolution and pixel dimensions of your image as well as the amount of detail or texture will dictate the blur settings you use. Try to create a soft image, but make sure you can still recognize the contents of the image; otherwise the result might have too obvious of a glow effect.

In this case, **Soft Light** mode was used with Blend If settings of 25/100. If you find the effect is too strong, you can either modify the Blend If settings, or simply lower the Opacity of the blurred layer.

High Key Glows

With this image, we'll use the same general methods we used in the Highlight Glow technique shown at far left, but to create a highly romantic effect, we'll use multiple blurred layers and convert the image to grayscale for more impact.

After creating the blurred layer and setting its blend mode to **Screen** (Overlay or Soft Light mode would have worked as well), we created a very smooth, subtle transition into the shadow areas by using 100/255 with the Blend If sliders.

Since those Blend If settings left only the lightest lights of the layer visible, we needed to duplicate the layer to exaggerate the impact of the highlight glow. In this case, we typed Command/Ctrl-J three times with the blurry layer active to end up with four layers set to Screen mode.

Finally, we removed all hint of color from the image by choosing Hue/Saturation from the Adjustment Layer pop-up menu a the bottom of the Layers palette **A** and moving the Saturation slider all the way to the left. 🔲

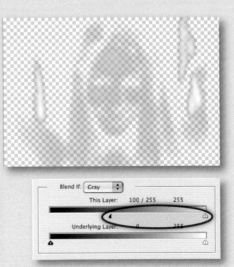

Popping Images with High Pass

Use this often overlooked filter to automatically "dodge and burn" around contours in a photograph.

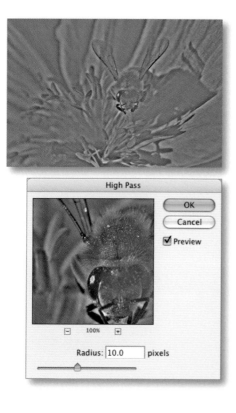

1. Duplicate and Apply High Pass

Start by typing Command/Ctrl-J to copy the original image onto its own layer. Then, choose Filter>Other>High Pass. If you choose the lowest setting available, you'll see that everything has become 50% gray; then as you raise the Radius setting, you'll start seeing the edges of objects showing up as dark and light halos. If your image contains a lot of fine detail that you want to emphasize, then use a low setting (2-20). If it's a simple image, on the other hand, then you can get away with using high settings to exaggerate the larger "shapes" (50-100), we used 10 for this 1000-pixel-wide image).

2. Choose Layer Blend Mode

No matter which setting you use in the High Pass filter, you're going to end up with a lot of 50% gray. Fortunately we can use blend modes to prevent the gray from showing up while allowing the lighter and darker "halos" of the layer to effectively "dodge and burn" the contours of the underlying image.

The Contrast blend modes (Overlay, Soft Light, Hard Light, etc.) cause 50% gray to become neutral, or invisible, while brighter areas brighten the underlying image and darker areas darken it. That will allow all that 50% to disappear and will use the remaining information to make the image "pop." In this case, Overlay or Soft Light is going to be your best bets (we used Soft Light in this example).

3. Dodge & Burn by Hand

Since we used a contrast blend mode, we can further brighten or darken the filtered layer to effectively dodge and burn the image by hand and control the brightness of individual areas.

Looking at this image, we'd be able to see a lot more detail in the bee's head if we were to brighten it (known as dodging). To accomplish that, change the foreground color to white; choose a large, soft-edged brush; set the Opacity low (somewhere between 10% to 20%) and you're ready to paint. With a low Opacity setting, you can paint over an area multiple times to slowly build up the brightening. With a large enough brush, you should be able to just tap a few times on top of the bee's head. You can also change your foreground color to black and paint to darken areas of the image. (A very large brush set to black is a great way to paint in some subtle darkening around the edges.) ▦

Selective High Pass Popping

Now let's expand on the technique used on the previous page to gain more control over how and where the High Pass filter affects the underlying image. Adding a Layer Mask to the filtered layer will provide the most versatility in controlling exactly where the image is affected.

Use a Layer Mask to Limit the High Pass Effect

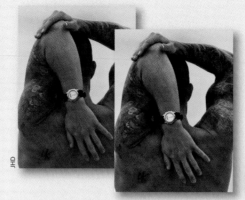

The above photo was taken in a light rain. Applying the High Pass technique described on the previous page would exaggerate the rain and distract from the subject. To prevent those areas from being sharpened, we'll mask the filtered layer so that it only applies to the surfer.

After 1) typing Command/Ctrl-J to duplicate the original image, 2) applying the High Pass filter to the duplicate layer and 3) setting its mode to Soft Light, 4) hold down the Option/Alt key and click on the Layer Mask button at the bottom of the Layers palette. Holding Option/Alt will cause the layer mask to be filled with black (rather than the default white) which will hide the entire contents of the active layer.

Now that the contents of the layer have been hidden, you can paint with white, which will cause the High Pass effect to be revealed. In this case, we chose a large, soft-edged brush, set the Opacity to 80% and painted over the surfer. If you accidentally paint in an area you didn't want the filter to apply to, then switch to paint with black to prevent the filtered image from showing up in that area.

You can also lower the opacity of the filtered layer to control how much the image will be effected. ▥

Gradient Fill Layers

Choose Gradient from the Adjustment Layer pop-up menu at the bottom of the Layers palette **A** to create a Gradient Fill layer. These special layers are much more versatile than using the Gradient tool in the Tools palette because they appear as a separate layer and can be edited in their own dialog box **B** at any time by double-clicking on the gradient thumbnail that appears on the left side of the layer.

Style

The Style menu offers five different types of gradients, from left to right:
Linear, Radial, Reflected, Angle, and Diamond.

Angle

The Angle setting determines the direction the gradient will run. You can either enter a number or click and drag on the angle graphic to change this setting.

Scale

The Scale setting determines how quickly the gradient will fade from the start color to the end color, which determines how soft of a transition you will achieve.

Position

You can adjust the positioning of the gradient by dragging within the main image window while the Gradient Fill dialog box is open.

Reverse

The Reverse checkbox will reverse the entire gradient making the starting color become the ending color and vice versa.

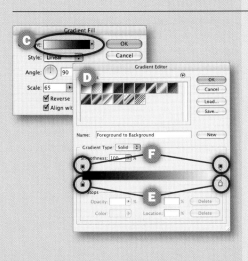

Gradient Editor

If you click on the gradient preview within the Gradient Fill dialog box **C**, you will be presented with the Gradient Editor **D**. The color swatches that appear below the gradient preview determine which colors will be used in the gradient **E**. You can reposition those colors by dragging their swatches, or add additional colors by clicking just below the gradient preview. To change a color, double-click on its swatch to access the color picker. The swatches that appear above the gradient preview **F** determine how opaque the gradient will appear. Click on a swatch and then adjust the Opacity setting near the bottom of the dialog box. ▥

Density Gradient "Style Filters"

Learn to simulate a traditional graduated neutral density filter to selectively darken areas of an image.

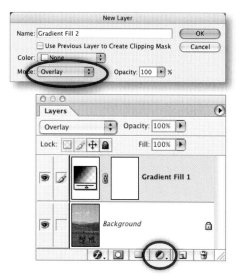

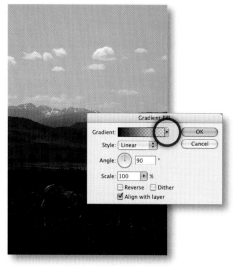

1. Create a Gradient Fill Layer

Start by typing D to reset the foreground/background colors to black/white. Next, hold Option/Alt and choose **Gradient** from the Adjustment Layer pop-up menu at the bottom of the Layers palette. In the New Layer dialog box, set the Mode pop-up menu to Overlay and click OK. The Overlay blend mode will darken the underlying image and saturate the colors in the image. When the Gradient Fill dialog box appears, click on the arrow next to the gradient preview and choose the second option, which is the Foreground to Transparent gradient.

Use Dither. When applying a gradient from black to white, Photoshop is limited to using 256 shades of gray (also known as 8-bit). With that few number of shades, you might notice banding in gradients that cover a large area. To prevent the banding and smooth your gradient, be sure to turn on the Dither checkbox in the Gradient Fill dialog box. We use it for every gradient we create.

2. Refine Gradient Settings

We're using black and white so that we don't introduce a color cast into the image. Now adjust the Angle and Scale settings until the sky darkens and the transition from top to bottom looks smooth. Finally, **click and drag within the main image window** to fine-tune the **positioning** of the gradient.

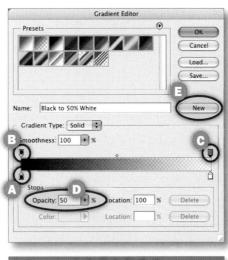

Graduated Neutral Density *What?*
Let's break it down into its parts: ***Filter*** simply means a traditional glass filter that you can attach to the front of a camera lens. ***Density*** in this case means to block some of the light entering the camera lens, thus darkening the image. ***Neutral*** means to not shift the color of the image. And finally, ***graduated*** simply means that the filter would have a gradual transition between the area that darkens and the clear area of the filter.

3. Access Gradient Editor

Since we used one of the contrast blend modes, areas of the gradient that are 50% gray have no effect on the image, while areas that are brighter are brightening the image and areas that are darker are darkening the image. In this case, the foreground of the photograph is becoming a little too bright. To adjust how much brightening and darkening is happening, click on the gradient preview (the horizontal preview seen in the Gradient Fill dialog box in step 2) to access the Gradient Editor dialog box. The gradient preview in *this* dialog box shows you which colors are used to make the gradient (bottom swatches **A**) and how opaque those areas should be (top swatches **B**). To lessen the brightening that is happening to the bottom of the photo, click on the swatch that appears above white **C** and then adjust the Opacity setting (we used 50%) **D**.

If you think you'll want to use this gradient on other images, give it a name and then click the New button **E** so it will show up as a preset in the Gradient Fill dialog box.

Color Gradient "Style Filters"

Simulate traditional graduated color photographic filters to darken and shift the color of a sky.

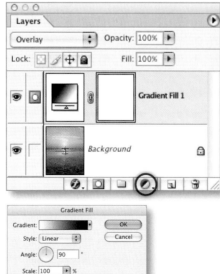

1. Create a Gradient Fill Layer

Start by typing D to reset the foreground/background colors to black/white, then hold Option/Alt and choose Gradient from the Adjustment Layer pop-up menu at the bottom of the Layers palette. When prompted for settings in the New Layer dialog box, set the Mode pop-up menu to Overlay and then click OK. Your Gradient Fill dialog box will then open and you can start adjusting the settings, such as Angle.

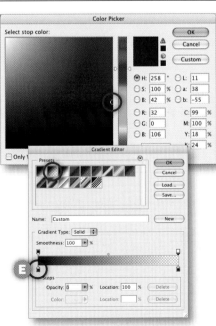

2. Change Gradient Fill Settings

You have many options when darkening a sky with a Gradient Fill layer:

- Use a low scale setting **A** and drag your cursor within the image (trust us, it works) so that the darkening effect hugs the horizon line.

- Use a high scale setting (150 or so) for a very subtle transition **B**.

- Use a reflected gradient style with the Reverse checkbox turned on **C** to brighten the center and darken the top and bottom.

- Use the Foreground to Transparent gradient (second one in the list **D**) to only darken the image.

For this project, we used the Foreground to Transparent gradient using the Reflected style with the Reverse checkbox turned on and a Scale of 150%. That allowed us to darken both the sky and the foreground while leaving the center of the image largely unchanged.

3. Add Color to the Gradient

To add color, click on the gradient preview in the Gradient Fill dialog to access the Gradient Editor. Next, double-click on the black swatch that appears just below and to the left of the large gradient preview **E**. When the color picker appears, experiment with different colors (try blues and purples). Since the Overlay blend mode is capable of both darkening and brightening the image, stay away from bright colors and stick with dark, saturated colors (we used dark purple).

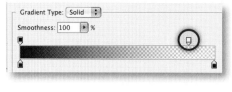

4. Adjust Gradient Opacity

To prevent too much of the central area of the image from being darkened, slide the opacity slider (above right of the gradient preview) toward the middle (we set the Location to 87%).

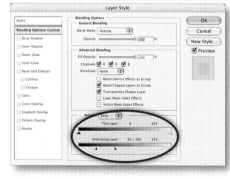

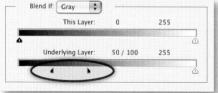

5. Bring Back Shadow Detail

To make sure we retain detail in the darkest area of the image, double-click *to the right of* the name of the layer you just created. Next, move the lower-left Blend If slider toward the right to reveal the dark areas of the underlying image. Finally, hold the Option/Alt key and drag the right edge of that slider to create a smooth transition (we used 50/100).

JHD

Customizing Gradient "Style Filters"

Go beyond the capabilities of a simple Gradient Fill layer to make a gradient precisely match a composition.

1. Create Gradient Fill Layer

We'll start with the same general steps that were used in the previous example. Type D to reset the foreground/ background colors, hold Option/Alt, and choose **Gradient** from the Adjustment Layer pop-up menu at the bottom of the Layers palette and use **Overlay** mode. Once the Gradient Fill dialog box appears, click on the first preset (also known as the Foreground to Background setting).

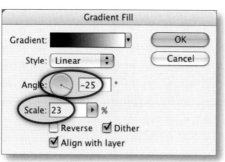

2. Fine-Tune Gradient Settings

To create a rather abrupt transition, set the scale to a low number (we used 23%). Next, to get the gradient to match the angle of the building, adjust the Angle setting until it corresponds with the angle of the buildings (–25 degrees in our case). Then click and drag *within the image* to position the gradient so that none of the buildings are being darkened.

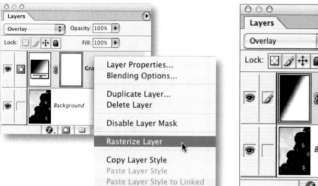

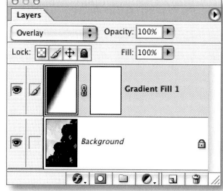

3. Rasterize Gradient Layer

Let's fix the transition so it more closely follows the shape of the buildings. Since we used a Gradient Fill layer, we are not able to paint directly on the layer because it's completely defined by the settings we specified when it was created (angle, scale, colors, etc.). In order to paint on the layer, we need to convert it from a collection of settings that dictate a result to a normal pixel-filled layer. This process is known as *rasterization* and can be done by Control-clicking (Mac) or right-clicking (PC or a Mac with a 2-button mouse) on the name of the gradient layer and choosing Rasterize Layer. This will convert it from a Gradient Fill layer to the same kind of gradient you'd get from the Gradient tool.

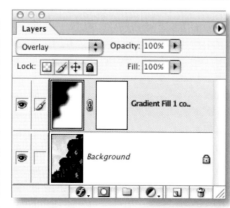

4. Paint to Fine-Tune Gradient

Change your foreground color to black, choose the Brush tool, set its Opacity to 50% and select a large, soft-edged brush. Now you're all set to paint on the layer that contains the gradient and paint in areas where you need more darkening. You can also paint with white to brighten the buildings. If the effect is too extreme, try changing the blend mode of the gradient layer to Soft Light and/or reduce the layer's opacity. ✏

Creative Focus Control

Create a Depth Map to expressively control the Lens Blur filter.

JHD

1. Create Alpha Channel

In this project, we'll explore methods to creatively blur an image. Our goal isn't to simulate the limited depth of field you'd get by using a low f-stop setting in your camera; instead, we want to create a dreamlike atmosphere where the out-of-focus areas appear as if they are almost in a mist.

Open the Channels palette by choosing Window>Channels and then click the New Channel icon to create an Alpha channel.

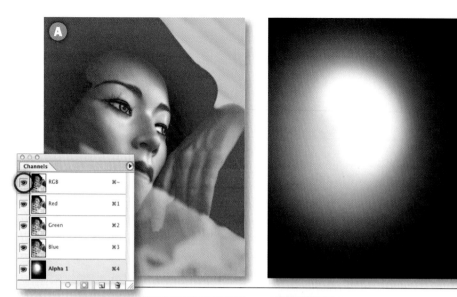

2. Paint a Depth Map

While keeping the new channel active, turn on the eyeball icon for the topmost channel which will show you the main image with the channel overlaid in red **A**.

Next, choose the Brush tool, with a large, soft-edged brush and set the Opacity to 50%. Now, paint with white across the areas you would like to keep in focus; in our case that would be the face. After painting over the face area, release the mouse button, choose a smaller brush and tap a few more times over the central portion of the face to make sure no red appears in that area.

3. Apply Lens Blur Filter

Now, click on the topmost channel (RGB) and click off the eyeball for the bottom channel. Then, move back to the Layers palette and type Command/ Ctrl-J to duplicate the active layer, and choose Filter>Blur>Lens Blur. Adjusting the Radius setting will blur the entire image. To limit the blurring to the areas that were covered in red when we were editing that channel, choose Alpha 1 from the Source pop-up menu. The Invert checkbox will allow you to easily swap the sharp and blurry areas **A**. Now you can adjust the Radius setting to your liking **B**.

4. Match Noise

Our final concern relates to noise. When you blurred the image, the effected areas became very smooth while the original sharp areas of the image still had some of their intrinsic film grain or digital noise. The image will look more realistic if we can get a more consistent amount of noise across the image. So, adjust the Noise Amount slider until the blurry areas have as much noise as the sharp areas. Finally, turn on the Mono- chromatic and Gaussian checkboxes.

More Lens Blur Examples

The Lens Blur filter is a truly dynamic and robust feature that we've grown to love. We just showed you how to use it in one example; now we want you to see how to work its magic on some other subject matter. We'll do this by exploring some additional uses for the creative focus control technique we used on the previous page.

> **TIP**
>
> **Fast Filtering.** If you run a filter and you don't like the result, type Command/Ctrl-Z to undo it. Then hold down the Option-Command/Alt-Ctrl keys and press F, and the dialog box for that same filter will open. You'll find the previous settings still there, waiting for you to adjust them.

Dreamlike Quality

The above image is of a small model photographed among some shrubbery. Let's say we'd like to use that image as an illustration for the travel section in a newspaper. To easily add a dream-like quality, we'll start by creating an Alpha channel and painting with a huge, soft-edged brush. Designating that Alpha channel as a Depth Map from within the Lens Blur filter will allow us to focus the reader's attention on the central portion of the image. To make the blurred area fit with the rest of the image, we used a noise setting of 10.

Romantic Aura

In this example, we'll use the Lens Blur filter to quickly add a romantic aura to this wedding photo. The Alpha channel shown below was created by painting at 50% Opacity with a very large brush and then switching to a much smaller brush and painting over the bride's face to make sure it remained in crisp focus. This image also needed some noise (about 20) in order to get the blurred areas to match the rest of the image. ▦

Depth of Field Altering

Simulate a limited depth of field using the Lens Blur filter.

	Channels	
👁	RGB	⌘~
👁	Red	⌘1
👁	Green	⌘2
👁	Blue	⌘3
👁	Alpha 1	⌘4

1. Create an Alpha Channel

To duplicate the look of a real-world limited depth of field, we'll need to be careful when creating the Alpha channel that will be used by the Lens Blur filter as a Depth Map.

In this image we want to keep the entire white flower sharp while allowing the foreground and background to realistically blur, so we'll need an Alpha channel that defines the exact area of focus.

First, duplicate your background image for safe keeping by typing Command/Ctrl-J, then open the Channels palette and click on the New Channel icon at the bottom of the palette. Next, turn on the eyeball icon for the topmost channel (RGB) to view the main image while you are editing the new alpha channel.

2. Apply Gradient tool to Channel

Choose the Gradient tool, set it to Foreground to Background, type D to reset your foreground/background colors to black/white, and then drag from the **middle** of the *flower* to its top edge **A**. To define where the bottom of the image should become blurry, change the mode of the Gradient tool to *Screen* so it can **only** lighten the image and then click at the *bottom* of the *flower* and drag straight down until you're just beyond the reflection of the flower in the water **B**.

3. Fill Areas for Sharp Focus

Using this current Alpha channel, the top portion of the flower would be blurred slightly. To make sure the entire flower is in focus, we need to select it and add it to our depth map. For this image we clicked on the topmost channel, so that any selection tool we use will look at the flower instead of our Alpha channel. Switch to the Magic Wand tool and click on the top part of the flower. Hold the Shift key and click on additional areas of the flower until the entire top portion of the flower is selected **A**. Then, to add that to our Alpha channel, click on the Alpha channel and then type Option/Alt-Delete to fill that area with the black foreground color **B**.

4. Apply Lens Blur Filter

Click on the topmost channel (RGB) to make it active, turn off the eyeball on the Alpha channel and choose Select>Deselect. Then blur the image by choosing Filter>Blur>Lens Blur, choosing Alpha 1 from the Source pop-up menu and adjusting the radius (we used 20). Finally, adjust the Noise settings until the blurry areas match the sharp areas. ▥

Motion Blurring & Variations

Introduce a dynamic component to your static image or minimize unwanted distractions by adding the illusion of motion.

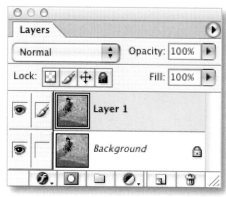

1. Duplicate the Original Layer

Before we start blurring, you'll want to duplicate the original image onto its own layer because we're going to blend the blurred image with the sharp one. Type Command/Ctrl-J to duplicate the layer, or if your document has multiple layers, make a "Merged Visible" layer by holding down the Shift-Option-Command/Shift-Alt-Ctrl keys and typing N and then E.

2. Apply Motion Blur Filter

Choose Blur>Motion Blur. In this case we want it to look as if the crashing wave and portions of the boy are in motion, while the foreground and the boy's face are in crisp focus. For our example, we used −30 for the angle and 15 for distance setting.

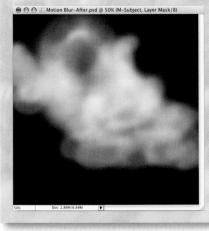

3. Revealing Through a Layer Mask

Now we need to control exactly where the blurring shows up in our image. To do that, hold the Option/Alt key and click on the Layer Mask icon at the bottom of the Layers palette. This will make a negative layer mask that as a default will **hide** (rather than reveal) whatever is on that layer. Next, choose the Brush tool; choose a large, soft-edged brush; set the tool opacity to 25%; and paint with white. Painting with white will make this blurred layer visible. After you've painted over all of the subject area, then type [(the open bracket key) a few times to get a smaller brush and paint more on the edges for a more dramatic blur effect. (Remember, in this sample, edges of the boy and the waves are in motion, and the relatively static foreground and background are in focus.) If you go a little too far, type the X key to swap your foreground/back-ground colors and then paint to remove the blur effect. ▨

Additional Motion Blur Effects

But wait, there's more! (Hats off to Russell Brown.) You can use the same ideas presented on the previous page to simulate many different motion effects. Let's take a look at four variations on that theme.

Camera Blur

In this effect we're going for the look of the camera being in motion and in sync with the motion of the subject. That will cause the subject to remain in focus while the background becomes blurry.

Just as with the last project, we're going to type Command/Ctrl-J to duplicate the image into a new layer. Then, choose **Filter>Blur>Motion Blur** and set the Angle to –30 and the Distance to 15 (same as the last project).

Once the image is blurry, it's time to click on the Layer Mask icon at the bottom of the Layers palette and then paint with black to *remove* the blur effect from just the subject of the photo.

Zoom Blur

Now let's simulate taking a photo while either zooming the lens or moving the camera away from the subject (which is more likely with a wave rushing toward the photographer)!

To begin, duplicate the image onto its own layer, then choose **Filter>Blur>Radial Blur**. This filter has a bit of guesswork involved since it doesn't have a preview. For this 1000-pixel-wide image, we'll use the **Zoom** setting, an amount of 10 and a Quality of Good. To keep the subject of the photo in focus, we'll need to center the zoom effect on the boy's face. Do that by dragging within the Blur Center area.

Next, Option/Alt-click on the Layer Mask icon and paint with white to paint *in the blur* around the subject.

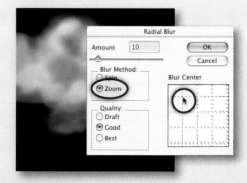

Spin Blur

In this technique, we'll simulate what happens if the subject or your camera spins while taking the photo, which will cause a circular blur.

As usual, we'll start by duplicating the image by typing Command/Ctrl-J. Then choose **Filter>Blur>Radial Blur**, and use the **Spin** setting. The Blur Center should still be set to the same point we used in the previous effect, but this time we'll need a lower Distance setting of somewhere around 6.

Now to control where the blurring affects the image, hold Option/Alt, click on the Layer Mask icon at the bottom of the Layers palette and paint with white to blur the image.

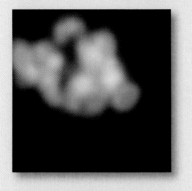

Combining Multiple Blurs for Optimal Realism

For the ultimate in motion blurring, try applying all four of the blur techniques to the same document.

Just duplicate the original image onto a new layer before applying each effect, then when you have all four effects applied, you can click on the individual layers and adjust their opacity settings to control which ones are strongest.

You can also click on the mask for each layer and paint to fine-tune the result. Combining the different types of blurs can give you a more realistic result; after all, in reality the waves, camera and subject would all be moving in slightly different directions.

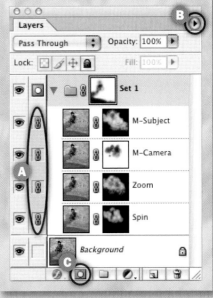

7

COLOR & TONE TREATMENTS

From Subtle to Extreme:
A Journey into Color

THIS CHAPTER is about a meeting of the past and future. Anyone who cares about photography has, at some point, been captivated by the images of long ago and spent time poring over old books, family albums, magazines and postcards. Pioneering photographers spent hours in stuffy darkrooms to produce and polish their art, but they were limited to monochromatic images. Until color film came along, the only way you could introduce some hue into your photograph was to actually paint on it. And so the process of hand-tinting became its own art form. But while its popularity has waxed and waned over the years, hand-tinting always seems to find an appreciative audience. As photography evolved, so did the techniques that darkroom masters used to express their unique vision. Now, with fewer of us in darkrooms and more of us sitting in front of flat screens, we find ourselves wanting to turn back the clock and re-create the type of imagery we associate with a time that seems (at least on the surface) much simpler and more straightforward than our own.

Photoshop gives us the power to produce all the retro effects reflective of the past but without all the fuss and mess. What's more, we can borrow from the artistry of the early masters, meld

it with the highly evolved techniques of today and leave the darkroom in the proverbial dust.

Starting Out with B&W

The earliest photographs were black-and-white with a sepia tint. For many of our effects, we'll start with a black-and-white image, but it's important to first show you how to properly transform your images from color to black-and-white. The key ingredients of this process involve:

- The indispensable Channel Mixer
- Blending adjustments for smooth transitions
- Using filters effectively

Precise Color Control

Before we let you loose with the paintbrush, you'll learn several automated techniques for tinting and introducing color into black-and-white images. You'll also learn how to match the colors between different photos. To do this, we'll explore:

- Single and multi-tone tinting
- Precision color matching
- Effective use of layer styles

Your Turn to Color!

You will be amazed at how easy it is to create the look and feel of antique

postcards and old hand-colored photographs. Once you've mastered the look of the past, you'll be ready to launch yourself into a new creative orbit that includes:

- The art of antique coloring
- The histogram you can't live without
- Effects beyond the darkroom

Color to B&W Conversions: Channel Mixer

Maintain absolute control over the quality and "personality" of your monochromatic masterpieces.

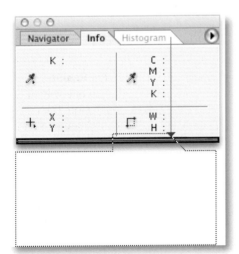

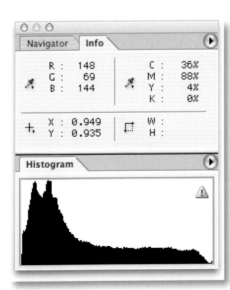

1. Open Info & Histogram Palettes

If your camera offers the ability to shoot in black-and-white, resist using it—you can have much more control by converting a color image to black-and-white in Photoshop using Channel Mixer.

Start by opening the Histogram and Info palettes by choosing them from the Window menu. In their default configuration, the two palettes will be grouped together, but since we're going to need to see them both at the same time, drag the Histogram tab to the bottom of the Info palette until you see a rectangle extending across the bottom of the palette, then release the mouse button to stack the palettes.

2. Inspect R, G and B Channels

Open the Channels palette and look at the Red, Green and Blue channels. Notice the dramatically different components that make up your image. In this case the Red channel has great contrast, Green has tremendous detail, and the Blue contains quite a bit of noise which is typical. After you've inspected the channels to get an idea of the raw material we'll use to create a grayscale image, click on the topmost channel (RGB) to get back to the full-color photo.

3. Adjust with Channel Mixer

Choose Channel Mixer from the Adjustment Layer pop-up menu at the bottom of the Layers palette and turn on the Monochrome checkbox to remove any hint of color. The Channel Mixer has to start somewhere, and it always starts at 100% of the Red channel. If you increase red (+118), watch what happens to the highlights in the Histogram palette—they're blown out! To compensate for the brightening, let's darken the image by lowering the green slider (−18). Even at those settings, we're still blowing out the highlights, so fine-tune the red slider until you still have highlight detail (+116). You can also mouse over your image and watch the Info palette to make sure you don't lose detail.

4. Create More Than One Result

There is always more than one way to interpret an image. To try more than one conversion, hide the Channel Mixer adjustment layer you created earlier and create a new one. For example, you could emphasize the greens in this image by making the Green channel the most prominent (+130) and to make sure the image isn't too bright, you can darken using blue (−26) and then adjust red to fine-tune the image (+4). The flower petals almost turn black! 🖬

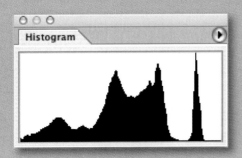

Histogram Palette

With Photoshop CS came the new Histogram palette, which is like an EKG machine attached to your image. It allows you to monitor how an adjustment is affecting the overall tonality and quality of your image. Among other things, you can find out if you've lost highlight or shadow detail, see how an adjustment affects the contrast of your image, or find out if your image is becoming posterized. Once you understand how to think about this palette, you'll start getting more control over your images.

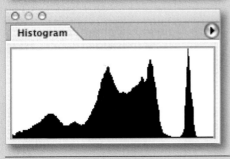

Brightness Levels

A histogram is a bar chart that reflects the brightness levels that make up your image. With any image open, choose Image>Adjustments>Levels and take a look at the histogram. At the bottom of the dialog box there is a gradient that runs from black to white. That gradient represents all the possible brightness levels you can have in an image (this gradient is not visible in the Histogram palette as it is in Levels, but it still applies). If you look above any one of those shades, you can find out if that particular brightness level is used in the current image. The height of the bars that appear directly above each shade indicates how prevalent that shade is compared to the others that make up the image. A gap (no bar) indicates that a shade is not found in the image. Tall bars indicate that a shade is dominant in the image, while short bars indicate the shade is not very prevalent.

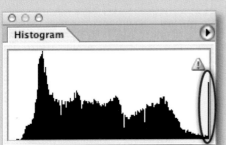

Clipping

Isolated tall lines (also known as *spikes*) in a histogram indicate that a particular brightness level takes up a large amount of space in your image. If a spike appears on the far left of the histogram, then a large area of the image has been forced to black, which means you've lost shadow detail. A spike on the far right of a histogram (as seen here) indicates that a large area has become white, which means that you've blown out some highlight detail (also known as clipping).

Contrast

The width of the material in a histogram reflects how much contrast the image contains. Wider histograms indicate higher contrast (having the full range of lights and darks), while narrow ones indicate a low contrast (with a limited range of tones). When adding contrast to an image, make sure the histogram doesn't get so wide that spikes develop on the right or left end. That's usually an indication that you're starting to lose highlight or shadow detail.

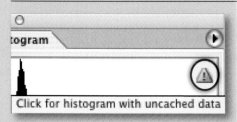

Cache Warning

A small triangle in the Histogram palette indicates that the histogram is not 100% accurate because it is being created from a scaled-down 8-bit version of your image (also known as a cached image). Cached images are used to allow Photoshop to update the histogram in real time as you adjust your image. Click the triangle symbol whenever you'd like a more accurate histogram.

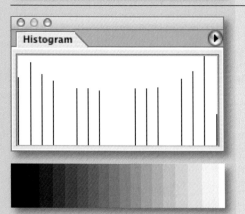

Posterization

Wide gaps in a histogram indicate that many brightness levels are nowhere to be found in the image. That is usually an indication of posterization (also known as stair stepping or banding). The wider the gaps, the more extreme the posterization. Once the gaps get to be larger than three or four pixels, you might start to notice the posterization in areas that should have a smooth transition between light and dark. Cached histograms are not accurate gauges of posterization, so make sure you click the small triangle that often appears in the upper right of the Histogram palette before looking for posterization.

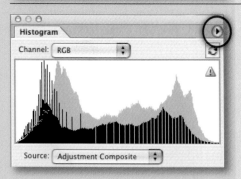

Pre and Post Adjustment Histograms

Choose Expanded View from the side menu of the Histogram palette to display a larger histogram that offers additional options. The Source pop-up menu determines what Photoshop will analyze when creating a histogram. Setting the Source menu to Adjustment Composite will cause Photoshop to display two overlaid histograms whenever you apply an adjustment. The gray histogram represents the image *before* the adjustment is applied, while the black one represents the image *after* the adjustment is applied. If you find that the black histogram obscures your view of the pre-adjustment histogram, then change the Source pop-up menu to Entire Image and then all you will see is the pre-adjustment histogram. You can also choose Active Layer from the Source pop-up menu to analyze a single layer.

JHD / MODEL: RACHEL SACHER

Color to B&W Conversion: Combining Options

Create a "no-compromise" black-and-white photograph by combining multiple conversions using Layer Masks.

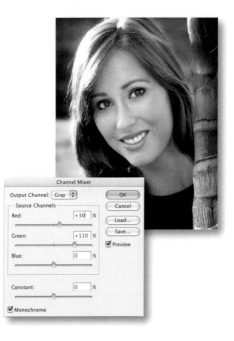

Channel Mixer

Output Channel: Gray

Source Channels

Red: +30 %
Green: +110 %
Blue: 0   %

Constant: 0   %

☑ Monochrome

OK
Cancel
Load...
Save...
☑ Preview

1. Create an Overall Conversion

Our goal in this step is to create a "grayscale" version of our photo which is optimized for the midtones and shadows, without worrying about holding the very lightest highlight detail.

For faces, the Red channel is usually the most subtle for making most skin types look lighter and softer. The Green channel will have more contrast, usually making the lips darker, while the Blue channel darkens the skin and has the most noise. For our first conversion, we used red +30, green +110, and kept blue at 0 to avoid introducing noise.

When combining different Channel Mixer conversions, it's best to do the lighter "mix" first, and the darker one second, as we will do in the next step.

Red

Green

Blue

Channel Mixer

Output Channel: Gray

Source Channels

Red: 0 %

Green: +100 %

Blue: 0 %

Constant: 0 %

☑ Monochrome

OK
Cancel
Load...
Save...
☑ Preview

2. Create a Highlight Conversion

With the conversion from step 1, we've blown out the highlights in the hair and behind her shoulder. Now let's create a second Channel Mixer conversion optimized specifically for those blown-out areas. Click on the eyeball icon for the original Channel Mixer adjustment layer (to get back to the full-color photograph), choose Channel Mixer from the Adjustment Layer pop-up menu at the bottom of the Layers palette, and finally turn on the Monochrome checkbox. Since we're going to do a mix just for the highlights, we don't need to be concerned with what happens to the rest of the image. Looking through the channels that make up the image, the Green channel has quite a bit of highlight detail, so we'll set the sliders to Red: 0; Green: 100; Blue: 0.

Layers

Normal   Opacity: 100%

Lock: ☐ ✐ ✦ 🔒   Fill: 100%

Channel Mixer 2

Channel Mixer 1

Background

3. Mask Two Conversions

Now that we have two separate conversions, let's combine them into an idealized image. If you make the bottom adjustment layer visible again (by turning on its eyeball icon), and then toggle the visibility of the top adjustment layer, you might notice that the top adjustment had no effect on the overall appearance of the image (since what is below is already monochromatic). We'll need to hide portions of the *underlying* Adjustment Layer in order to allow the top adjustment to apply to the image. So, grab a large, soft-edged brush; set the foreground color to black; lower the opacity of the Brush tool to 50%; and with the first Channel Mixer layer active, paint over the background and hair to allow some of the second conversion to show through. Trust us and try it! 🎨

Color to B&W Conversion: Faux Infrared

Simulate the look of traditional infrared photography (where greens become light and blues become dark) using Channel Mixer and the Diffused Glow filter.

1. Create a Generic Conversion

We're going to follow the same steps that we've used for the past two conversions, but this time we'll use a special mix of red, green and blue.

Within the Channel Mixer Adjustment Layer dialog, start by moving the green slider all the way to the right (+200) to make the green areas in the image white. Next, move the blue slider all the way to the left (–200) to force the blues to black. Then move the red slider until you end up with a R+G+B sum of 100% (+200 green plus –200 blue equals 0, so use +100 for red).

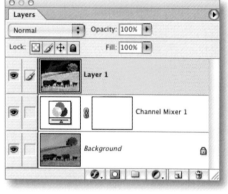

2. Fine-Tune the Adjustment

Before you click OK, you'll need to adjust the settings for your specific image. In our example, the generic infrared simulation produced blown-out highlights. To prevent that, we lowered the green and blue settings to +150 and −150 and then fine-tuned the red slider and ended up with +90 red. Once the conversion looks acceptable, click OK. Remember to have your Histogram palette open during these adjustments (Windows>Histogram) so you know when you have arrived at the desired balance of contrast and detail.

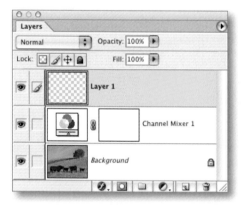

3. Create a Merged Copy Layer

To finish the infrared effect, we're going to need to apply a filter to the overall image. The only problem is that the image is made out of two layers, the original image and our Channel Mixer adjustment layer. Photoshop's filters can only apply to a single layer, so we're going to need to create a special layer that contains the result of our adjustment. So, with the top layer active, hold down the Shift-Option-Command/Shift-Alt-Ctrl keys and type N and then E.

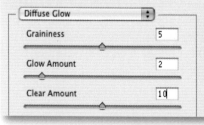

4. Apply the Diffuse Glow Filter

Traditional infrared film is very high-speed which makes it grainy, and it also has a glow due to long exposures. To simulate that effect, choose Filter>Distort>Diffuse Glow and then click the arrow that appears to the left of the OK button so you can get a larger view of your image. The Clear Amount determines how much detail we'll end up with; you'll want it to be high (we used 10). The Glow Amount determines when the glow will kick in; you'll want to keep it low (we used 2). Finally, the Graininess setting will add noise to the image (we used 5).

Layer Style Tinting

Quickly tint and vignette a photograph using Photoshop's Layer Styles.

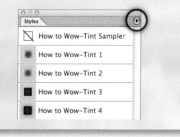

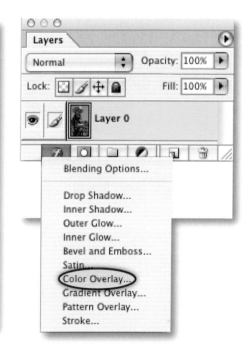

1. Convert the Background Layer

Layer styles are effects that are applied to a single layer where there is a transition between opaque and transparent. Since it's not possible to create transparent areas when working with the Background layer, we'll need to convert it to a normal layer before we can apply styles. To convert the background into a normal layer, double-click on its name in the Layers palette, then click OK in the following New Layer dialog. After you've done that, you will be able to access the Layer Style pop-up menu at the bottom of the Layers palette. In this case we'll begin by selecting Color Overlay.

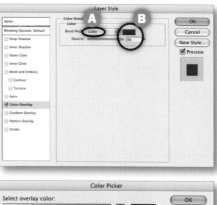

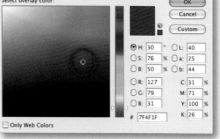

2. Add a Color Overlay Layer Style

With default Color Overlay settings, the color you apply will completely cover your photo. If you change the Blend Mode pop-up menu to Color **A** then the color will be applied to the brightness of the original image. Now, click the color swatch **B** and experiment with different colors until you find a pleasing color (we used H: 30, S: 75, B: 50). If you'd like to experiment, try lowering the opacity slider a small amount (we used 90%) to bring back hints of the original colors **B**.

3. Add Inner Glow Layer Style

Now let's spice things up a bit by brightening the edges of the image. While still in the Layer Style dialog, choose Inner Glow from the options on the left-hand side **A**. Now, to make sure our glow fits in with the tint color we've used, click on the color swatch **B** and type in the same Hue setting we used for the previous step (H: 30) and then experiment with different saturation and brightness settings until you like the result (we used S: 30, B: 100). After you click OK in the color picker, adjust the Size slider **C** to control how the glow encroaches into the image (we used 70px).

Finally, if you'd like to apply this effect to other images, then click the New Style button in the upper right of the dialog box **D** so these settings will be added as a preset at the bottom of the Styles palette. ▦

Tinting Variations

When using layer styles to tint an image, you're not at all limited to creating a traditional sepia look. Let's explore a few alternatives that are just as easy to create and apply.

A Cool Tint

JHD / MODEL: SARA GRACE

The only difference between this technique and the one shown on the previous page is that a cool color was used (H: 216, S: 16, B: 50) for the Color Overlay layer style. This style is called How to Wow-Tint 2 and is one of the zillions of **How to Wow Presets** that cam on this book's companion CD. See page 19 for more on loading these presets.

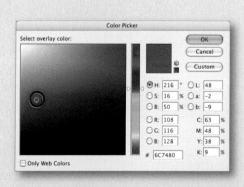

Almost B&W

JHD / MODEL: NICOLE KRUEGER

In this version, we'll make the image become almost black and white and darken the edges instead of brightening them. The steps to create this image are the same as those used on the previous page, except we substituted an Inner Shadow style for the Inner Glow style. The black-and-white effect was created by choosing black for the Color Overlay and slightly reducing its opacity. This style is called How to Wow-Tint 3 and is part of the **HTW-Styles Sampler** library.

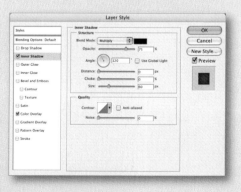

Textured Tint

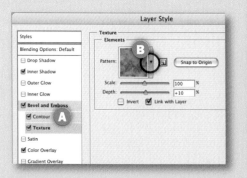

Now let's add some extra pizzazz by applying a texture to the image. We'll start off with the same steps that we covered a few pages ago by double-clicking on the background layer, adding a Color Overlay layer style in Color mode (using H: 47, S: 19, B: 39), and just as with the previous image, using Inner Shadow instead of Inner Glow.

What really distinguishes this image is that a Bevel and Emboss layer style was added and some special settings were used to add texture to the image. The default Bevel and Emboss settings will add a bevel around the edge of your image. Since that's not what we're looking for, click on the **Contour** option that

appears just below the Bevel and Emboss option on the far left of the dialog box **A**. Next, click on the contour preview image to access the Contour Editor, where you can specify the bevel shape to be applied to the edge of your photograph. Since we don't want the bevel to show up, click on the anchor point that appears in the upper right of the diagram and drag it all the way to the bottom to completely flatten the shape, and click OK.

Now to add the texture, click on the **Texture** option on the far left of the dialog box and click the pulldown arrow next to the pattern preview to choose a texture **B**. Finally, adjust the Scale and Depth settings to control how the texture is applied to your image.

An alternative method for adding texture to an image is to apply a *Pattern Overlay* style using Soft Light mode and an opacity of 50%. Check out How to Wow-Tint 4 for all the settings that make up this style, including the custom pattern contained within it.

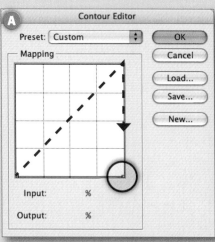

Drop Shadow

So far, the images we've used have completely filled the frame. We can add additional interest by increasing the canvas size and then applying a drop shadow to the image.

To add space to your image, choose Image>Canvas Size, turn on the Relative checkbox and then enter how much space you'd like to add to the width and height of the image.

Now that you have extra space around your image, choose Drop Shadow from the Layer Style pop-up menu at the bottom of the Layers palette and experiment with the Size and Opacity settings until you like what you see.

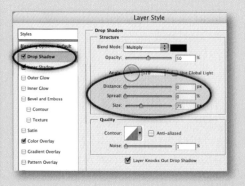

JHD / MODEL: BREEZEE REIFLER

Advanced Multi-tones

Create a tinted image utilizing separate color controls for both highlight and shadows.

1. Remove All Color

We'll start by creating a great black-and-white image by using the Channel Mixer technique that was used earlier in this chapter. In this case we're emphasizing a surfer girl look with light hair and freckled skin. So, create a Channel Mixer adjustment layer; turn on the Monochrome checkbox, set Red to 25%, Green to 50% and blue to 50%; then adjust the Constant slider until the highlights retain sufficient detail (we used –4).

2. Apply Color Balance

Now let's add a bit of contrast to the image to make the image pop a little more. **_Hold down the Option key and choose Color Balance_** from the Adjustment Layer pop-up menu at the bottom of the Layers palette. When the New Layer dialog box appears, set the blend mode of the layer to Soft Light, and click OK.

3. Tone Highlights and Shadows

Color Balance will allow us to apply different colors to the shadows, midtones and highlights of the image. The Preserve Luminosity checkbox is meant to ensure that the brightness of the image doesn't change, but in this case it actually does the opposite, so turn it off before adjusting the image. Let's start by choosing Highlights and moving the Cyan/Red slider to +10, the Magenta/Green slider to −10, and the Yellow/Blue slider to −50. Now in the same adjustment, click on Shadows and use the following settings: Cyan/Red: +20, Magenta/Green: −5, and Yellow/Blue: −20. Then click OK. That should create a very subtle tinting with neutral midtones.

Finally, if the tinting you've created is a little too strong, change the opacity of the adjustment layer to lessen its effect on the image. ▥

TIP

Strong Tints. If you'd like a more dramatic effect for your image, then leave the blend mode of the Color Balance adjustment layer set to Normal. That will cause the full force of the adjustment to apply to your image. Just remember that you can also adjust the opacity of the adjustment layer to control how much of a change you make to the image.

In the examples on the left use the following settings:

Top Image–Shadows: C/R −43; M/G +41; Y/B +65; Highlights: C/R +4, M/G +23, Y/B +38.

Bottom Image–Shadows: C/R +81; M/G 0; Y/B −90; Highlights: C/R +10; M/G −15; Y/B −31.

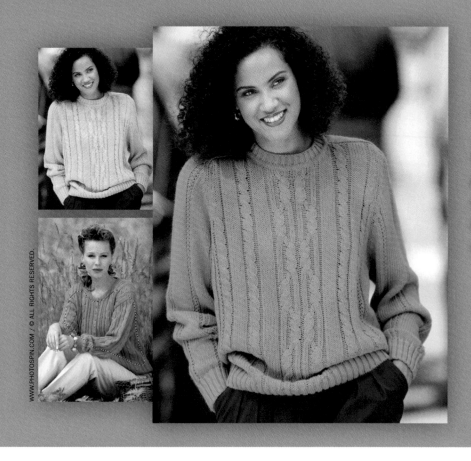

Matching Color: Product to Product

Shift the color of one garment to match the color of another using two images and the Match Color command.

INSIGHT

Neutralize for Extreme Casts.

The Neutralize checkbox in the Match Color dialog box will attempt to remove any unwanted color casts from the area you are shifting. We leave that checkbox turned off the vast majority of the time, since it doesn't usually help when matching two colors.

We occasionally use the Neutralize checkbox when working with images that contain extreme color casts (like underwater photography). To remove a color cast, choose Image>Adjustments>Match Color and simply turn on the Neutralize checkbox (without specifying an image to match). If the adjustment is too extreme, then adjust the Fade slider.

1. Select Area in Reference Image

Start by opening *the image that contains the color you'd like to match—the Source file.* If the image contains more than one color, then make a basic selection that includes the full brightness range of the particular color you'd like to match. This selection should include both the highlights and the shadows of the color you're attempting to match, but does not need to be a precise selection of the object (as you can see here).

2. Select Area in Original Image

Next, open *the image that contains the area of color you'd like to shift—the Destination file.* It's important to make a very precise selection of the object that we want to work on (we used the Magnetic Lasso tool). If you're using the image found on the book's CD, you can load a pre-saved selection by choosing Select>Load Selection.

Now that you have carefully selected the area you want to shift the color of, type Command/Ctrl-J to copy that area to its own layer. By copying the layer, you will never be stuck with an undesired end result since you'll always have the original image safely kept at the bottom of the layers stack.

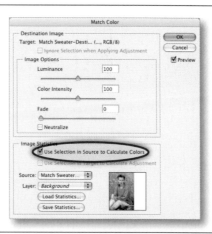

3. Apply Match Color

With the layer you just created active, choose Image>Adjustments> Match Color. The Source pop-up menu near the bottom of the dialog box determines what Photoshop will attempt to match, so change that menu so that it corresponds with the name of your open Source file. Next, turn on the Use Selection in Source to Calculate Colors checkbox so Photoshop ignores all the areas outside of the selection.

4. Fine-tune Adjustment

Now that we have a basic match, let's fine-tune the settings used while visually comparing the two images. Adjust the Luminance slider if the image is too bright or dark (we used 120). If the colors vary too much, try adjusting the Color Intensity slider. Lowering it will leave you with less variation (we used 1). Finally, the Fade slider allows you to lessen the shift that was being made (we used 20). █

Matching Color: Product to Swatch

Match colors from a custom swatch rather than from an existing product.

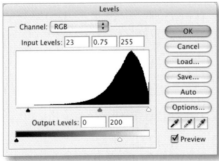

1. Adjust Brightness with Levels

We'll begin by adjusting the object we want to shift so that it roughly matches the *brightness* of our target color, in this case a printed PANTONE swatch book. To do that, make a precise selection of the area that needs to shift and choose Levels from the Adjustment Layer pop-up menu at the bottom of the Layers palette. This existing selection will be used to automatically make a restricting layer mask on this new adjustment layer. The Input sliders will increase contrast (which can blow out detail), while the Output sliders will decrease contrast. It's best to adjust the general tonality using the Output sliders so you don't lose detail and then tweak the result using the Input sliders.

2. Add a Solid Fill Layer

Now hold Option/Alt and choose Solid Color from the Adjustment Layer pop-up menu at the bottom of the Layers palette. When the New Layer dialog box appears, set the mode to **Color** and then, to limit the changes to the same area that we adjusted with Levels, turn on the **Use Previous Layer to Create Clipping Mask** and click OK.

If you look at the Solid Color layer in the Layers palette you'll notice a small arrow pointing down. That arrow means the layer is being clipped using the contents of the layer the arrow points to. That way the Color Fill layer uses the existing mask that is attached to the Levels adjustment layer.

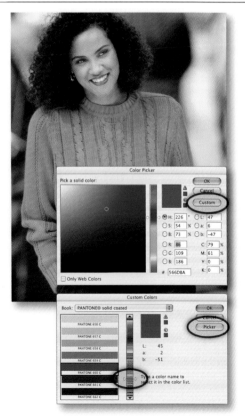

3. Choose Color from Reference

When you add a Solid Color layer you'll be presented with the standard Color Picker dialog. Now click on the Custom button in the upper right. In the new dialog box, either drag the arrows that appear next to the vertical bar to cycle through the colors, or type a number to jump to a specific PMS (PANTONE Matching System) color. Once you've specified a color, click the Picker button to get back to the standard color picker and adjust the Saturation (S) setting until the image looks like the printed sample that you are trying to match.

Finally, double-click on the left side of the Levels Adjustment Layer to reopen its dialog box and fine-tune the brightness settings.

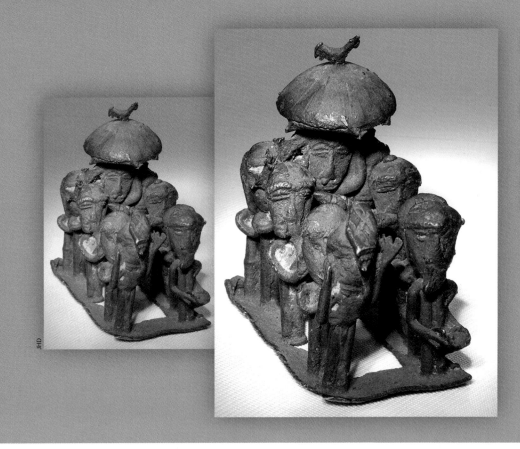

Matching Color: Lighting & Color Casts

Use Match Color to match the overall color cast or white balance of two images.

1. Duplicate Layer

These photographs were taken by two different people using different lighting and camera settings. The detail image on the left accurately portrays the patina'd colors of this antique bronze sculpture; the problem was that the image on the right, which shows the full sculpture, has an overall color that doesn't accurately reflect the color of the original.

Start by opening both the Source image (with the desired color), and the "Destination" image (that needs to be adjusted). Then type Command/Ctrl-J in the Destination file to duplicate the image onto its own layer.

2. Select Source in Match Color

There is no need to make any selections in either image since we are attempting to match the overall lighting and color in two very similar objects.

With the layer you just created active, choose Image>Adjustments>Match Color and change the Source menu to the name of the image that has accurate color. Right off the bat, you'll see a dramatic change to the image.

3. Fine-tune Match Color Settings

Now that the overall color is close to what we're aiming for, we can adjust the Luminance, Color Intensity and Fade sliders to fine-tune the image. The Luminance slider adjusts the overall brightness of the image. If you think you might be losing detail in the brightest areas of the image, then choose Window>Histogram and then move the Luminance slider until the histogram is as wide as possible without developing a tall spike on either end. If you'd like to achieve more color variation in the image, try moving the Color Intensity slider (we used +119 to make the patina on the sculpture more apparent).

4. Desaturate the Background

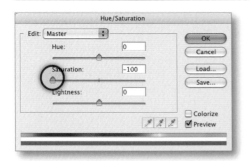

The background of this particular image has a slight color cast that the Neutralize checkbox isn't capable of removing. To remove the cast, manually select the background, create a Hue/Saturation adjustment layer, and move the Saturation slider all the way to the left to remove all color from that area. ▥

Quick Antique Coloring

Create the impression of an antique hand-tinted photograph by quickly adding back some of the color of the original image to a custom black-and-white conversion.

1. Remove Color from Image

Let's start by making a customized black-and-white conversion. We'll use the Channel Mixer technique that was covered at the beginning of this chapter. Inspecting the channels, you'll find that the Red channel is a little flat but has a lot of detail, the Green channel is very dramatic but does not have much shadow detail, and the Blue as usual has a bit of noise but will be useful for darkening the sky. In this case we'll use +100 red, +100 green, and −100 blue, which produces a nice detailed image without being too dark.

2. Duplicate Original in Soft Light

Now to start creating the feel of a hand-tinted photo, click on the background layer that contains the original full-color image, duplicate it by typing Command/Ctrl-J, and move it to the top of the layers stack. Then change the blend mode at the top of the Layers palette to Soft Light, which will start to give us our antique coloring effect.

3. Blur the Duplicate Layer

We've got a tinted look to our image, but since we're going for an antique look, the color here is too precise. Traditional hand-tinting is often done using a Q-tip-like tool, which produces very soft transitions in color. To simulate that look, choose Filter>Blur>Gaussian Blur to soften the color transitions (we used 10 for this 1000-pixel-high image).

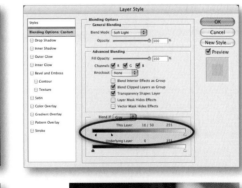

4. Apply Advanced Blending

Now we're left with just one problem: We've lost some shadow detail in the process of tinting the image. To get back our shadow detail, choose Blending Options from the Layer Style pop-up menu at the bottom of the Layers palette. In the Blend If area, move the upper left slider to something like 50, then hold Option/Alt and drag the left edge of that slider to 10.

This technique can be used with all sorts of images. The steps are always the same. The only variations occur with the Channel Mixer settings **A** (which depend on the content of the original image) and the advanced blending settings **B** used to retain shadow detail. To get fancy, paint with a low-opacity, soft black brush on the Channel Mixer's Layer Mask to selectively allow a little more of the original color to show through, as we did with the flower bouquet in the wedding photo. 🖐

Selective Recoloring

Reintroduce subtle color to an optimized black-and-white conversion.

1. Remove Color from Image

We'll start with our favored black-and-white conversion method. Choose Channel Mixer from the Adjustment Layer pop-up menu at the bottom of the Layers palette, turn on the Monochrome checkbox and start by moving the red slider to +50 and the green slider to +50, which is usually a good default starting point for a "grayscale" conversion.

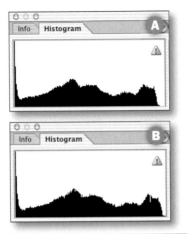

2. Check the Histogram

Let's make sure we have a nice bright shirt without blowing out any highlight detail. Do that by choosing Window> Histogram while the Channel Mixer is still open **A**. To brighten the shirt, nudge the green slider to the right until the histogram extends all the way to the right without developing a spike **B**.

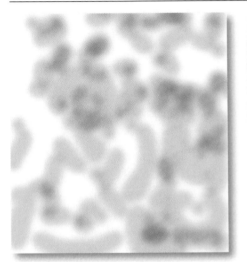

3. Paint with Black on Mask

Now that the image looks black and white, let's start to paint back some of the color. With the Channel Mixer adjustment layer active, choose a large, soft-edged brush; set the opacity of the Brush tool to 20%; and paint with black across the areas where you'd like to see color. The hand-tinting effect we're trying to mimic was usually done very quickly, so make sure you don't spend more than about 30 seconds painting and try not to be too precise; otherwise it will look like a faded photograph instead of a hand-tinted image.

4. Adjust Mask with Levels

We're going for a look that was created long before the sharp, vivid colors of present-day photography, so take it easy when painting. You can fine-tune how colorful the image is by choosing Image>Adjustments>Levels *while the Channel Mixer adjustment layer is active.* Moving the upper-left slider will darken the mask, causing more color to show through; moving the lower-left slider will lighten the mask, which will lessen the color.

JHD / MODEL: MARY DAVIS

Hand Coloring

Add color to an antique black-and-white photograph by manually tinting it with selected colors.

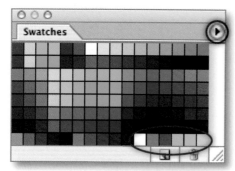

1. Add Colors to Swatches Palette

If your image is starting life in Grayscale mode, then be sure to choose Image>Mode>RGB Color before proceeding. To prepare for painting, let's pick and store the colors we'll be using. Click on the Foreground color, define a skin color, then choose Window>Swatches and click in an empty area of the Swatches palette to save your color. Do this four more times to define colors for lips, hair, clothes and the wall (Option/Alt-click to delete an existing color).

The swatches here (called ***HTW-Swatches Sampler***) can be loaded from the Swatches palette's pop-out menu in the upper right.

The Postcard Look. Here's a traditional infrared photograph that was tinted to look like an antique postcard. A total of four colors were used: three shades of green and one of blue. The total amount of time spent was less than 60 seconds. Nothing really follows the edges: it's about as sloppy as you can get—that's the key to making it look like an image that was created decades ago.

2. Create Layers to Hold Colors

We'll use five layers, one for each color. Option/Alt-click the new layer icon, set the name to "Skin," set the Mode pop-up menu to Color and set the opacity to 50%. Create one layer for each area you'll be colorizing (hair, clothes, wall, etc.). By starting with a 50% opacity, we'll be able to easily intensify the colors if necessary after we're done painting.

3. Paint with Low Opacity

Now choose a large, soft-edged brush, and set the Brush tool's opacity to 50%. Next, click on the skin layer, choose the skin color from the Swatches palette, and paint on the face, being careful not to paint over the eyes. If you get too much overspray, just type X to switch to black or white and paint to remove the color. The soft edges and spilling of color is a feature, not a bug.

4. Switch Layers and Paint Again

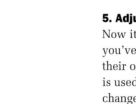

Once you've finished with one color, choose the next color from the Swatches palette, click on the appropriate layer and then start painting. Continue this process until you've colorized the entire image. Notice we used a touch of the lip color to add a hint of blush to the cheeks.

5. Adjust Layer Opacity

Now it's time to click through the layers you've been painting on and fine-tune their opacity to control how much color is used in each area. In our case, we changed the Lips layer to 25% and the Wall layer to 60%.

Colorizing & Cross-Processing

Apply creative coloring by simulating a cross-processing effect (which is conventionally achieved by developing a slide as a negative, or a negative as a slide) using Gradient Maps.

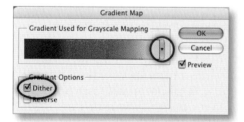

CAUTION

Always Dither. Gradient Map adjustments are limited to 256 colors, which has the possibility of looking posterized. Be sure to turn on the Dither checkbox so Photoshop smooths the gradient to reduce posterization or "banding."

1. Create a Gradient Map Layer

We'll start by choosing Gradient Map from the Adjustment Layer pop-up menu at the bottom of the Layers palette. A gradient map replaces the brightness levels in your image with the colors found in a gradient. The shadows in the image become the color that appears on the left of the gradient, the highlights become the color that's on the right of the gradient, and the midtones become what appears in the middle of the gradient. You can click on the pulldown arrow next to the gradient preview to try different preset gradients. It's also a good idea to turn on the Dither option in the Gradient Map dialog box to lessen the possibility of color banding.

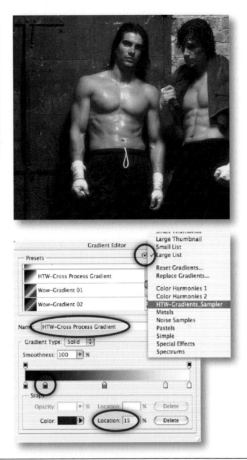

2. Customize the Gradient

You're going to need to create a custom gradient if you want to simulate the look of a traditional cross-processed image. Cross-processing can produce all sorts of strange color artifacts, but often it produces cool tones in the shadows, greens in the midtones and peach/yellows in highlights. To create your own gradient, click on the gradient preview to access the Gradient Editor.

The square-shaped color swatches below the gradient preview are the ones that make up the gradient. You can drag each color to control where it appears in the gradient or double-click on a color to change it, or click where there is no square to add one. To prevent "solarization," try to keep dark colors on the left and bright ones on the right. To maintain the overall tonality of the image, watch the Location setting for each color and then adjust the brightness (the B in HSB) to match the location setting. In our case, we placed color at the following locations: blue at 15%; green at 50%; and yellow at 85%.

3. Lower Opacity of Adjustment

The colors in a cross-processed image may still resemble the colors in a normal photograph. So, to bring a hint of the original colors back into the image, lower the opacity of the Gradient Map adjustment layer to around 40%. You can also try different blend modes like Multiply or Overlay. If you'd like to try all the blending modes, then switch to the Move tool and type Shift-Option/Alt-+ (plus sign). ▥

Solarizing & Sabatier Effects

Simulate an expressive darkroom technique using Blurs, Curves and Colorizing.

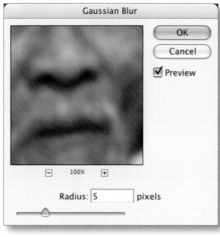

1. Duplicate and Blur

The solarizing/Sabatier effect was one of the first expressive special effects of traditional photography. The effect can occur in the darkroom when an image is exposed to light while it is being developed; but you get to experiment with the process without the chemical fumes!

We'll start by typing Command/Ctrl-J to place the original image onto a new layer. Next, choose Filter>Blur>Gaussian Blur, use a low setting (we used 5 for this 1000-pixel-tall image) and then lower the opacity of the layer to 50%. Blurring the image will add a slight halo effect and help prevent a pixelated result later on.

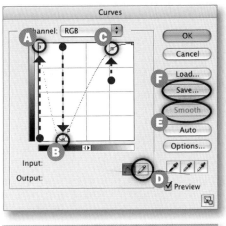

2. Apply Curves Adjustment Layer

Now choose Curves from the Adjustment Layer pop-up menu at the bottom of the Layers palette. Click on the anchor point appearing directly above black and move it all the way to the top to invert black areas to pure white **A**. Then create a U-shaped curve by adding a point above 75% gray and moving it down, adding points as needed to control the angles **B**. Next, transform that U into a V shape by adding a point to the curve above 25% gray and move it as far up as you can, making sure the curve doesn't flatten out over the highlights **C**.

If you have trouble creating a V-shaped curve, then click the Pencil icon at the bottom the Curves dialog box **D** and draw the shape you desire. When using the Pencil, you can also click the Smooth button after drawing a curve to smooth out its shape **E**. This "V" shape is just one of millions of possible arrangements. When you get a curve that you like, you may want to save it for use later **F**.

C A U T I O N

Careful What You Click On! As a default, the lower-left corner of the Curves grid defines the shadows of a file. Be careful not to click the arrows in the middle of the gradient below the grid, or the orientation of the shadows and highlights will be reversed. See page 55 for more on Curves.

3. Apply Hue/Saturation Layer

Now that we have manipulated the overall tonality of the image, let's start adjusting the color (we're feeling especially expressive right now). ***Click back on the blurred layer,*** and choose Hue/Saturation from the Adjustment Layer pop-up menu at the bottom of the Layers palette. When the Hue/Saturation dialog box appears, turn on the Colorize checkbox, and experiment with the Hue slider (to 55) and lower the Saturation setting (to 10). These particular settings would usually cause the entire image to take on a green tint, but the Curves adjustment layer above is causing that green color to be inverted to purple in the shadow areas.

JHD / MODEL: KARA GRIMSLEY

Expressive Shading & Halos

Use Blurs, Blend Modes and Advanced Blending for creative "tonality shaping."

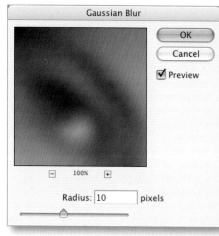

1. Duplicate and Blur Layer

We're not limited to just simulating traditional darkroom techniques. So let's free ourselves from the constraints of the darkroom and go for an effect that is best performed digitally, such as exaggerating (or "haloing") the middle tones of an image, while leaving the shadows and highlights unaffected. This technique is effective for still lifes, landscapes, and portraits.

Start by typing Command/Ctrl-J to copy the original image onto its own layer. Then soften that duplicate layer by choosing Filter>Blur>Gaussian Blur (we used 10 for this 1000-pixel-high image).

2. Blend Using Multiply Mode

Next, change the blend mode at the top of the Layers palette to Multiply, which will cause the blurred layer to darken the underlying image.

3. Apply Advanced Blending

Now let's limit the darkening effect to the midtones. To bring the shadow areas back to their original brightness level, choose Blending Options from the Layer Style pop-up menu at the bottom of the Layers palette, and in the Blend If area, drag the upper-left slider to 70. Then to soften the transition, Option/Alt-drag the right edge of that slider to 100. To bring back the highlights, drag the upper-right slider to 125 and then create a soft transition by Option/Alt-dragging the right edge of the slider to 200.

4. Duplicate Layer and Use Overlay

With the Multiply layer active, type Command/Ctrl-J to create a duplicate and change the mode to Overlay, which will lighten and saturate the image. Once you've completed all the steps of this technique, you may want to experiment with the opacity or Blend If settings of each layer to fine-tune the effect.

8

ARTISTIC EFFECTS & OVERLAYS

Adding That Extra Expressive Flair

THERE ARE MANY WAYS to tell a story through photography. A photograph may speak entirely for itself, or you can embellish it, whether subtly or boldly, in order to enhance its essence. This chapter focuses on taking the *less* subtle route – transforming an original photo into a unique and personalized image with attention-getting edge effects, highly stylized frames and textures, and the romantic brush strokes of expressive paintings.

Many of the techniques described here have roots in traditional art forms that were developed long before our world went digital. Just as a sidebar, did you know that the word "pixilated" (slightly different spelling) was originally defined as mentally unbalanced or drunk? Some of the terms we use in this chapter have their own history as well, but their definitions have held up better through the years.

Vignetting

Vignetting is the darkening of a photograph around the edges. It originally occurred unintentionally when a picture was taken and the lens couldn't capture consistent lighting out to the edges of the image. Now it's often achieved deliberately by using opaque or translucent masks held in front of the lens. Vignetting can also be achieved during the printing or enlarging process. In Photoshop you can get a vignetting effect almost instantly, and you'll be able to play with a few interesting variations that we'll give you.

Mezzotint

We'll also show you how to create *Mezzotint*-like effects. Mezzo tinting was originally a reverse-engraving process used on a copper or steel plate to produce illustrations in relief with effects of light and shadow. It was widely used in the 18th and 19th centuries to reproduce portraits and paintings, but eventually lost out to photo-engraving. Later, the term "mezzotint" came to simply mean any irregular or textured pattern that was used in place of a traditional round halftone dot to reproduce a photograph or illustration. In Photoshop, you'll be able to apply these texture, grain or faux-mezzotint treatments with ease.

Deckling

Rooted in book-making history is the term *deckle.* A deckle edge was the rough, untrimmed edge of a sheet of handmade paper. You see this type of edge in many older books, and it evokes a sense of a different time, when "browsing" meant flipping through the pages of a book, rather than Googling your way through cyberspace. For our deckling purposes, we will be showing you how to make a photograph look like it has a torn edge, which will give it a certain realism and dimension that it wouldn't have otherwise.

Imitating Natural Media

And while we'll work through an inspiring collection of other effects, we feel that the jewel of this chapter is the technique that shows you how to turn a photo into an expressive painting. You might be thinking…"So, what's the big deal? Photoshop has lots of built-in filters that can turn a photo into a painting!" This is true, but at closer inspection you'll find that any of these filters (used alone or in combination) will not give you the kind of personal control and creative flexibility that an artist would want when they are working on their masterpiece. Working with the *Pattern Stamp* tool and some custom Wow paint brushes, this technique takes a bit of time to work through (minutes compared to seconds!), but we think you'll find the results well worth it.

So, whether you're aiming for the roughened patina of the Mezzotint era, or the vivid, bold strokes of the French Impressionists, we hope you'll enjoy this chapter's tour through art history.

JHD / MODELS: ISMAEL & VIVIAN

Soft-Edged Framing

Create a personalized soft-edged framing effect.

1. Duplicate and Create Backdrop

The background layer does not support transparency, so we'll have to duplicate it before we start. Type Command/Ctrl-J to duplicate the Background layer into a new transparency-ready layer.

Now to create a backdrop for our edge effect, let's fill the old Background layer with white. Click on the Background layer, type D to reset the foreground/background colors to black/white and then type Command/Ctrl-Delete. For this sample we'll use white, but to fill with any color—or even a pattern—type Shift-Delete to bring up the fill dialog box.

2. Create "The Frame"

Choose the Rectangular Marquee tool and click/drag within your image to define the area you'd like to keep, leaving a little bit of space between the selection and the edge of the document. Then to "crop" the image so it only shows up within that selection, click on the image layer and then click on the Layer Mask icon at the bottom of the Layers palette.

3. Soften Edge of the Image

With the Layer Mask thumbnail still active, let's soften that edge with a filter. Choose Filter>Blur>Gaussian Blur and experiment to find the setting you prefer (we used 20 for this 1000-pixel-wide image).

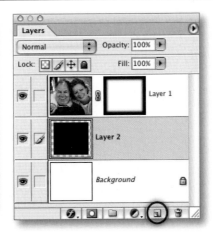

4. Create Black Edge Effect

Now let's do some extra credit tricks by adding a dark haloing interior edge to the framing effect. Choose Select>Reselect to get back the last selection that you had. Add a new empty layer *above the background* then type Option/Alt-Delete to fill with your foreground color, which is currently black. Since the selection was not feathered, we'll end up with a crisp edge. Now you are seeing this dark inner halo through the semitransparent soft edge of the photo above. Finally, type Command/Ctrl-D to get rid of the selection. If you like, you may then apply Gaussian Blur to the layer that contains black to soften its edge (we used a setting of 2).

Soft-Edged Framing Variations

When you consider that Photoshop comes with over 100 filters, and that you can combine them with a heap of textures and nearly a dozen layer styles, each with their own unique set of variations, well, you do the math. The number of effects you could conjure up is exhilarating and would probably take a room full of monkeys using Photoshop for the next thousand years to even come close to exhausting the possibilities. The five images shown on this page can be created by adding one additional step to the technique that's demonstrated on the previous page.

Color Halftone

Start by Clicking on the Layer Mask that is attached to the main image layer and then choose Filter>Pixelate>Color Halftone. Set all the Channel settings to 45° and experiment with the Max Radius setting to control the size of the largest circles used on the edge of the image. We used 8.

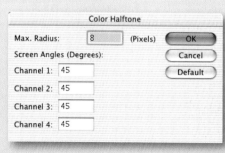

Ocean Ripple

Start by Clicking on the Layer Mask that is attached to the main image layer and then choose Filter>Distort>Ocean Ripple. We set the Ripple Size to 1 and the Ripple Magnitude to 12.

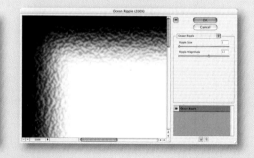

Sprayed Strokes

Start by Clicking on the Layer Mask that is attached to the main image layer and then choose Filter>Brush Strokes>Sprayed Strokes. For this image, we set the Stroke Length to 12, the Spray Radius to 20 and the Stroke Direction pop-up menu to Right Diagonal.

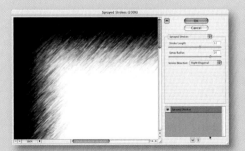

Texturizer/Canvas

Start by clicking on the Layer Mask that is attached to the main image layer and then choose Filter>Texture>Texturizer. We set the Texture pop-up menu to Canvas, the Scaling to 125, the Relief to 5 and the Light pop-up menu to Top Left and turned off the Invert checkbox.

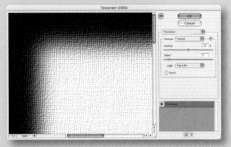

Grain

Start by clicking on the Layer Mask that is attached to the main image layer and then choose Filter>Texture>Grain. We set the Intensity to 60, the Contrast to 75 and the Grain Type pop-up menu to Horizontal. Then to exaggerate the edge effect, we chose Inner Shadow from the layer style pop-up menu at the bottom of the Layers palette and set the Opacity to 50%, the Distance to 5px and the Size to 40px.

Brush Stroke Borders

Quickly add a little personality to a photo using a hand-painted brushed edge effect.

1. Enlarge the Canvas Visually

We'll need to add some extra space around our image in order to make room for a painted border. The added space will be filled with the current background color, so type D to set the background to white. Next, type F to enter full screen mode, choose the Crop tool and drag across the image. After releasing the mouse button, hold down the Option/Alt key and drag one of the corners beyond the image boundaries to the new desired size, and then press Enter.

2. Load Presets and Paint

Before we can start painting, we'll need to load some tool presets by choosing View>Tool Presets and then choosing HTW-Tool-Presets Sampler from the menu in the upper right of the palette (for more about loading presets, see page 19). Now choose the Brush tool, turn on the Current Tool Only checkbox at the bottom of the Tool Presets palette and click on the Wow-BT Oil-X Large preset. Now that we're ready to paint, create a new layer by clicking the New Layer icon on the bottom of the Layers palette, change the foreground color to white, then paint around the edge of your image.

3. Add Layer Styles

We could end it at this point, but let's add a little "oomph." Try choosing Drop Shadow from the layer style pop-up menu at the bottom of the Layers palette. In this case, set the opacity to 50, the distance to zero and adjust the size until you like the result (we used 30). This makes the details much more visible, thus creating a more elaborate edge effect.

4. Apply Unsharp Mask Filter

Finally, to make the paint layer pop even more, choose Filter>Sharpen>Unsharp Mask. We used the following settings: Amount: 100, Radius: 1, Threshold: 0.

After you've gone through all the steps, you're welcome to turn off visibility for the current painted frame layer, create a new empty layer above it, and create another variation. Just click on a different tool preset and start painting. The examples on the left were created using the Wow-BT Chalk-Large Chalk, and Wow-BT Watercolor-Large presets. 🖑

Creating a Deckled Edge

Create a realistic looking torn paper edge using masks, brushes, patterns and styles.

1. Convert Background to a Layer

We're going to be using a Layer Mask to limit where the image shows up. The only problem is that the Background layer does not support Layer Masks (or any kind of transparency), so we'll have to convert the Background into a normal layer. You can quickly do that by double-clicking on the Background layer and changing its name.

2. Load Tool and Pattern Presets

Before we can start painting, we'll need to get our special brushes loaded. Choose Window>Tool Presets and then choose HTW-Tool-Presets Sampler from the menu in the upper right of the palette (for more about loading the Wow presets that are included on this book's companion CD, see page 19). Then to see the presets you just loaded, click on the Brush tool, and turn on the Current Tool Only checkbox at the bottom of the Tool Presets palette.

3. Add Mask and Start Painting

Now to limit where the photo shows up, click on the Layer Mask icon at the bottom of the Layers palette. But, before you start to paint, choose the "Wow-BT Watercolor-Large" preset from the Tool Presets palette, type D and then X to change the foreground color to black. Now if you start painting around the edge of the image, you'll start to hide areas of the active layer. The brush preset we're using creates a semi-transparent look, so go over the edge several times.

4. Check the Mask for Black

Before we move on, Option/Alt-click in the middle of the *Layer Mask thumbnail* that shows up to the right of the layer thumbnail for the active layer. That will display the Layer Mask in the main document window. This is your chance to double-check that you've got black all the way around the image. Look out for areas that are light gray because they will cause the image to show up slightly, so paint over those areas until they are dark gray or solid black. To get back to viewing the main image again, Option/Alt-click on the Layer Mask thumbnail one more time.

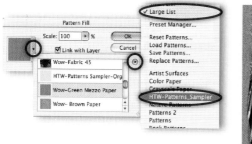

5. Add Pattern Fill Layer

Now that we have masked away the edge of the photo, let's place something behind the image to show in the transparent areas. Choose Pattern from the Adjustment Layer pop-up menu at the bottom of the Layers palette, click on the down-pointing arrow next to the pattern preview, then load the HTW-Patterns Sampler Set from the pop-out menu in the upper-right. Now choose the HTW-Green Mezzo Paper pattern from the bottom of the list and click OK. Then drag the name of the pattern layer you just created to the bottom of the layers stack.

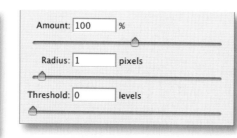

6. Sharpen the Mask

Now let's adjust the edge of the mask to make it look a bit more defined. Click on the *Layer Mask icon* of the top layer to make it active and then choose Filter>Sharpen>Unsharp Mask. Use the standard default settings of Amount: 100, Radius: 1, and Threshold: 0.

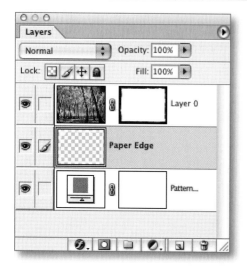

7. Add White Edge

Now let's make it look like this is really torn paper by adding a white edge that will represent the areas where the photo emulsion was torn away, but some of the paper stock remains. Command/Ctrl-click on the Layer Mask on the top layer to load it as a selection. Create a new layer **under** the image layer by Command/Ctrl-clicking on the new layer icon. Choose Select>Modify>Expand; for this 1000-pixel-wide image, we'll use 4 pixels. Set the foreground color to white, type Command/Ctrl-H to hide the selection and paint around the edge of the image. Keep the brush on the *inside* of the photo with just a little bit of the brush extending beyond the edge of the image. You don't want to add a white edge to the entire image because the effect wouldn't look realistic.

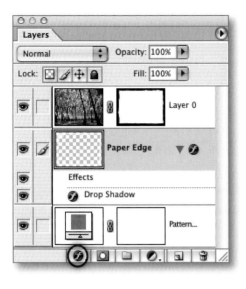

8. Add a Drop Shadow Layer Style

With the white paper edge layer still active, choose Drop Shadow from the layer style pop-up menu at the bottom of the Layers palette (we used the default settings). If the drop shadow isn't showing up around the entire photograph, then go back to the Brush tool and continue painting with white around the edge of the image. On this round of painting, you're not trying to add white that will stick out beyond the edge of the photo; instead you're adding white that is *hidden* under the photo but the drop shadow it's casting *is* visible beyond the edge of the image. Try it, and you'll see what we mean.

9. Sharpen the Paint Layer

There's just one step left before we're done with our masterpiece. With the paper edge still active, type Command/Ctrl-D to deselect the hidden selection, and then type Command/Ctrl-F to apply the last filter you used (which is Unsharp Mask in this case). That will give the paper edge a nice crisp look.

Now that the effect is complete, you're welcome to double-click on the pattern preview thumbnail for the bottom layer and experiment with different patterns until you find the best complement to the image. Or, you may want to try a solid color, or even another photograph, that you copy and paste and place at the bottom of the layer stack. ▦

JHD / MODEL: KENNEDY ROSE

Canvas Texture Treatments

Create a textured overlay combination with variations on the previous brush edge techniques.

Layers

Normal | Opacity: 100%

Lock: | Fill: 100%

Layer 0

Preset Type: Tools

Wow–BT Oil-Medium
Wow–BT Oil-Small
Wow–BT Oil-X Small
Wow–BT Watercolor-Large
Wow–BT Watercolor-Medium

1. Convert Background & Load Presets

Since we're going to be using a Layer Mask to hide the edge of the image, we'll need to convert the Background layer into a normal layer by double-clicking on its name. Then, before we move on, let's load a few of our custom How to Wow presets. Choose Edit>Preset Manager, choose Tools from the Preset Type pop-up menu, click on the right-pointing arrow and choose HTW-Tool Presets Sampler. Before exiting the Preset Manager, choose Patterns from the Preset Type pop-up menu and click on that arrow again and choose HTW-Patterns Sampler from the side menu (for more on presets, see page 19).

2. Create a Pattern Fill layer

Now choose Pattern from the Adjustment Layer pop-up menu at the bottom of the Layers Palette, click on the down-pointing arrow next to the pattern preview and choose the Wow-Canvas Background pattern. Now drag the pattern layer you just created below the original image layer so we have something to see when we mask the image.

3. Add Mask and Paint

Click back on the original image layer, click the Layer Mask icon at the bottom of the Layers palette, switch to the Brush tool and choose the Wow-BT Oil- X Large preset from the Tool Presets palette. Now change the foreground color to black and start painting around the edge of the image to hide the photograph and reveal the texture below. This brush uses the same texture that we have on the underlying layer, so they match up wonderfully.

4. Add Inner Shadow Layer Style

Choose Inner Shadow from the layer style pop-up menu at the bottom of the Layers palette, set the distance to zero so we get a little bit of a halo, set the size to 25, and the opacity to 25.

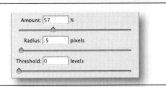

5. Sharpen the Mask

Once you finish painting, choose Filter>Sharpen>Unsharp Mask. We used Amount: 57, Radius: .5, and Threshold: 0.

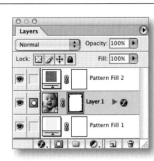

6. Add a Pattern Fill Layer

To add a little texture over the photo itself, hold down Option/Alt, choose Pattern from the Adjustment Layer pop-up menu at the bottom of the Layers palette, set the Mode to Soft Light and the Opacity to 50%, then click OK and choose the same Wow-Canvas Background pattern we used in step 2.

Texture & Noise Overlay Treatments

Add some natural-looking texture, patterns, or noise to your image, and give it a whole new personality.

1. Duplicate Original Layer

In this technique, we're going to apply different filters to copies of our image, then change the blend mode so that these filtered layers interact with the original image in an interesting way. We'll start off by duplicating the image onto its own layer by typing Command/ Ctrl-J. That will leave the original image on the underlying layer and the duplicate at the top of the layers stack.

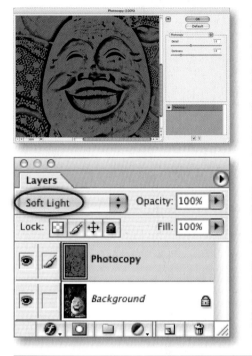

2. Apply Photocopy Filter

We're going to end up using the Photo-copy filter to add an exaggerated edge effect to the image. The filter uses the current foreground and background color as part of its effect. So, type D to reset the foreground/background colors to black/white, click on the back-ground color (white) and choose H: 0, S:0, B:50 to get 50% gray. Now choose Filter>Sketch>Photocopy, set the Detail to 10 and the Darkness to 10 and then click OK. It's a personal preference; you can use whatever you think looks good—just use our settings as a start-ing point. Now change the blend mode at the top of the Layers palette to Soft Light. Since the layer contains a lot of 50% gray, you could use any of the con-trast blend modes which will make the 50% gray areas disappear.

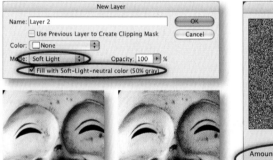

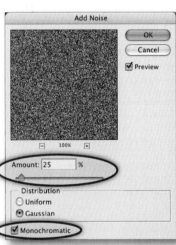

3. Add Grain

Hold Option/Alt and click on the New Layer icon at the bottom of the Lay-ers palette, set the Mode to Soft Light, turn on the Fill with Soft-Light-Neutral Color (50% gray) checkbox and click OK. Then to add some noise, choose Filter>Noise>Add Noise, set the Distri-bution to Gaussian, turn on the Mono-chromatic checkbox and set the Amount to 25. If the result looks a little too digi-tal, choose Filter>Blur>Blur. That will make the noise look much more organic and more like film grain.

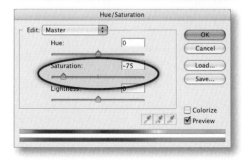

4. Lower Saturation

To add to the weathered-image effect, let's make the image less colorful. With the top layer active, choose Hue/Satura-tion from the Adjustment Layer pop-up menu at the bottom of the Layers palette and reduce the saturation of the image (we used −75%).

Texture & Noise Variations

You can open up a veritable Pandora's box of variations by replacing Step 3 of the previous technique with the following: hold Option/Alt and choose Pattern from the Adjustment Layer pop-up menu at the bottom of the Layers palette, set the Mode pop-up menu to Soft Light and then click OK. In the Pattern Fill dialog box, click on the down-pointing arrow next to the pattern preview, then click on the right-pointing arrow in the upper-right of the pop-up palette that appears and choose the How to Wow-Patterns Sampler set. Once you've done that, you can click on one of the patterns in the list and use the up and down arrow keys to cycle through the patterns. The patterns that are mainly gray will produce the best results.

The 225 dpi samples on these pages do not have the Photocopy filter or the reduced hue and saturation we used with the previous project so you can see how a single Wow pattern in Soft Light mode affects a photograph.

There are three variables to consider when applying the Wow-Patterns: Blend mode; Layer Opacity, and the Scale of the pattern itself.

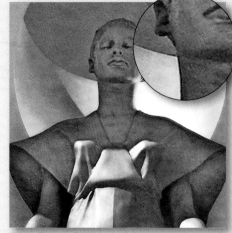

Wow-Brown Paper

Wow-Abstract Texture 06

Wow-Brushed Stucco

Wow-Canvas Texture 01

Wow-Granite 01

Wow-Pebble Board 02

Wow-Reticulation

Wow-Reticulation Blotched

Wow-Sandstone

Wow-Watercolor Salt Overlay

Wow-Watercolor Texture 01

Wow-Weave 03

Wow-Weave 04

Wow-Weave 06

Wow-Wood 06

Turning a Photo into a Painting

Transform a photograph into a watercolor using custom Tool and Pattern presets, along with your personal artistic style.

1. Prepare the Source Image

Since paintings usually are aiming for an idealized interpretation of a scene, we'll want to start off by removing any distracting detail from our source image. In this case we used the techniques covered in Chapter 4 "Retouching & Repairing" to remove a branch from the top of the image, a little cloud from the right edge and a bunch of leaves from the sand; we also simplified the waves.

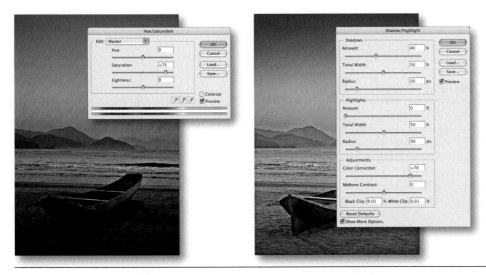

2. Adjust Color and Contrast

The source image will mainly be used to define the colors we will be painting with. To create a more impressionistic look, we'll choose to use overly saturated colors. So, choose Image>Adjustments>Hue/Saturation and adjust to your liking. Then, to make sure you can see a lot of color in the darkest areas of this exaggerated image, choose Image>Adjustments>Shadow/Highlight, move the Shadows Amount slider (we used +40) and then adjust the color correction setting until the image is very colorful (we used +70).

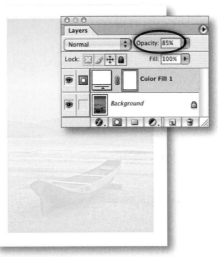

3. Prepare Your "Paper" Surface

Now that the color and detail in our image has been idealized, it's time to get the file ready to accept paint. We'll start by adding some extra white space around the image. Choose Image>Canvas Size, turn on the Relative checkbox, set the Canvas Extension Color to White and enter 130 pixels for both the width and height settings. Then to add a "paper" layer, choose Solid Color from the Adjustment Layer pop-up menu at the bottom of the Layers palette, choose white and lower the opacity of the layer to 85%. This will help with the tracing we'll do later.

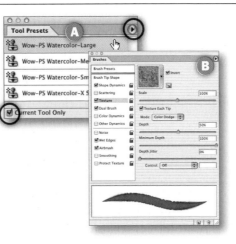

4. Load Tool & Pattern Presets

Before we start to paint, we need to set up the Pattern Stamp tool so that it simulates a water color brush. First, choose the Pattern Stamp Tool in the toolbox (it's hidden under the Clone Stamp Tool), then choose Window>Tool Presets, turn on the Current Tool Only checkbox at the bottom of the Tool Presets palette **A** and choose a Tool Preset called Wow-PS Watercolor-Large **B**. See page 19 for more information on loading the Wow Presets.

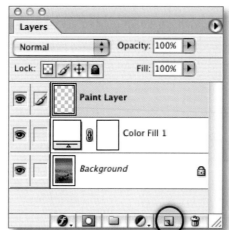

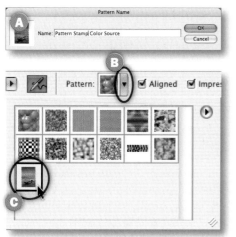

5. Define the Image as a Pattern

Let's set things up so that Photoshop will use the image we've prepared to define the colors we'll be painting with. Do that by turning off the eyeball icon on the white paper layer we created earlier, click on the layer that contains the photograph and choose Edit>Define Pattern **A**. Then to make the Pattern Stamp tool use that pattern as our color source, click on the down-pointing arrow next to the pattern setting in the Options bar **B** and choose the pattern you just defined **C**. Now let's create a paint layer. Turn the eyeball back on for the white "paper" layer and with that layer active, click the New Layer icon at the bottom of the Layers palette.

6. Begin Painting

We've got everything set up and we're ready to paint, but we need to go over a few ground rules:

- Never paint across two contrasting colors with one stroke (with real watercolor paints you'd usually need to switch paints to accomplish that).

- Never let two colors touch, otherwise the colors will start to bleed together.

- Painting fast will allow the paper texture to show through; painting slow will "flood" the paper with color.

- You may want to occasionally leave little white spaces between some of your paint strokes (common in a quick watercolor "sketch"). These gaps can cause the colors to appear more vivid in contrast to the white.

With these tips in mind, make the paint layer active and use your Pattern Stamp tool (using the Wow-PS Watercolor-Larger preset) to paint in the sky. Work very quickly, as if doing a "wash" of color and once you get to the edge of the mountains, stop.

TIP

Brush Size. We're using a Wacom graphics tablet to control the size of the brush. The *pressure* we use when painting with the pen controls the *size* of the brush. If you don't have a pressure-sensitive graphics tablet, then use the bracket keys] and [to interactively change your brush size on the fly.

INSIGHT

Tracing Paper. The reduced-opacity white "paper" layer is there so you can see a hint of the original image. This allows you to follow the regions within the original image as if you were painting on a sheet of tracing paper. Occasionally, you'll want to change the opacity of that layer back to 100% so you can see only the final paint layer and none of the original image.

7. Complete the Painting

When the sky is complete, work your way down the image, reducing your brush size as you encounter areas of finer detail, remembering to release the mouse button each time you run into a different line, shape, form or color. Keep in mind, you're not going for photo-realism, so you don't want to make things perfect; rather you should give the impression of the shapes and colors that make up the image. As you get to areas of finer detail, you might want to try lowering the opacity of the "paper" layer so it's easier to see the detail in the original image. As you are working, occasionally bring the opacity of the "paper" layer back to 100% to check your progress. Then reduce it again, select the paint layer, and continue painting.

There is no such thing as erasing in traditional watercolors, but you can use a paper towel to blot up the mistakes. To simulate that technique around the edges of your painting in Photoshop, start a paint stroke while your brush is over the white border and move in to cover the color and clean up the edges of your masterpiece.

8. Add Density and Touch Up

Now let's add density to the image by typing Command/Ctrl-J once or twice to create duplicate layers, which will triple the density of the paint. Then, with the top layer active, touch up areas of your painting that need it, such as any gaps that are too distracting. You might also want to do a bit of a wash to mix some of the colors. Since we're painting on only one of the layers, it's a subtle effect. (Which means you now you have permission to blend the colors.)

9. Imitate Paint Pooling

In real watercolors, while the paint is drying, the pigments tend to pool toward the edges causing them to become darker. To imitate that effect, duplicate the top paint layer by typing Command/Ctrl-J, type D to reset the foreground/background colors and choose Filter>Sketch>Photocopy. We set the Detail to 20 and the Darkness to 5 and then clicked OK. Now change the blend mode at the top of the Layers palette to Color Burn and lower the opacity of the layer to somewhere around 50%.

10. Add Paper and Salt Texture

Now let's add paper texture and a special "salt stain" texture. With the HTW-Patterns Sampler loaded, choose Pattern from the Adjustment Layer pop-up menu at the bottom of the Layers palette, click on the down-pointing arrow next to the pattern preview **A** and choose Wow-Watercolor Overlay and click OK. Change the blend mode at the top of the Layers palette to Soft Light and then repeat the process to add another Pattern Fill layer, this time using the Wow-Watercolor Salt Overlay pattern **B**. Finally, to make sure that second texture is subtle, lower the opacity of its layer to around 25%.

11. Apply Unsharp Mask filter

In real watercolor painting, the pigments can accentuate the texture of the paper. To simulate that look, click on the top layer of the image and make a merged visible layer by holding Shift-Command/Ctrl-Option/Alt and then typing N and then E. Then choose Filter>Sharpen>Unsharp Mask, set the Amount to 100, the Radius to 1 and the Threshold to 0. ▥

Painting Past Reality

If you think about it, the last technique is all about taking a realistic photo and removing the realism and transforming it into something more *expressive*—putting the "documentation" of the captured moment aside and instead focusing on your "impression" (thus the term *Impressionism)*. Since that's the case, you don't even need to start with a single photograph. You could start with just about any image!

So, while we're still on the subject, we think this a golden opportunity to put this technique to the test on a composited image. We combined multiple photographs into an idealized composite and because the painterly approach conceals most problems we'd usually encounter when combining multiple images, we were happy to throw precision out the window.

JHD / SURFER: JOHN OGBURN

The source image for this painting was created by combining two photos. The first photo features a friend of Jack's, surfing **A**. The second photo has a better composition and was taken of a different surfer, with a much better wave **B**. Wanting the best of both worlds, the photos were combined to create an idealized image using the techniques we covered in Chapter 4, "Retouching & Repairing."

Then, using the same techniques detailed in the previous project, this idealized image was prepared for painting **C**. After completing the transformation from plain reality into a luminous waterscape, the final "painting" was printed out on ink jet-compatible watercolor paper, framed, and presented as a gift to the delighted friend **D**.

COMBINING & COLLAGING

Combining Multiple Elements into Elegant Presentations

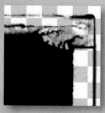

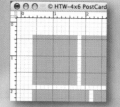

YOU'RE STARING AT a bare stage, your photo elements are the players and you are the set designer. You have an important story to tell. You want your presentation to be clean, focused, attention-grabbing and pleasing to the eye. Because you're working with Photoshop, your options stretch out like a highway that extends all the way to the moon and back. How are you going to put the pieces together so they don't just look like a random bunch of elements thrown haphazardly on the page? Need a place to start? Well, you've come to the right place. We'll even do some of the work for you.

In this chapter we'll make it easy for you to combine your images into a polished and highly professional end result. We'll run the gamut from basic combining of elements and photographs to some bold, splashy treatments that will make your images jump off the page. Here's what this chapter has to offer the burgeoning collagist:

- Working with premade templates to quickly create collages

- Learning how to create your own templates from scratch

- Using graphic-based Layer Masks to create cool edge effects

- Using custom shapes to create unusual and eye-catching frames

- Tricks for combining dissimilar elements into a unified presentation

- Creating the look of a professional photo-studio backdrop for your subject

- Mastering the classic Photoshop collage; the art of soft-edged combining

- Seamlessly stitching together multiple images to create a panorama

Getting Friendly with the CD

This chapter depends heavily on the files provided on the CD at the back of the book. So if you haven't already done so, you'll want to go to the beginning of the book (page 19) and brush up on how

to load the files provided on the CD. We will be working with various images, presets and templates, all of which are enormous timesavers.

Striking Out on Your Own

In addition to getting the "fast food" satisfaction of using our premade shapes, templates and graphic-based masks, you'll also learn how to create your own templates and masks, so you aren't limited to what's provided on the CD. Our intention here is to give you a jumpstart as you explore new territory in Photoshop. We hope you'll find our prefabrications pleasing, but strongly encourage you to take the time to work through the sections where we teach you how to build your own inventory. It will be time well spent, with big pay-offs later.

Template-Based Collaging

Using premade templates for quick, easy and consistent collages.

Keep Template Hidden. The HTW template files use a distinctive green color for each Shape layer so that you can easily see if any of your images are not large enough to cover the shape. If you'd like to resize any of the shapes, type Command/Ctrl-' to view the underlying grid and then with a Shape layer active, type Command/Ctrl-T to scale the Shape layer.

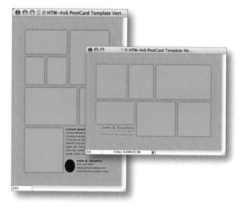

1. Open Template

Start by opening either of the "HTW-4x6 PostCard Template" files that are found on the CD at the back of this book. Both of those files were created using Shape Layers, Text and Layer Styles. Since none of those tools are dependent on the resolution of your image (they are just settings that define the visual appearance of the image instead of being made out of pixels), they can be scaled to any size without degrading their quality.

Use Bicubic Sharper. To maintain the highest quality when scaling down images, choose Preferences>General from the Photoshop menu (Mac), or Edit menu (Win) and set the Image Interpolation pop-up menu to **Bicubic Sharper.** That setting will produce much sharper images when reducing the size of images, which allows you to quickly create collages without having to apply sharpening to each layer.

Image Interpolation: Bicubic Sharper

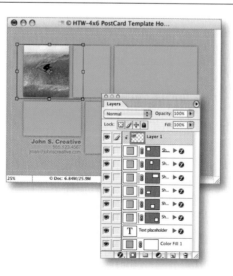

2. Add Images, Mask and Scale

Open a photograph and use the Move tool to drag the image to the template document. Now drag the layer within the layers stack so it is directly above the Shape layer you'd like to use and type Command/Ctrl-G so that it is clipped by the underlying layer. Type Command/Ctrl-T, then click near the middle (but not on the crosshair) and drag to reposition the image, or hold Shift and drag one of the corner handles to scale the image. If the photo is overly large, you might need to type Command/Ctrl-0 (zero) to see the corner handles.

3. Load & Mask Remaining Images

Now repeat the last step for the remaining images you plan on using. The process is: click on the Shape layer, drag over an image, type Command/Ctrl-G to group, type Command/Ctrl-T to reposition and scale image, repeat. If you need to flip an image (we flipped the bird image), Control/right-click and choose Flip Horizontal while scaling and positioning the image. Then, after you have everything in place, go back and adjust the positioning of each image.

4. Adjust for Alternate Layout

To rotate an image *within* its mask, type Command/Ctrl-T, move your mouse beyond one of the corner handles and drag. To rotate the image *along with* its clipping mask below, then with the photo layer active, click to the right of the eyeball icon for the Shape layer that is directly below the photo layer to link the layers together so they move as a unit, and type Command/Ctrl-T.

5. Choose a Background

Now that the layout is looking good, we can start to customize the overall look of the image by choosing a new background. With the HTW-Patterns Sampler Set loaded, click on the bottom layer of the template, choose Layer>Change Layer Content>Pattern and choose Wow-Rice Paper Black.

INSIGHT

Crisp Edges. If you'd like to retain the extremely crisp edges of the text and photo cropping, then save the image in either EPS or PDF file format. Turning on the ***Include Vector Data*** checkbox when saving in those formats will include the paths needed to reproduce the razor sharp edges.

☑ Include Vector Data

6. Refine Text

To change the color of the text, change the foreground color and then with the Type layer active, type Option/Alt-Delete. We also changed the Layer Style applied to the text. Control/right-click on the black circle on the right of the Type layer and choose Clear Layer Style, and then choose Drop Shadow from the Layer>Layer Style menu.

Creating Quick Collage Templates

Let's take a look at how to create grid-based templates like the one used in the previous technique. Investing your time now can really pay off later when time gets tight and your creativity isn't at its peak. For example, using a template makes it incredibly easy to create a monthly promotional postcard without having to reinvent the wheel each time.

Think of how much time you'd save if you used templates for those lengthy annual reports, product catalogs, or the proverbial wedding album. For more ideas on creating a library of collage templates for your work, see the Custom Mask Collaging project later in this chapter.

Create New Document

Start by choosing File>New to create a new document. When setting the Width and Height, think about the final size of the printed piece you'd like to have. If the project will be printed on a commercial printing press, you might need to take bleed into consideration. Bleed is needed anytime you plan on printing all the way up to the edge of the sheet of trimmed paper. If you add an extra .25 inch to the width and height of the document, the printing company will have enough leeway to cut the paper just where you want it, and if the cropping is a little off, the extra bleed removes the risk of white gaps appearing on the edge of your printed piece. So, if you plan on having a 6x4 inch postcard printed commercially, you'll actually want to create a 6.25x4.25 inch document. We like to create most of our collage templates using a resolution of 300 pixels per inch, in RGB mode.

Set Up Rulers & Guides

If you added bleed to your document size, you'll need a few guides to indicate where the trimmed paper edge will be by doing the following:

Let's set up our rulers by typing Command/Ctrl-R, and Control/Right-clicking on the ruler to choose a unit of measurement. The measurement system you use for the design process is a personal choice. We typically work in inches, but sometimes use percent.

Add your first guide by choosing View>New Guide, then choose Horizontal and enter ".125 in" in the Position field. Next create another guide using the same settings except set the Orientation to Vertical. Those two guides define the upper-left corner of the trimmed image.

Before we move on, let's get the zero point of the rulers lining up with the corner of the trimmed image. To accomplish that, drag from the far upper-left corner of the rulers and place the zero point where the upper-left guides cross.

Now let's set up the lower-right corner. Choose View>New Guide once again and this time create a Vertical guide with the position set to the final width of your image (the non-bleed size) and add .125 for bleed. So for a six inch wide image, enter "6.125 in." Now repeat that process to add a Horizontal guide to represent the trimmed height of the image. For a 4-inch-high image, enter "4.125 in." You can also create custom guides by clicking and dragging out from one of the rulers.

Define Grid

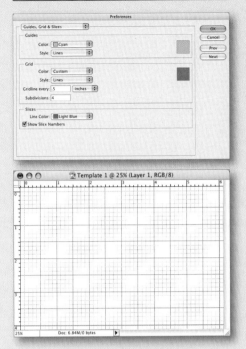

Now let's define the grid that will be the foundation of our layout. Choose View>Show>Grid to see the preexisting grid, then double-click on the ruler and click the Next button to get to the Guides, Grid & Slices preferences. The exact setting you use will vary from document to document. You're looking for the choice that will give you a lot of versatility while defining enough structure so that the design doesn't look thrown together. For a 6x4 inch postcard, we might set the Gridline Every setting to 0.5 inches and Subdivisions to 4. Or if the document is an odd size, try setting the Gridline Every setting to 10 or 15 percent. Since we made the grid visible before changing the preferences, you can let your eyes be your guide in determining which settings to use.

Create Layout

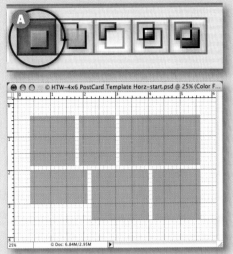

With the grid visible, it's time to create the structure that will determine where images appear in the layout. Start by changing the foreground color to something that sticks out. That will help once we start placing images into the template because we'll be able to see when a photo isn't large enough to completely cover the shape that will be masking it. Next, choose the Rectangular Shape tool and start to draw out boxes that define where you'll later place photographs (making sure the New Shape Layer option is chosen in the Options bar **A** so you end up with separate layers for each rectangle). Try to keep a consistent empty border around the entire document and use the grid lines to define the space between rectangles. For our 6x4 inch postcard, we left a 3/4 inch border around the entire card (plus 1/8 inch for bleed) and 1/8 inch between each rectangle. Remember, it's *always* best to work out your design on paper before translating it to the computer.

Add Layer Styles

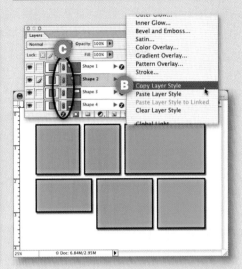

Now it's time to spice up the design by adding a background, drop shadows and other visual accoutrements. With one of the Shape layers active, choose Drop Shadow (or any other style) from the Layer Style pop-up menu at the bottom of the Layers palette. For this template we set the Distance to 0, the Size to 25, the Opacity to 25, and the Noise to 1. This style is just an example you might try (in the image above we used Drop Shadow, Inner Glow and Stroke styles). Be creative; don't be afraid to experiment!

Once you've added a few Layer Styles to one of the Shape layers, you can apply the same styles to the other Shape layers by doing the following: Control/right-click on the black circle that appears on the right side of the active layer and choose Copy Layer Style from the menu that appears **B**. Next, drag down the empty column to the right of the eyeball icons in the Layers palette to link all the Shape layers together **C**, then Control/right-click on that black circle again and this time choose Paste Layer Style to Linked. ▥

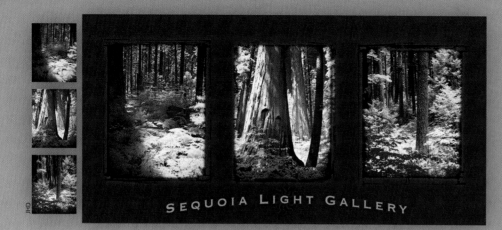

Custom Mask Collaging

Create dynamic compositions by adding custom photographic edges, custom Layer Styles and modified type.

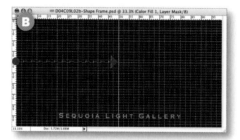

1. Setup Document

Open all the files in the chapter 9 folder: *C09-224 Mask Collage,* starting with *C09-224 Mask Background.psd,* then type Command/Ctrl-R to make the rulers visible, Control/right-click on the ruler and choose Percent. Next, double-click on the ruler to access the Preferences dialog box, click the *Next* button, set the *Gridline Every* setting to 10, change the *Measurement* pop-up menu to *Percent* and set the *Subdivisions* to 4 **A**. Now choose View>Show>Grid to see the grid you just created, then click on the left ruler, drag out a guide and place it at the 50% position **B**.

2. Add and Position First Image

Now switch to the document named *C09-224 Mask Sequoias.psd* which contains three infrared photos. Use the Move tool to drag one of the images to the template document. As you move the image within the template document, it will snap to the grid lines. Position the image so that the upper-left corner is two grid lines from the left edge and four grid lines from the top of the document. Next, type Command/Ctrl-T and scale the image while holding Shift until its bottom edge is seven grid lines from the bottom.

3. Add and Position Other Images

Now drag over a second image and position its upper-right corner two grid lines from the right edge and four grid lines from the top of the document. Type Command/Ctrl-T, hold Shift and drag the lower-left corner of the image until the bottom is seven grid lines from the bottom of the document and then press Return/Enter. Next, drag over the last image, position it four grid lines from the top and then type Command/Ctrl-T and scale it to the same height as the other images.

4. Distribute Images

With one of the end image layers active, click to the right of the eyeball icons for the other two image layers to link them to the active layer **A**. *With the Move tool active,* click on the Distribute Horizontal Centers icon **B** in the Options bar. That will center the middle image between the other two images. Now you need to unlink the images to avoid problems in the next steps, so click the link symbols next to the eyeballs of each layer to toggle them off.

5. Add and Scale Border

We're done using the grid, so type Command/Ctrl-H to hide the grid and Command/Ctrl-R to hide the rulers. Now click on the Background layer to make it active, switch to our scanned edges image *(Graphic Auth ExtEdges-all 3.psd)* and use the Move tool to drag one of the borders over to the template document. Back in the template document, type Command/Ctrl-T to transform the image, and type Command/Ctrl-0 (zero) so you can see the transformation handles and scale down the graphic until it's a tiny amount smaller than the image it's under (no need to hold Shift). *Now click on the layer above* and type Command/Ctrl-G so it's masked by the border layer below.

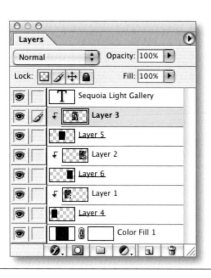

6. Add Additional Masks

To mask the right-hand image, click on the layer below it, switch to the scanned edges document, and drag over the second border using the Move tool. Then type Command/Ctrl-T and scale it down until it's just smaller than the image it will be masking (since this is a high-res image, you might have to type Command/Ctrl-0 [zero] in order to see the transformation handles). Then click on the layer above the border and type Command/Ctrl-G to mask it. Repeat this process with the third border image to mask the center image in the template.

7. Add Layer Styles

Now let's tweak the results by adding some Layer Styles. Click on one of the border layers, and choose Inner Shadow from the Layer Style pop-up menu at the bottom of the Layers palette. In the Layer Style dialog box, set the Distance to zero, the Size to 15 and the Choke setting to 35. To create a grainy look, bring up the Noise setting to somewhere around 20. Before leaving the Layer Style dialog box, click on the Outer Glow choice on the left of the dialog box. Click on the color swatch and choose white, set the Opacity to 20, set the Noise to 5 and then set the Size to 25.

8. Copy/Paste Styles to Linked

To apply that style to the other borders, Control/right-click on the black circle that appears on the right side of the active layer in the Layers palette and choose Copy Layer Style. Then click to the right of the eyeball icons for the other two other border layers to link them to the active layer **A**, Control/right-click on the black circle **B** a second time and this time choose Paste Layer Style to Linked.

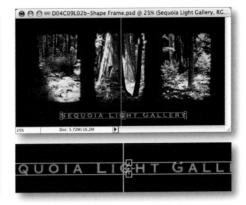

9. Center the Text

Now we'll finesse the text at the bottom of the document. First, let's make sure it's centered in the document. You can do that by typing Command/Ctrl-H to make the grid and guides visible again and then typing Command/Ctrl-T while the Type layer is active. If the text is centered, the center point of the transformation box should line up with the guide in the center of the image. If it doesn't line up, use the right and left arrow keys to nudge it into place and press Return/Enter when it's centered.

10. Add Custom Shape

Now let's spice up our "Sequoia Light Gallery" logo by adding a custom shape. Choose the Custom Shape tool **A**, click on the down-pointing arrow that appears next to the Shape preview in the Options bar at the top of the screen **B**, choose Nature from the side menu of the drop-down palette that appears **C** and then choose the shape that's called Sun 1. Click on the color swatch on the right side of the Options bar **D** and set the color to H: 85, S: 35, B: 25 **E**. Now click on the center of the guide near the text, and drag while holding Option/Alt to start from the center and Shift to keep it proportional. Finally, change the stacking order of the layers so that the sun appears under the text.

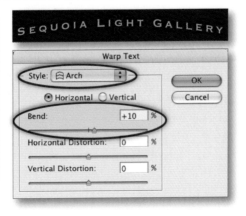

11. Warp the Text

If you don't have Copperplate in your personal font library, just select another font. To finalize our logo, choose Layer>Type>Warp Text while the Type layer is active, choose Arch from the Style pop-up menu and change the Bend setting to +10. Finally, position the text so that the G in "LIGHT" lines up with the center of the sun. ▥

Converting Scanned Images into Masks

Let's look at how you can prepare a scanned image to be used as a quick clipping mask. The border images (Graphic Auth ExtEdges-all 3.psd) used in the previous technique had to go through this process to be converted from black-and-white artwork to transparency-endowed masking material.

From White to Transparent

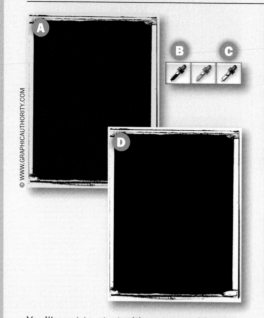

© WWW.GRAPHICAUTHORITY.COM

You'll want to start with a scanned image that contains mainly black and white with very few intermediate grays. This could be a splat of black ink on white paper, a photo of the white lines that are painted on the black asphalt of a parking lot or anything else that is primarily black and white. In our case, we'll use a special image from our friends at *graphicauthority.com*. It's part of the Extreme Edges collection. This particular image (Graphic Auth ExtEdges-start.psd) has been degraded so that it represents what you might get when scanning an image (no pure blacks or whites) **A**. Our goal is to keep the black areas of the image opaque while transforming the white portions into transparent areas.

The first thing we need to do is to ensure that we mainly have solid black and solid white, so choose Image>Adjustments> Levels, click on the black eyedropper **B** and then click on the darkest area of the image. Before you leave the Levels dialog

box, click on the white eyedropper **C** and then click on a bright area of the image. That will force the areas you click on to solid black and solid white, which is just what we need **D**.

Now let's select all the areas that are solid white by holding down the Option/Alt and Command/Ctrl keys and pressing ~ (that squiggly looking symbol is known as a *tilde* that is located in the upper-left of most keyboards). We actually want the black areas selected, so choose Select>Inverse. At this point, create a new empty layer and drag the original image layer to the trash can at the bottom of the Layers palette.

Finally, with the selection still active, type D to reset the foreground color to black and then type Option/Alt-Delete to fill the selected area with black.

That gives us our graphic on a transparent background **E**. This technique prevents the white halo you would normally get when trying to remove the background. ▥

Importing Custom Shapes from Illustrator

As you'll see with the technique demonstrated on the following page, using custom shapes to mask a photograph can have a dramatic effect on an image. But before we get into that nifty trick, let's look at how you can get your favorite Adobe Illustrator clip art, logo or "dingbats" transformed into custom shapes in Photoshop.

1. Create Outlines in Adobe Illustrator

Photoshop is only capable of using paths from Illustrator to create custom shapes. That means that certain features in Illustrator will need to be modified before they can be brought into Photoshop. For instance: Text will need to be converted to a path by choosing Type>Create Outlines. To get strokes to transfer choose Object>Path>Outline Stroke. And for custom brush strokes choose Object>Expand Appearance.

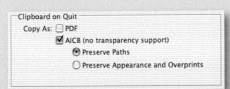

2. Set Preferences & Copy to Clipboard

Before you attempt to copy and paste between Illustrator and Photoshop, be sure to choose Preferences>File Handling & Clipboard from the Illustrator menu (Mac), or Edit menu (Win). You'll need to turn on the AICB option (which stands for Adobe Illustrator Clip Board) and choose Preserve Paths to get Illustrator to use a format that is compatible with Photoshop's custom shapes (otherwise it will be imported as a PDF file).

3. Paste as a Custom Shape

Now that you have your Illustrator artwork made out of paths and have set up the preferences properly, it's time to transfer the artwork into Photoshop. In Illustrator, type Command/Ctrl-A to select all the paths that make up your artwork and then type Command/Ctrl-C to place that art on the clipboard. Next, switch to Photoshop and open or create the document you'd like to use. Type Command/Ctrl-V to paste the artwork, and when prompted, choose Shape Layer. Then to name this shape so you can access it later, choose Edit>Define Custom Shape (be careful not to click anywhere before doing this as you might accidentally deselect the paths that are needed to create that custom shape).

4. Save New Shape as a Preset

Now that a custom shape is defined, let's save it into its own custom shape presets file so we can get back to it even after loading a different set of preset shapes. Choose Edit>Preset Manager, choose Custom Shapes from the Preset Type pop-up menu, click on the shape (or Command/Ctrl-click on multiple shapes to save a "library" of your favorite shapes) you just created from within the list and then click the Save Set button on the far right of the dialog box. By saving the preset into the Presets folder within your Photoshop folder, the next time your restart Photoshop, your newly saved preset will be available from the side menu of the Custom Shapes drop-down palette in the Options bar. ▥

Custom Shape Framing

Sandwich images between two custom shapes to create dynamic collage templates that can be used over and over again.

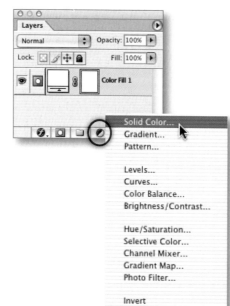

1. Create New Document

Start by creating a new document in which you'll create your collage. We used an 800 by 1000 pixel RGB image with a resolution of 300 pixels per inch and a transparent background. When this document first opens, it will be empty (which looks like a checkerboard in Photoshop). We'll start with a simple backdrop, so choose Solid Color from the Adjustment Layer pop-up menu at the bottom of the Layers palette and choose white (R: 255, G: 255, B: 255). Using a Solid Color layer instead of a standard Background layer will allow us to quickly change the background later.

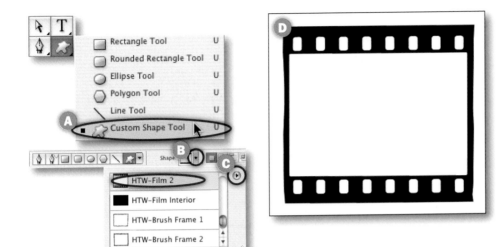

2. Load Presets and Draw Shape

Choose the Custom Shape tool in the Tools palette **A**. Now click on the down-pointing arrow next to the shape preview in the Options bar **B**, choose HTW-Custom-Shapes-Sampler from the side menu of the drop-down palette that appears **C** and then choose the HTW-Film 2 shape from the preset list. Click on the color swatch on the right side of the Options bar, choose black and click OK. Now click and drag within the image while holding Shift to create a film shape **D**. Then before moving on, turn off the link icon in the Options bar.

3. Add Drop Shadow Style

Now let's add a drop shadow to our film shape. With the Film Strip layer still active, choose Drop Shadow from the Layer Style pop-up menu at the bottom of the Layers palette. Set the Distance to zero, the Size to 7 and click OK.

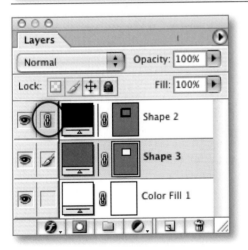

4. Draw Film Base

Click on the bottom layer, with the Custom Shape tool still active, choose the HTW-Film Interior shape preset, click on the color swatch in the Options bar, choose a light shade of gray and click OK. Now click and drag to create a rectangle that is slightly larger than the photo area in the film strip but not so large that it shows through any of the sprocket holes. This shape will be used to mask the images that we'll be loading in a moment (we'll call it the Film Base layer). Before we move on, *click to the right of the eyeball icon for the Film Strip layer to link it to the active Film Base layer.* By linking these two layers together, you'll make sure that the Film Base will always line up with the Film Strip even if you move, rotate or scale the Film Strip layer.

5. Load and Mask First Image

With the film base layer active, use the Move tool to drag an image over from another document so it appears directly above the gray layer. Then to get the image to only show up where the gray Film Base layer is, type Command/Ctrl-G. Now type Command/Ctrl-T and resize the image (while holding Shift) so that most of the image is visible within the frame.

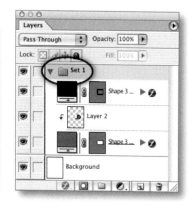

6. Create Layer Set

Now that we have one image masked, let's prep the image in such a way that it will be easy to mask additional photos. With the photo layer active, click to the right of the eyeball icons next to both the Film Strip layer and the Film Base layer to link them to the photo layer. Next, choose New Set From Linked from the side menu of the Layers palette, which will place those three layers into a Layer Set (which looks like a folder).

7. Load and Mask Other Images

Before dragging over another image, drag the Layer Set you just created to the New Layer icon at the bottom of the Layers palette **A** which will duplicate the set. Next, click on the *photo layer* within the new Layer Set and then Option/Alt-click on the trash icon to delete it. Now, click on the Film Base layer within that set to make it active, and then use the Move tool to drag in another photo. Just as before, type Command/Ctrl-G to make the photo only show up where the Film Base layer is and then type Command/Ctrl-T and scale the image while holding Shift to maintain its proportions. You can repeat this process (duplicate set, delete photo layer, drag in new photo, mask photo to Film Base, transform) with any additional images.

> **TIP**
>
> **Linked Rotation.** If any of the images you want to frame in a film strip are vertical, then click on the film strip layer and choose Edit>Transform Path>Rotate 90° CW to create a vertical frame. Since the film base layer is linked to the film strip layer they will rotate together.

8. Load Background Image

Now that you have all of the images framed, let's set up the background. Click on the bottom layer and drag over the last image while holding Shift to center the image within the document. If you'd rather use a simple patterned image for the background, then choose Pattern from the Adjustment Layer pop-up menu at the bottom of the Layers palette and experiment with the preset patterns. Remember that we have supplied the **HTW Patterns Sampler** Library on the CD.

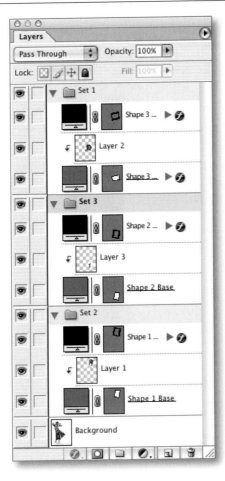

9. Fine-Tune Layout

Now that we have all our elements in place, it's time to fine-tune the layout. Because you're working with Photoshop, you have an abundance of options:

- If you want to move or rotate any of the framed photos, just click on the appropriate *Layer Set* and type Command/Ctrl-T to access Free Transform.

- If you'd like to rotate the film border while leaving the photo stationary, then click on the film strip layer, turn off the link symbol for the photo layer and start rotating.

- If you'd rather rotate the photograph and leave the frame stationary, click on the photo layer and turn off any link symbols that appear to the right of the eyeball icons in the Layers palette. You can also click on one Layer Set and then link it to the other Layer Sets to move them all as a group.

- You can change the stacking order of the Film Strips by dragging the Layer Set up or down the layers stack.

Unifying a Series with Styles

Instantly unify a series of varied photographs—within a single collage or across multiple files—using custom Layer Styles.

1. Create the Base Collage

For this project we started a collage for you *(C09-234 Unifying Styles.psd)* by creating a new document and dragging each photo into it using the Move tool. Then we scaled each image (by typing Command/Ctrl-T) and arranged them into a nice composition. The images were shot using inexpensive disposable cameras and they vary in quality, color and sharpness, which is what makes them suitable for this kind of treatment.

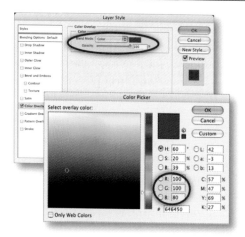

2. Add a Color Overlay Layer Style

Let's unify the color of the images by adding a sepia-toned effect. With any photo layer active, choose Color Overlay from the Layer Style pop-up menu at the bottom of the Layers palette, set the Blend Mode pop-up menu to Color and click on the color swatch. In the color picker, choose a not-so-vivid brown-yellow color (we used R: 100, G: 100, B: 80). You can also lower the Opacity setting of the Color Overlay if you'd like to see a hint of the original colors (we left ours at 100%).

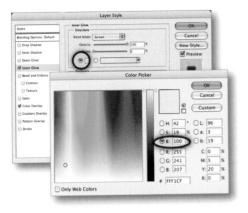

3. Add an Inner Glow Layer Style

Next, we'll create a more interesting edge so the blacks in the various images don't blend together. To accomplish that, choose Inner Glow from the Layer Style pop-up menu at the bottom of the Layers palette, set the Size to 25 and then click on the color swatch. When the color picker appears, type in the same numbers that you used for the previous step (R: 100, G: 100, B: 80 in our case), then set the B in the HSB area to 100 to get a bright version of that color.

TIP

Copying Layer Styles. When you Control/right-click on the Layer Style icon on the active layer and choose *Copy Layer Style,* you're not limited to pasting the style within the active document. You can switch to any open document, Control/right-click any layer name within the Layers palette and choose *Paste Layer Style,* or *Paste Layer Style* to Linked to apply the style to the active or linked layers.

4. Add a Drop Shadow Layer Style

Now, let's give the image a little more dimension by adding a subtle drop shadow "halo" to the image. Choose Drop Shadow from the Layer Style pop-up menu at the bottom of the Layers palette, set the Distance to zero, the Size to 25 and the Opacity to 25.

5. Copy/Paste Layer Styles

Now that one image looks good, let's apply those settings to the other layers. Control/right-click on the black circle that appears on the right side of the active layer **A** and choose Copy Layer Style from the menu. To apply those style settings to the other layers, drag down the column to the right of the eyeball icons in the Layers palette (to link all the image layers **B**), then Control/right-click on that black circle again and this time choose Paste Layer Style to Linked **C**. If you'd like to use this style in the future, choose Window>Styles, click on the Create New Style icon at the bottom of the palette **D** and give the style a name **E**. 🔲

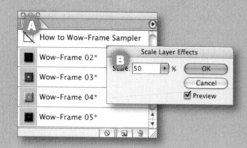

Working with Preset Layer Styles

In the last technique, we combined a few simple Layer Styles. Now let's expand our horizons by learning to effectively apply preset Layer Styles. First, a word of caution—whenever you apply Layer Styles to every layer of an image, it's tempting to overdo it: When the style takes center stage and the photographs are secondary, that's a pretty good clue that you've gotten carried away.

Applying Preset Styles

Choose View>Styles to open the Layer Styles palette **A**. You can load a group of preset styles by choosing the set's name from the side menu of the Layer Style palette. We've created some custom frames and mattes as Layer Styles; they are under the How to Wow-Frame Sampler label, which is part of the **HTW Styles Sampler** library (see page 19 for more on loading and working with the Wow presets). To apply a style, click on a style within the Styles palette to apply it to the active layer, or drag a style to a layer within the main image window. Once you have a style applied to one layer, you can copy the style by clicking the arrow that appears next to the Layer Style icon (a black circle with an f inside) on the active layer and dragging the individual styles to another layer, or dragging the word "Effects" to copy all the styles from that layer.

Modifying Styles

When you apply certain preset styles, you may find that the settings that make up the style cause it to overwhelm your image. That usually happens when the style was designed for a higher resolution image than what you are currently working on. You can adjust the setting for all the styles applied to a layer by choosing Layer>Layer Styles> Scale Effects **B**. You can also customize a style by double-clicking on the Layer Style icon that appears on the right side of the layer. For instance, you might apply the Wow-Frame 04 preset **C**, use the Scale Effects dialog box to reduce the width of the frames and then add the same Color Overlay style that was used in the previous technique to add a sepia-toned effect. Once you've chosen a frame and tint, you can copy and paste that style to all the linked layers in that file using step 5 from the previous page **D**.

Styles as Backgrounds

Layer Styles are not available when you're working on the **Background** layer. The *Background* layer does not allow for transparency and Layer Styles depend on transparency to determine exactly where their effects should be applied. If you'd like to use a style to define the background of your image, simply double-click on the *Background* layer to change its name, which will convert it into a normal layer. Once you've done that, the Layer Style pop-up menu will become available at the bottom of the Layers palette. In the image to the left, a Pattern Overlay style using the Wow-Green Mezzo Paper pattern was used to define the overall background, and then an Inner Glow style was added **E** to create a distinctive edge.

Frame Style Samples

The images to the right are examples of what can be created using the Layer Styles that are available in the **HTW Styles Sampler** library on the CD at the back of this book (see page 19 for more on loading presets). Remember to use the Layer>Layer Styles>Scale Effects command any time the frame or edge effects are too large for the image they are being applied to.

Above is the sample image and its Layers palette before we applied the HTW frame styles. You'll notice that a Layer Mask was added to the palm photograph layer and black circles were painted in the four corners to create a scalloped shape effect.

How to Wow–Tint 2

How to Wow–Tint 4

Wow–Edges 09

Wow–Edges 10

Wow–Frame 03

Wow–Frame 08

Walking On Water

Lorem ipsum dolor sit amet, hac consectetuer adipiscing elit. Quisque augue.

Aenean blandit. Cras purus orci, ultricies sed, blandit aliquam, condimentum eget, est. Nunc ac odio. Morbi orci nisl, sollicitudin et, frin Curabitur magna nulla, placerat eget.

Text Panel Overlays

Create custom tool presets and work with hidden features of the Type tool to quickly add polished text and graphic elements to an image.

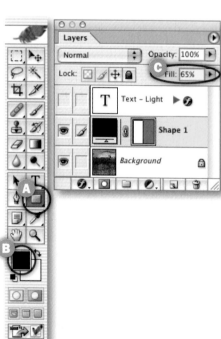

1. Create Shape Layer

Let's start off by making a panel on which to place some text. Choose the Rectangular Shape tool **A**, set the foreground color to Black **B** and then click and drag over the left side of the image to add a black rectangle. Now let's make the rectangle partially transparent so that you can see a hint of the underlying image showing through. Since we're going to end up adding Layer Styles to this layer, change the *Fill* setting at the top of the Layers palette to 65% **C**. By using the Fill setting you can partially see through the rectangle that we've made, but any edge-based Layer Styles we add later (like shadows or glows) will appear at full strength. Using the *Opacity* setting affects both fills and edge styles.

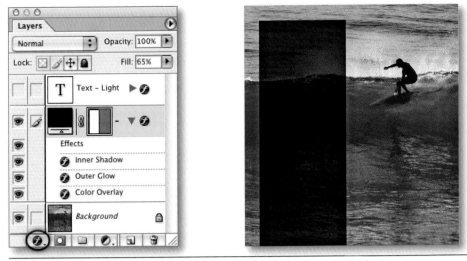

2. Add Layer Styles

Now let's make the panel pop off the background a bit by adding an Outer Glow Layer Style. Choose Outer Glow from the Layer Style pop-up menu at the bottom of the Layers palette, click on the color swatch, choose white, set the Size to 15 and the Opacity to 10%. Then before we leave the Layer Style dialog box, darken the *inside* edge of the rectangle by choosing Inner Shadow from the left side of the Layer Style dialog box and setting the Distance to zero and the Size to 40px.

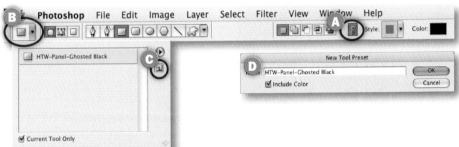

3. Create Tool Preset

We should save all the settings we just used as a Tool Preset so we can easily re-create this effect in the future. With the Rectangular Shape tool still active, click on the Link icon in the Options bar at the top of your screen **A** to make sure the tool preset includes the Layer Styles that are applied to the active layer. To save these settings as a preset, click on the Tool icon on the left of the Options bar **B**, click the New Tool Preset icon **C**, give the preset a name **D** and click OK.

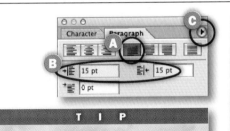

4. Add Text Within the Custom Shape

With the Shape layer still active, choose the Type tool, click within the black rectangle you drew earlier to use it as a text column and enter some text. Then to add some space between the text and the edges of the black rectangle, choose Window>Paragraphs, click on the Justify Last Left icon **A**, and set the Indent Left and Indent Right settings to 15pt **B**. Finally, to make the justified text more professional-looking (with fewer gaps in the word spacing), choose *Adobe Everyline Composer* and *Roman Hanging Punctuation* from the side menu of the palette **C**.

TIP

Justification. Choosing Justification from the side menu of the Paragraph palette and setting the Maximum Letter Spacing to 20% usually improves the look of justified text.

	Minimum	Desired	Maximum
Word Spacing:	80%	100%	133%
Letter Spacing:	0%	0%	20%
Glyph Scaling:	100%	100%	100%

Text Panel Variations

In the previous technique, we created a tool preset so that we could easily re-create the effect we just made. We encourage you to create your own collection of presets, but for now we've provided over a dozen presets designed specifically to work as backdrops for text. They are part of the *HTW-Tool Presets Sampler* file included on the CD at the back of the book. See page 19 for more on loading and using presets and page 249 for suggestions on customizing them. HTW

Panel – Ghosted Black

Panel – Ghosted White

T-B: Top to Bottom; **B-T:** Bottom to Top;
L-R: Left to Right; **R-L:** Right to Left

Panel – Recessed Dark

Panel – Raised Light

Panel – Gradient Desaturate T-B

Panel – Gradient Desaturate B-T

Panel – Gradient Desaturate L-R

Panel – Gradient Desaturate R-L

Panel – Gradient T-B Black

Panel – Gradient B-T Black

Panel – Gradient T-B White

Panel – Gradient B-T White

Panel – Gradient L-R Black

Panel – Gradient R-L Black

Panel – Gradient L-R White

Panel – Ghosted Black

Panel – Ghosted White

Quick Collaging Overlays with Tool Presets

Apply and modify tool presets to create quick and easy collages, backdrops and framing effects.

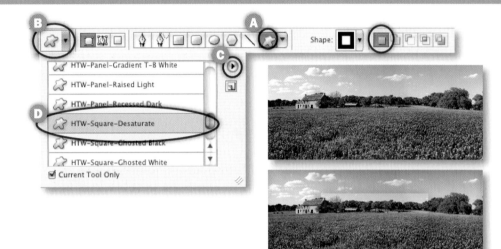

1. Draw Rectangle with Preset

We'll start by crafting a backdrop upon which we can overlay other images. Choose the Custom Shape tool **A**, then in the Options bar click on the Tool icon on the far left **B**, choose *HTW-Tool Presets Sampler* from the side menu of the drop-down palette that appears **C**, and choose the *HTW-Square-Desaturate* preset **D**. Now create a Shape Layer that covers the whole image by clicking in the upper-left corner of the image and dragging to the lower-right corner (press spacebar if you need to move the shape while dragging).

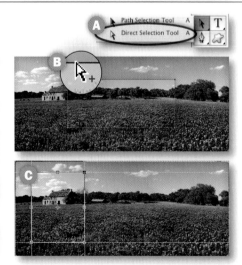

INSIGHT

Transforming Shapes. When a Shape Layer is active, typing Command/Ctrl-T will only work when the **paths** that make up the Shape Layer are **visible**. To toggle the visibility of the path, either click on the Shape thumbnail for the active layer in the Layers palette, or type Return/Enter while any of the path selection tools are active **A**. Free Transform Path will only transform the **points** that are selected (black instead of hollow). If no points are selected, then the entire shape will be transformed.

2. Transform Shape

Let's modify the shape we just created so that the house is in full color while the surrounding area is grayscale—drawing the viewer's attention to the house. Type Command/Ctrl-H to view the guides that we have created to define the house area. Choose the Direct Selection tool **A** and Option/Alt-click on the *edge* of the path that defines the color area of the image **B** (but be careful not to click on any of the corner points). Now type Command/Ctrl-T, drag each of the **corner handles** so they match up with the position of the guides **C** and then press Return/Enter.

3. Draw & Transform 2nd Shape

Now let's ghost back the surrounding area as well to create a lighter backdrop upon which we can overlay multiple images. Choose the *HTW-Square-Vignette White Ghosted* preset from the Tool Presets drop-down palette, draw a rectangle that covers the entire image **A**, select the central rectangle and transform it just as we did in steps 1 and 2 **B**.

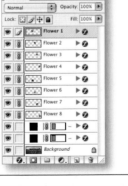

4. Scale Effects

The vignette effect we just added is a little too soft, so choose Layer>Layer Styles>Scale Effects, enter 50% and click OK. Then complete the overall composition by turning on the eyeball icons for the flower layers in our sample file.

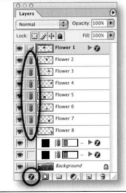

5. Add Styles to Flower Layers

Now to add a little "pop" to the flower layers, click on one of the flower layers to make it active, choose Outer Glow from the Layer Style pop-up menu at the bottom of the Layers palette, set the color to white, the Size to 10 and the Opacity to 75. Now let's apply that same style to the other images. With the style-applied flower layer active, link the flower layers together by clicking and dragging down the empty column to the right of the eyeball icons for those layers. Then to apply the styles to the linked layers, choose Layer>Layer Styles>Copy Layer Style and then Layer>Layer Styles>Paste Layer Style to Linked.

6. Create Layer Set

Now that the image is visually complete, let's simplify the organization of the Layers palette view by placing the flower layers into a Layer Set. With the flower layers still linked together, choose New Set From Linked from the side menu of the Layers palette. ▥

Panel Overlay Variations

In the previous technique, we used a tool preset to quickly customize a backdrop upon which we overlaid multiple images. To the right, you'll find examples of what can be done using the other shape tool presets that are available in the *HTW-Tool Presets Sampler* file included on the CD at the back of the book (see page 19 for more info on loading and using presets).

(see page 19 for more info on loading and using presets)

Original

Panel – Gradient L-R Black

Panel – Gradient R-L White

Panel – Ghosted Black

Panel – Graduated Desaturate B-T

Panel – Graduated Desaturate L-R

TIP

Example Files. We've provided a Photoshop file with examples of each of the tool presets on the next five pages. Each preset is a separate layer so that you can drag it into another file. You can use the layers in the sample file when you don't feel like using the tool presets. You can also combine them by making more than one layer visible.

T-B: Top to Bottom; **B-T:** Bottom to Top;
L-R: Left to Right; **R-L:** Right to Left

Panel – Ghosted White

Panel – Gradient B-T Black

Panel – Gradient B-T White

Panel – Gradient Desaturate T-B

Panel – Gradient L-R White

Panel – Gradient R-L Black

Panel – Gradient Desaturate R-L

Panel – Gradient T-B Black

Panel – Ghosted T-B White

Frame Overlay Variations

To the right are examples created using the *How to Wow Frame Tool Presets* that are available on the CD at the back of this book (see page19 for more on loading presets). The framing presets are divided into three groups that represent their shape or edge—Oval, Square and Brush.

To access these presets, choose Window>Tool Presets, then select *HTW-Tools Presets Sampler* from the pop-out menu in the upper-right of the palette. If the Current Tool Only checkbox is turned on at the bottom of the Tool Presets palette, then you'll need to have the *Custom Shape tool* active in order to see the presets.

Oval Frame Overlays

Frame Oval –
Desaturate

Frame Oval –
Ghosted White

Frame Oval –
Ghosted Black

Frame Oval –
Vignette Black

Frame Oval –
Vignette Desaturate

Frame Oval –
Vignette Ghosted Black

Frame Oval –
Vignette White

Frame Oval –
Vignette Ghosted White

**Frame Square –
Desaturate**

**Frame Square –
Ghosted Black**

**Frame Square –
Ghosted White**

**Frame Square –
Vignette Black**

**Frame Square –
Vignette Desaturate**

**Frame Square –
Vignette Ghosted Black**

**Frame Square –
Vignette White**

**Frame Square –
Vignette Ghosted White**

Using the HTW Frame Presets. The *HTW Frame Presets* are based on rectangular shapes that have various "holes" (ovals, squares, or brush edges) punched into the centers of those shapes, thus allowing an image to show through. These customized shapes were saved as Tool Presets, along with their associated Layer Styles which create the Desaturating, Ghosting, and Vignetting effects.

To use one of these HTW Tool Presets, type F to enter Full Screen Mode, then zoom out so you can see plenty of gray area around your image. Now, with the Custom Shade Tool active in the Tool palette, select the desired HTW Frame Preset from the Tool Presets palette and click in the gray area above and to the left of your photograph **A**, and drag down **B** past the lower-right of your image, trying to center the inner shape (the oval, square, or brush edge) in your file. Without releasing the mouse button, adjust the position of the entire shape *while* you are drawing it out by holding down the space bar. You can go back and forth between *scaling* the shape (by dragging) and *repositioning* it (space bar while dragging) as many times as necessary to get its size and position as you like it **C**. Release the mouse button to complete the stylized shape **D**.

INSIGHT

Styles & Resolution. When applying Layer Styles (including the ones that are part of tool presets), they will be scaled based on the resolution of your image. That means that the size of a drop shadow will vary depending on the resolution of the image. You can quickly scale the Layer Style that is applied to the active layer by choosing Layer>Layer Style>Scale Effects. All the WOW styles that are available on the CD at the back of this book are optimized for 225ppi images (which is ideal for commercial printing with a 150-line screen). Any WOW styles that include patterns will look best at 225ppi because they will not be degraded by scaling the pattern.

CAUTION

Computationally Instensive. The vector-based edge used for these pre-sets is very complex and might cause your screen redraw to slow down. We hope you'll find it worth the extra time once you see the results!

Brush Frame Overlays

Brush – Desaturate

Brush – Ghosted Black

Brush – Ghosted White

Brush – Vignette Black

Brush – Vignette Desaturate

Brush – Vignette Ghosted Black

Brush – Vignette White

Brush – Vignette Ghosted White

Panel As Backdrop

The panel presets shown on page 240 are also useful as backdrops for simple collages. In the images above, we've used the HTW-Panel-Ghosted White preset and covered the entire background, then a second image was placed on a layer above and a Drop Shadow Layer Style was added. This can be done with multiple images as shown in the left example, or with a close-up of a single image as shown on the right. Once you've created a Shape Layer using one of the tool presets, you can adjust the Opacity and Fill settings at the top of the Layers palette to control the strength of the effect.

Editing Style Settings

The effects that you apply with a tool preset are not locked in stone. Once you've created a Shape Layer, you can double-click on the Layer Style symbol for the active layer and edit the settings used to create the effect. For instance, you can select the *Gradient Overlay* style in the Layer Style dialog box and then click and drag within the image to reposition the gradient, or change the Scale setting to control how abrupt the transition is from white to transparent.

Scaling Effects

The tool presets are optimized for images that have a resolution of 225 pixels per inch. If the size of drop shadows, glows and other effects overwhelm your image, then try Control/right-clicking on the Layer Style icon on the right side of the active layer and choosing Scale Effects. In the image above, we used the HTW-Brush-Desaturate preset to add the frame effect and then scaled the effects to make sure the shadow didn't dominate the image.

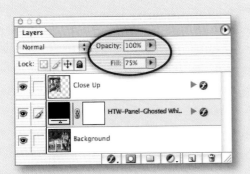

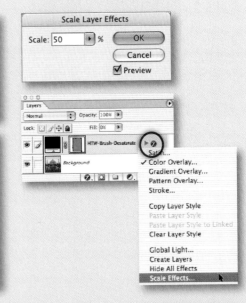

Instant Backdrops & Cast Shadows

Learn to create cast shadows and dimensional backdrops for quick "studio" portraits.

TIP

Controlling the Edge. When viewing the subject in its new background, if the edge seems a little too abrupt, then Command/Ctrl-click on the subject layer to load the contents of the layer as a selection. Next, choose Select>Feather and use .5. Now click the Layer Mask icon at the bottom of the Layers palette, which will soften the edge.

1. Combine Subject and Background

Start by opening this project's two sample images, (*C09-250 Subject.tif* and *C09-50 Background.tif)*. With the subject image active, make a selection of the subject of the photograph and choose Edit>Copy. Then switch to the background document and choose Edit>Paste.

The sample PhotoSpin stock image used here (located with the rest of this book's working files in the ***HTW Project Images*** folder on the CD) has a built-in Alpha Channel that can be loaded as a selection. To do this, choose Select>Load Selection, then set the Channel pop-up menu to Alpha Channel and click OK.

2. Create a Cast Shadow

With the subject layer active, choose Drop Shadow from the Layer Style pop-up menu at the bottom of the Layers palette. Since there is no such thing as black drop shadows in nature (shadows take on the color of the ambient light in the environment), click on the shadow color swatch and then click on a very dark area of the background image (make sure the image is active instead of the layer mask). That will help blend the faux shadow into the new background. Let's leave the edge rather crisp (Size 5px), and set the Noise to 1.

3. Convert Shadow into a Layer

Now let's get the drop shadow onto its own layer so we can manipulate separately from the subject layer. Control/right-click on the Layer Style icon that is attached to the active layer **A** and choose Create Layer from the menu **B**. When prompted with a warning dialog box, click OK. This step placed the drop shadow onto a separate layer, which means we are no longer limited to the *Drop Shadow* setting we used to create it.

4. Cast the Shadow

With the shadow layer active, choose Edit>Free Transform, hold the Command/Ctrl key and drag the top center anchor point down and to the right to turn the drop shadow into a cast shadow. You can also hold the Command/Ctrl key and pull on one of the corners to distort the shadow. Then double-click within the bounding box to finalize the transformation.

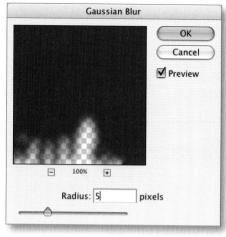

5. Blur the Shadow

Now let's make our cast shadow softer as it gets further from the subject. Choose the Lasso tool, *change the Feather setting* to 20 in the Options bar at the top of your screen, then hold the Option/Alt key (to allow us to select outside of the current canvas) and select all of the shadow layer, except the bottom edge. Now choose Filter>Blur>Gaussian Blur and use a Radius of 5 and click OK. Next, click and hold in the middle of the area that is selected and move the selection up and then type Comamnd-F to apply the blur filter a second time. Repeat this move then blur process until you have a gradually-softening cast shadow.

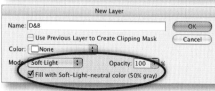

6. Change Background Lighting

Create a separate Dodge & Burn layer by holding down Option/Alt and clicking on the New Layer icon at the bottom of the Layers palette and setting the Mode to Soft Light. Now turn on the Fill with Soft-Light-Neutral Color (50% gray) checkbox and name the layer "D&B" for Dodge and Burn. Even though this layer is full of 50% gray, nothing shows up because Soft Light mode causes 50% gray to disappear (also known as being neutral). Now, choose the Brush tool with a large, soft-edged brush set to a low opacity (like 10%), choose black to paint with and paint over the areas you'd like to darken. Darken the edges to draw the eye toward the model and imitate subtle light and shadow variations. You can type X to switch to white paint so you can quickly lighten (or "dodge") your background as well. Remember to keep the basic lighting direction of your subject in mind when adjusting your background.

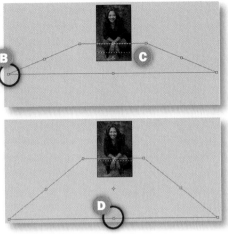

7. Add Perspective to Background

Now that we have a nice shadow and a "lit" background, let's duplicate the background so we can easily change its perspective. Click on the Background layer and then type Command/Ctrl-J to duplicate the layer. With the duplicate layer active, use the lasso tool to select the bottom portion of the image (hold Option/Alt so you can extend your selection beyond the edge of the document **A**). Type F to enter full screen mode, choose Edit>Transform>Perspective, and drag one of the lower corners toward the outside edge of your screen **B**. But after doing that, the background has been foreshortened and does not cover the bottom of the photograph **C**. To compensate, Control/right-click and choose Free Transform from the menu and then move the bottom center control point until the image covers the entire bottom portion of the image **D**.

Swapping Backgrounds. If you don't have a library of seamless backgrounds just waiting to be used, then you can create your own by doing the following: Create a new layer and then choose Filter>Render>Difference Clouds. Apply that filter multiple times until you've got a texture you like, then you can colorize the texture using one of the methods found in Chapter 7, "Color & Tone Treatments."

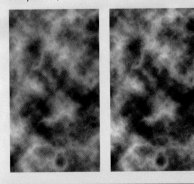

8. Exaggerate Depth of Field

To further make the model pop off the background, choose Select>Inverse to select the "back wall" of the background, choose Filter>Blur>Gaussian Blur and use a low setting like 1. If you'd like to darken the background even more, while the selection is still active, click on the D&B layer, choose Image>Adjustments>Levels and move the lower-right output slider to darken the background without losing detail. ▦

TIP

Unify with Lens Blur. You can enhance the illusion of unification between two images by applying the Lens Blur filter to the overall image. By shortening the apparent depth of field in the photo, the images will appear to belong together (see page 151 for more details on applying the Lens Blur filter).

Soft-Edged Combining

Here are techniques for creating an editorial or marketing photo illustration using soft-edged Layer Masks.

1. Drag Over First Image and Scale

To follow along with this project, open the base file *C09-254 Chang Background.psd* and the images file *C09-254 Chang Photos.psd.* Our base image has already been scaled to size, so use the Move tool to drag the "shave ice" photo from the images file into the base file. Next, type Command/Ctrl-T and scale the image (while holding Shift to maintain its proportions) until it fits in the upper-right of the base image.

2. Select and Add Layer Mask

Let's vignette this image into a soft-edged circle. Choose the Elliptical Marquee tool, hold Shift, and drag out a circle that covers the central portion of the image (you can select right up to the edge of the image because of our next step). Choose Select>Modify>Contract, use 20 pixels and click OK. Then choose Select>Feather and use 10 because it uses the same amount on both the inside and outside of the selection for a total of 20. Now click on the Layer Mask icon at the bottom of the Layers palette.

T I P

Circle marks the spot. When attempting to center a selection on an object, use the following keyboard shortcuts after you've started to create the selection:

- Shift constrains a selection to a perfect circle.
- Option/Alt causes the selection to start from the center instead of the edge of the circle.
- Spacebar allows you to reposition the selection as you are creating it.

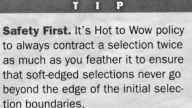

3. Add and Mask Second Image

Use the Move tool to drag over the second image. Type Command/Ctrl-T and scale the image down so that it fits in the lower-right of the document. Now let's create a soft rectangular edge. This time Command/Ctrl-click on the active layer's icon to get a selection, choose Select>Modify>Contract, use 20 pixels, then choose Select>Feather with a setting of 10. Now click on the Layer Mask icon at the bottom of the Layers palette and then change the stacking order of the layers so the round image is on top. Next, choose Edit>Transform>Flip Horizontal so the woman in the photo is looking into the image.

4. Hand Paint the Third Mask

Use the Move tool to drag over the last image. Type Command/Ctrl-T, move the image to the lower-left corner and scale it so it is no taller than the central figure of the collage. Next, click on the Layer Mask icon at the bottom of the Layers palette, choose a small, soft-edged brush, and paint with black around the edges of the image. Now choose a larger brush, lower the opacity to 50% and paint some more to get a softer edge. Since the priority is to market the bathing suit, we won't be concerned with the surfboard. Switch to white if you need to bring areas back.

5. Add and Style Custom Logo

Our last element is a Custom Logo: "No Ka Oi," or "the best." Use the Move tool and drag it over from the images file. To add a style, choose Window>Style, click on the side menu of the palette, choose *HTW-Styles Sampler* and then click on the Wow-Stroke 21 style preset. (The Fill Opacity setting of 0 at the top of the Layers palette is responsible for the transparent interiors of the letters.)

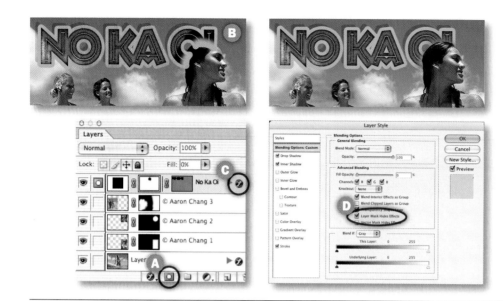

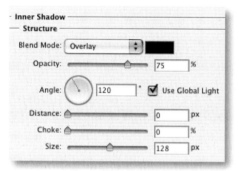

6. Mask the Logo and Style

Now let's mask the type so it looks like it's fading out behind the woman's head. With the logo layer active, click on the Layer Mask icon at the bottom of the Layers palette **A**, and paint with black using a soft-edged brush to hide the text. Things will look rather weird because the Layer Style is trying to apply to this "semi" soft edge that we've created **B**. To fix that, double-click on the black circle that appears on the right side of the active layer **C** and turn on the Layer Mask Hides Effects checkbox **D** so the painting we've done hides the effects as well as the text. Now you can continue painting to fine-tune the transition.

7. Add Inner Shadow

To finish off our collage, double-click on the Background layer to change its name (thus allowing it to have transparency, which will make it possible for it to receive a Layer Style) and choose Inner Shadow from the Layer Style pop-up menu at the bottom of the Layers palette. Set the Distance to zero, the Size to 128, and change the mode to Overlay. That will add a darkened vignetting effect to the edge of the image, effectively drawing the eye away from the edge and toward the middle of the composition.

C A U T I O N

Check Transitions. It's easy to end up with a semi-abrupt edge on a layer if you don't have enough image to cover the transition from opaque to transparent. You can check for an abrupt edge by hiding the Background layer, choosing the Magic Wand tool, setting its Tolerance to 0, turning off its Anti-aliasing, and clicking within the checkerboard area so you can see how far out the fading goes (to make sure you have enough image available). As long as the selection looks smooth and rounded, then everything is fine.

Panorama Stitching

Maintain precise control by manually stitching two images together to create a seamless panorama.

1. Combine with Difference Mode

With the two images you'd like to stitch together open, drag one image onto the other using the Move tool. In the combined document, double-click on the *Background* layer to change its name and turn it into a normal layer that can be moved around. Then to see where the images align, click on the top layer and change the blend mode at the top of the Layers palette to Difference. In Difference mode, images will turn black as they become closer to being aligned. If things don't line up then you'll see grays and colors.

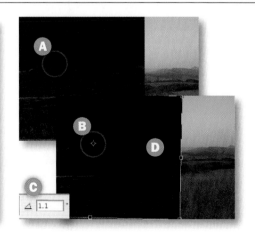

2. Align Images

Use the Move tool to line up a distinctive element in both images (we used the mountain peak) **A**. To better align the rest of the image, type Command/Ctrl-T to invoke Free Transform and drag the center crosshair to where the two images line up **B**. Click on the Angle field in the Options bar **C**, use the up and down arrow keys until the rotating image turns as close to black as possible **D**, then press Return/Enter twice to apply the change.

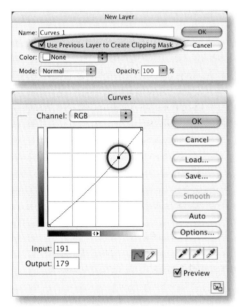

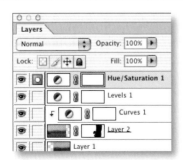

3. Mask Image

Now let's get the two images to seamlessly blend together. Choose Image>Reveal All so you can see the entire image **A** and then click on the Layer Mask icon at the bottom of the Layers palette. Next, with a large, soft-edged brush and the foreground color set to black, paint over the right edge of the blackish area and work your way left until you get close to the area that is closest to solid black (the areas in the two photos that most closely match up) **B**. Now change the blend mode of the top layer to Normal, choose a smaller brush and fine-tune the mask to make sure everything looks right (no seams) **C**.

4. Match Color & Tone

Now let's get the brightness of the two pieces to match. With the top layer active, hold Option/Alt and choose Curves from the Adjustment Layer pop-up menu at the bottom of the Layers palette. When the New Layer dialog box appears, turn on the Use Previous Layer to Create Clipping Mask checkbox and then click OK. That will cause the adjustment that we apply to only affect the top layer. Move your mouse over the image and Command/Ctrl-click on the sky in the center part of the image right before the transition **A** to automatically add a Curves anchor point. Now use the up and down arrow keys to adjust the brightness and make the images match.

5. Crop and Tweak the Image

Now to finish off the image, choose the Crop tool and click and drag across your image to get rid of any irregular edges. At this point, you might want to consider adding another Adjustment Layer or two (this time with the Use Previous Layer to Create Clipping Mask checkbox turned off) and adjust the overall tonality and/or color of the entire image.

Index

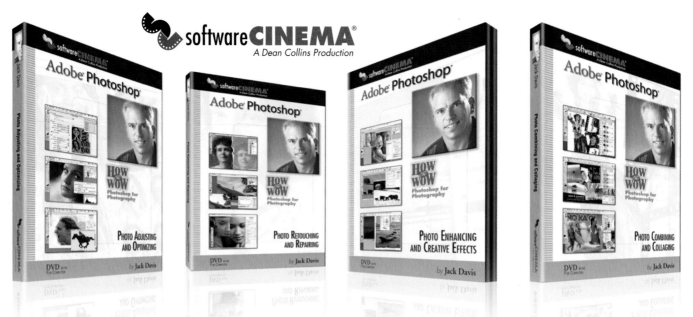

Photo Retouching & Repairing   DVD 2

Chapter 1 Retouching & Repairing
- Dust & Scratch Removal
- Using the Healing Brush & Patch Tools
- Sky Replacing & Manufacturing
- Tonal Rescue
- Color Resuscitation
- Photo Repair & Restoration

Chapter 2 People & Portraits I
- Controlling Blemishes & Wrinkles
- Manual Patching Techniques
- Pore & Skin Softening
- Skin Conditioning & Shaving
- Skin smoothing for a porcelain glow

Chapter 3 People & Portraits II
- Unifying Skin Color & Tone
- Eye & Teeth Tweaking
- Feature Enhancing
- Body Reshaping
- Body Part Swapping

software**CINEMA**®
A Dean Collins Production

Photo Enhancing & Creative Effects DVD 3

Chapter 1 Enhancing & Embellishing
- Adding Density with Blend Modes
- Diffused Glows
- Popping Images with Highpass
- Edge, Gradient & Color "Style Filters"
- Creative Focus Control
- Depth of Field Altering
- Motion Blurring & Variations

Chapter 2 Color & Tone Treatments
- Color to Black-and-White Conversions
- Layer Style Tinting
- Advanced Multi-tones
- Matching Color
- Quick Antique Re-coloring
- Hand Tinting
- Solarizing & Cross-Processing Effects

Chapter 3 Artistic Effects & Overlays
- Soft-edged Vignetting
- Brush Stroke Edge Effects
- Creating a Deckled Edge
- Canvas Texture Treatments
- Texture & Noise Overlay Treatments
- Turning a Photo into a Painting

Photo Combining & Collaging   DVD 4

Chapter 1 Collaging with Templates
- Template-Based Collaging
- Custom Mask Collaging
- Custom Shape Framing
- Unifying a Series with Styles

Chapter 2 Combining with Control
- Text Panel Overlays
- Quick Collaging Overlays
- Framing Overlays
- Instant Backdrops & Cast Shadows
- Soft-Edged Combining
- Panorama Stitching

Jack Davis is best known as the coauthor of the best-selling guide to Photoshop, **The Photoshop Wow! Book**, as well as being an award-winning designer, photographer, and contributing editor to numerous other books and magazines on digital tools and the creative process. These discs showcase his techniques with photography, and the process of going beyond what was captured to what was experienced—always emphasizing Quality, Flexibility and Speed.

For over 20 years Jack has been an internationally recognized creative spokesperson on digital imagery. Jack is part of the "Dream Team" at the National Association of Photoshop Professional's Photoshop World Conferences, where he was recently inducted into the Photoshop Hall of Fame for his lifetime contributions in the field of education and digital imagery.